THE SECRET LIVES OF BUILDINGS

EDWARD HOLLIS is an architect and designer who teaches at the Edinburgh College of Art. Trained at Cambridge and Edinburgh universities, he worked for five years in the United Kingdom as a practising architect, specializing in alterations to historic buildings. This is his first book.

THE SECRET LIVES OF BUILDINGS

FROM THE PARTHENON TO THE VEGAS STRIP IN THIRTEEN STORIES

Edward Hollis

Portobello
BOOKS

Published by Portobello Books Ltd 2009

Portobello Books Ltd
Twelve Addison Avenue
Holland Park
London
W11 4QR

A CIP catalogue record is available from the British Library

9 8 7 6 5 4 3 2 1

ISBN 978 1 84627 4

www.portobellobooks.com

Text designed and typeset in Van Dijck by Patty Rennie

Printed and bound in Great Britain by
The Cromwell Press Group, Trowbridge, Wiltshire

TO MY MOTHER AND MY BROTHER,
without whom this book would
never have been undertaken;

AND TO PAUL,
without whom it would
never have been completed.

Acknowledgements

My thanks are due firstly to those whose insights have inspired me to write this book: Tom Muir, Peter and Brigid Hardwick, Anthony John, Geoffrey Bawa, Channa Daswatte, Peter Besley, Richard Murphy, Matthew Turner, Jason Orringe, and many more.

Secondly I owe a debt of thanks to my travelling companions, who tolerated treks to obscure shrines long after cocktail hour: Rachel Holmes (née Findlay) and Jonathan Hart.

Thirdly, I must thank the people who agreed to read, as experts or amateurs, some of the stories this book comprises, and provided invaluable feedback: Professor Ian Boyd White, Brendan de Caires, Inge Foeppel, Miles Glendinning, Emine Gorgule, Peter Hardwick, Nicholas King SJ, Edward Leigh, Caroline and David Mitchell, David Neuhaus SJ, Heather Tyrrell, and the interior design students of Edinburgh College of Art.

Thanks fourthly to Edinburgh College of Art for their support in the form of research leave, without which the book would never have been completed.

Instrumental in this regard were the good offices of Willie Brown, Alex Milton, Alan Murray and Susie McCorquodale.

And lastly to those who helped edit, design, and produce the book; and to my agent Patrick Walsh, without whose silver tongue this work would still be gathering digital dust.

Contents

ix

Illustrations

INTRODUCTION

The Architect's Dream.
Thomas Cole, 1838.

The Architect's Dream

Once upon a time an architect had a dream. The curtain of his bourgeois parlour was rent, and he found himself reclining on top of a colossal column overlooking a great port. On a nearby hill, the spire of a Gothic cathedral rose above pointed cypresses in a dark wood; on the other side of the river, a Corinthian rotunda and the brick arches of a Roman aqueduct were bathed in golden light. The aqueduct had been built on top of a Grecian colonnade, in front of which a procession led from the waterside to an elaborate Ionic shrine. Further away the form of a Doric temple crouched beneath an Egyptian palace, and behind them all, veiled in haze and a wisp of cloud, was the Great Pyramid.

It was a moment of absolute stillness. A perspective in time had become a perspective in space, as the past receded in an orderly fashion, style by style, from the parlour curtain of the present all the way back to the horizon of antiquity. The Dark Ages partially obscured classical splendour; Roman magnificence was built on the foundation of Grecian reason; the glory that was Greece lay in the shadow of the ur-architecture of Egypt. The array of buildings formed an architectural canon, each example dispensing inspiration, advice, and warning to the architect from the golden treasury of history.

All the great buildings of the past had been resurrected in a monumental day of rapture. Everything had been made new, and neither weather nor war nor wandering taste had scarred the scene. Everything was fixed just as it had been intended to be: each building was a masterpiece, a work of art, a piece of frozen music, unspoiled by compromise, error, or disappointment. There was nothing that could be added or taken away except for the worse. Each building was beautiful, its form and function held in perfect balance.

The scene was what architecture was, and is, and should be. But just before he awoke, the architect realized that he was dreaming, and he recalled the words of Prospero renouncing his conjured dominion at the end of The Tempest:

> *The cloud-capp'd towers, the gorgeous palaces,*
> *The solemn temples, the great globe itself,*
> *Yea, all which it inherit, shall dissolve,*
> *And, like this insubstantial pageant faded,*
> *Leave not a rack behind: We are such stuff*
> *As dreams are made on, and our little life*
> *Is rounded with a sleep.*

THE ARCHITECT'S DREAM WAS DREAMED BY AN ÉMIGRÉ FROM THE OLD World to the New. Thomas Cole was born in Lancashire in 1801, but he spent his adult life among the crags and forests of the Hudson Valley north of New York City, where he painted pictures of an arcadia not yet buried under towers and palaces and temples. Cole could not prevent himself from thinking about the Old World he had left behind, and he knew that one day the New World would come to resemble it. His cycle of paintings entitled *The Course of Empire* depicted the Hudson Valley at five different stages: in *The Savage State*, *The Arcadian or Pastoral State*, at *The Consummation of Empire*, at *The Destruction of Empire*, and in *Desolation*. In these five images, a virgin forest at dawn becomes a great city at noon. By dusk it is a broken heap of stones, whited under a watery moon.

In 1840 the architect Ithiel Town commissioned Cole to paint *The Architect's Dream* and paid him in pattern books. Town didn't much like the painting, but it came to be regarded as Cole's masterpiece. Cole's funeral eulogy extolled it among the 'principal works ... of his genius', as 'an assemblage of structures, Egyptian, Gothic, Grecian, Moorish, such as might present itself to the imagination of one who had fallen asleep after reading a work on the different styles of architecture'.

Cole's vision still haunts architects. Pick up any classic work on architecture, glance at the pictures, and you will find yourself lost in a similar panorama of 'the different styles'. Crisp line drawings describe the masterworks of antiquity as new and fresh as the day they were born; and blue skies, clean streets, and a complete absence of people lend architectural photographs the timeless quality of *The Architect's Dream*. It's not just the illustrations: the written history of architecture is also a litany of masterpieces, unchanging and unchanged, from the Great Pyramid of Giza to its glass descendants in Paris or Vegas. The great buildings of the past are described as if the last piece of scaffolding has just been taken away, the paint is still fresh on the walls, and the ribbon has not yet been cut – as if, indeed, history had never happened.

It is a timeless vision because timeless is just what we expect great architecture to be. Nearly a century ago, the Viennese architect Adolf Loos observed that architecture originates not, as one might expect, in the dwelling, but in the monument. The houses of our ancestors, which were contingent responses to their ever-shifting needs, have perished. Their tombs and temples, which were intended to endure for the eternity of death and the gods, remain, and it is they that form the canon of architectural history.

The very discourse of architecture is a discourse on perfection, a word which derives from the Latin for 'finished'. The Roman theorist Vitruvius claimed that architecture was perfect when it held commodity, firmness, and delight in delicate balance. A millennium and a half later, his Renaissance interpreter Leone Battista Alberti wrote that perfect beauty is that to which nothing may be added, and from which nothing may be taken away. The Modernist architect Le Corbusier described the task of his profession as 'the problem of fixing standards, in order to face the problem of perfection.'

In the discourse of architecture, all buildings, in order to remain beautiful, must not change; and all buildings, in order not to change, must aspire to the funereal condition of the monument. The tomb of Christopher Wren in the crypt of St Paul's Cathedral in London is a simple affair for so great a man, but the inscription on the wall above the sarcophagus belies its modesty. 'Si monumentum requiris, circumspice,' it reads: 'If you seek a monument, look around you.' All architects hope that the buildings they have designed will memorialize their genius, and so they dare to hope that their buildings will last for ever, unaltered.

* * *

But *The Architect's Dream* is just that: a dream, an illusion, a flat picture imprisoned in a frame. Imagine, for a moment, that the architect woke up from his dream, stepped out of the painting, and walked out of the museum where it is exhibited.

He might still find himself on top of a colossal column, but it wouldn't command some monumental prospect. Instead, he might be looking into a tenement stairwell, which is just what he would see if he'd climbed to the summit of the surviving columns of the temple of Augustus in Barcelona. The Gothic cathedral would not be in some dark forest but right next door, and the walls of its crypt might be made from the foundations of a shrine to Apollo, as they are in Girona. The columns of that structure might form the cathedral porch, as they do at Syracuse; and the altar would be an upturned Roman bathtub, just as it is in the church of Santa Maria in Cosmedin in Rome. The cathedral would, like Chartres or Gloucester, have taken hundreds of years to build, and it would be a chaotic collage of different styles, overlaid with Victorian restorations of great enthusiasm and dubious accuracy. The Ionic temple, like that of Diana in Ephesus, would have been burned down by indignant Christians in the fifth century, while the Corinthian rotunda would have been turned into a fortress, just as the Pantheon was in medieval Rome. The Doric temple would have flitted away: its sculpture would be on display in London, like the Elgin marbles, and the building itself would have reappeared elsewhere, as the altar of Pergamene Zeus has been reconstructed in Berlin. The arches of the Roman aqueduct would be buried under the crowded slums of Jerusalem or Naples, its vaults now hiding places for criminals and the secret police. Only the tomb, the Great Pyramid, would have remained unaltered – marooned, monumentally useless, in the suburban sands of Giza.

The Architect's Dream would have become a Jazz Age Manhattan, a twenty-first-century Shanghai, an Ottoman Istanbul, a medieval Venice: a noisy, dirty entrepôt of multitudinous architectures in the process of constant change. This city would be anything but still. In the process of its perpetual and simultaneous construction and decay, buildings would appear and disappear; they would be built on top of one another, out of one another, or inside one another. They would do battle and then they would mate and produce monstrous offspring. Not a single building would survive as its makers had intended.

And the architect, who might be excused for finding his awakening a nightmare, would realize that the real world is stranger and more dreamlike than a painted dream. Before returning to his column within the picture frame, he might cast one last glance at the stormy scene outside, and recall another passage from *The Tempest*:

> *Full fathom five thy father lies;*
> *Of his bones are coral made;*
> *Those are pearls that were his eyes;*

Nothing of him that doth fade,
But doth suffer a sea-change
Into something rich and strange.

* * *

This is a book of tales about the lives that buildings lead, in the course of which they all change into 'something rich and strange'; and it is their cumulative argument that the history of architecture is nothing like *The Architect's Dream*. Indeed, these tales are told as the waking antidote to Cole's vision and its hypnotic hold over architectural orthodoxy. That is why these buildings have secret lives: all too often, the existence of their stories has been either overlooked or wilfully ignored.

At the heart of architectural theory is a paradox: buildings are designed to last, and therefore they outlast the insubstantial pageants that made them. Then, liberated from the shackles of immediate utility and the intentions of their masters, they are free to do as they will. Buildings long outlive the purposes for which they were built, the technologies by which they were constructed, and the aesthetics that determined their form; they suffer numberless subtractions, additions, divisions, and multiplications; and soon enough their form and their function have little to do with one another. The architect Aldo Rossi, for example, observed of his own northern Italian milieu that 'there are large palaces, building complexes, or agglomerations that constitute whole pieces of the city, and whose function now is no longer the original one. When one visits a monument of this type ... one is struck by the multiplicity of different functions that a building of this type can contain over time, and how these functions are completely independent of form.'

More often than not, the confident *dicta* of architectural theory are undermined by the secret lives of buildings, which are capricious, protean, and unpredictable; but all too often the contradiction is treated as the object of interest only to specialists involved in heritage conservation or interior design. We know all about the biographies of Le Corbusier or Frank Lloyd Wright, but much less about the biographies of the buildings they designed. It is more difficult by far to find studies that talk about the evolution of buildings themselves, as the wonderful and chimeric monsters that they are, than to find gossip about the monsters who designed them.

There are a few exceptions. In the nineteenth century, Eugène-Emmanuel Viollet-le-Duc in France and John Ruskin in England founded rival schools of conservation philosophy, whose twentieth-century exegesis has been undertaken by such writers as Alois Riegl and Cesare Brandi. In the modernist era, obsessed as it was with the future, only Jože Plečnik and Carlo Scarpa seriously addressed themselves to the alteration of the buildings of the past, designing fascinating hybrids where modern architecture is collaged over the layered substrates of previous historical epochs. In more recent times, Fred Scott's *On Altering Architecture* and Graeme Brooker and Sally Stone's *Rereadings* have addressed the practice from the point of view of the interior architect, whose profession consists almost exclusively of the alteration of existing buildings.

Still, the fact that all great buildings mutate over time is often treated as something of a dirty secret, or at best a source of melancholy reflection. This book has been written to insist not only that buildings will change, but perhaps, also, that they should. It is both a history of the alteration of buildings and a manifesto for the same.

✳ ✳ ✳

The buildings whose secret lives are related here are a familiar cast, some of whom are more or less directly recognizable from *The Architect's Dream*. The book begins, as all European architectural narratives must, with the Parthenon, which is followed, in orthodox fashion, by a textboook parade of masterpieces, from San Marco in Venice to a version of Le Corbusier's *Ville*

Radieuse. All of these are firmly situated in the orbit of European culture, whose *Ultimae Thules* in this context are the Strip in Las Vegas to the west and the Western Wall in Jerusalem to the east. (The architecture of the rest of the world is less afflicted than that of the West by an obsession with permanence – the ancient buildings of Japan, for instance, are made of paper – and has less need, therefore, of an antidote.)

But the orthodox frame of this study is an ironic one, for these master-pieces, so called, are too capricious to answer to any one master. They are ruined, stolen, or appropriated. They flit away and reproduce themselves, evolve and get translated into foreign languages, simulated, prophesied, and restored. They are transformed into sacred relics, empty spectacles, and *casus belli*. It is the contention of this book that their beauty has been generated by their long and unpredictable lives. As the American theorist Christopher Alexander has argued, 'when a place is lifeless or unreal, there is almost always a mastermind behind it. It is so filled with the will of its maker that there is no room for its own nature.' Timeless beauty 'cannot be made, but only gener-ated indirectly, by the ordinary actions of the people, just as a flower cannot be made, only generated from a seed'.

The buildings described in this book shapeshift from century to century, so the traditional chronologies of style that order architectural history are useless here. Instead, if there is an overarching structure to the sequence of stories, it derives from the ways in which attitudes towards architectural alteration have changed over time. The Visigoth, the medieval monk, and the modern archaeologist have all stood in front of the same classical building with wildly divergent proposals for its future, ranging from a good sacking to iconoclastic exorcism to careful excavation; and each one of these approaches represents a commentary, if not necessarily an improvement, upon the atti-tude it has inherited.

All histories are in some sense commentaries on their predecessors, and so are acts of architectural alteration, which are in themselves critiques of what they alter. 'Anyone can be creative,' Bertolt Brecht once said; 'it's rewriting other people that's a challenge.' Every performance of every play or piece of music is a reinterpretation, a rereading and rewriting of a script or score, and these performances take place without any of the anxiety we associate with the alteration of existing buildings. Musicians and actors are regarded as creative heroes without ever having had to produce a new work from scratch. It is accepted that their interpretations of Bach or Brecht are as valid a contribution to our culture as any original composition.

There are analogies here to the alteration of existing buildings. The problems that face early music ensembles or 'period' performances of Shakespeare, for example, are very similar to those that faced the preservationists of the nineteenth century. Meanwhile, 'modern' performances, from Karajan's renditions of Beethoven to Hollywood reinterpetations of Jane Austen, may be compared to the operations of a Renaissance architect trying to translate a Gothic church into the classical idiom.

It may be objected that the difference between architecture and literature or music is that while scripts and scores exist independently of performances, buildings are not independent of the alterations wrought upon them. These are always irreversible, and can therefore destroy their 'hosts' in a way that dramatic or musical productions of a classic work cannot. But there is one field in which the performance and the thing performed are inseparable: the oral tradition. If a story is not written down, then the only script that exists for the next performance is the previous telling. This means that the development of every tale is iterative: each retelling sets the conditions for the next, and stories from the *Iliad* to *Little Red Riding Hood* have been both preserved and altered by every narrator until they arrived on the written page. The classic case is the story of Cinderella, which first appears in the European written record in the Middle Ages. The glass slipper on which much of the plot turns is made of gold in German, and is a rubber galosh in Russian. In the German telling of the tale, the ugly sisters even cut off their toes to fit their feet into the slipper, and spatter it with their blood. There is a ninth-century Chinese telling of the tale in which the fairy godmother is a fish, and the palace ball a village fête; but Cinderella is still Cinderella all the same.

Buildings are less portable than stories, but there are significant parallels between their modes of transmission. As Christopher Alexander observed, 'No building is ever perfect. Each building, when it is first built, is an attempt to make a self-maintaining whole configuration. But the predictions are invariably wrong. People use buildings differently from the way they thought they would.' Accordingly, people have to make changes in order to maintain the fit between a structure and the events that take place in it. Each time this happens to a building 'we assume we are going to transform it, that new wholes will be born, that, indeed, the entire whole which is being repaired will become a different whole as a result.' Each alteration is a 'retelling' of the building as it exists at a particular time – and when the changes are complete it becomes the existing building for the next retelling. In this way the life of the building is both perpetuated and transformed by the repeated act of alteration and reuse.

This is exactly how stories are transmitted from generation to generation, preserved and remade again and again. Indeed, the buildings whose secret lives are recounted here have undergone metamorphoses that have the character of fairy tales or myths. The story of the transformation of the Berlin Wall into precious relics always makes me think of Rumpelstiltskin's captive, trying to spin straw into gold, while the tale of the Wondrous Flitting of the Holy House of Loreto always provokes the question: 'but what *actually* happened?'

I do not know what actually happened, and to answer such a question would be as useful as identifying the real Little Red Riding Hood. It is not the purpose of this book to deconstruct the stories (or the buildings) we have inherited from our forebears, but to narrate them, so that others can do the same in the future. Stories are like gifts: they must be accepted without scepticism and shared with others.

For stories and for buildings alike, incremental change has been the paradoxical mechanism of their preservation. Not one of the buildings whose secret lives are recounted here has lost anything by having been transformed. Instead, they have endured in a way that they would never have done if no-one had ever altered them. Architecture is all too often imagined as if buildings do not – and should not – change. But change they do, and have always done. Buildings are gifts, and because they are, we must pass them on.

THE PARTHENON, ATHENS

In Which a Virgin is Ruined

THE DESTRUCTION OF THE GRAND MOSQUE OF ATHENS.

Ruin

*T*he Parthenon is the architect's dream. It is perfect. It is what architecture was, is, and should be.

Or so they say. To Pericles, under whose aegis it was built, the Parthenon symbolized an Athens that was 'the school of Hellas'. Thucydides, who opposed its construction, commented that the Parthenon would cause future ages to imagine that Athens was a far greater civilization than it had ever been. Thucydides was closer to the mark, for Athens became the school not only of Hellas but of the whole Western world, and the Parthenon has been the model of architecture ever since.

Just as Vitruvius prescribed, the Parthenon holds commodity, firmness, and delight in perfect balance. The Parthenon is beautiful in the Renaissance sense: nothing may be added to it, or taken away, but for the worse. For the dilettanti who visited it in the eighteenth century, the Parthenon was the model for all civilized art; and for the citizens of the new nation who stood before it in 1837, the Parthenon was the symbol of Grecian liberty. The French architect Viollet-le-Duc described it as the perfect expression of its own construction, and Le Corbusier compared its refinements to the exhilarating styling of sports cars, calling it 'architecture, pure creation of the mind'.

There are Parthenons everywhere. There is one in Nashville, Tennessee, constructed for an exposition of the arts and industry in 1897, and another one by the banks of the Danube, near Regensburg. The High Court of Sri Lanka is lent an air of gravitas by the expedient of attaching a Parthenon to it as a porch, while Edinburgh College of Art in Scotland was designed to house casts of the sculptures that once adorned the Greek temple. Everywhere it appears, the Parthenon is used to symbolize art and civilization, liberty and eternal fame.

The Parthenon is what architecture is, and should be; but the perfect Parthenons of architecture have been conjured from a heap of broken stones that are anything but perfect. The Platonic philosophers of ancient Athens would have argued that the Acropolis was crowned by a maimed relic from the very beginning: that the physical Parthenon could never be more than a dim shadow of the ideal temple, which exists only in the mind's eye. Today, then, this model of architecture is but a phantom of a shadow of an idea: a ruin.

circa *460*

ONCE UPON A TIME, A PHILOSOPHER OF ATHENS HAD A DREAM. AS
Proclus slept in his little house below the Acropolis, a goddess armed with a
shield and spear appeared to him. 'Make your house ready,' she said. 'They
have turned me out of my temple.'

Proclus knew exactly who she was, for he had spent his life waiting for her.
Every day he would take his students up to the hill above his house, where he
would show them the goddess and her temple, and he would tell them stories
about the marble figures that were carved across the building.

He would point up at the figures in the eastern gable of the temple. These
figures showed the birth of the goddess Athene, he would say, for Athene was
not conceived of a womb but sprang from her father's head, fully armed, when
the god Hephaestus split it open with an axe. Because Athene was not born of
a sexual union, she vowed to abstain from such union, and for this reason she
was called *Parthenos*, which means 'virgin'. But Hephaestus, who had given her
being with his axe, attempted to ravish Athene. He was so excited that his seed
made it no further than her thigh. Disgusted, she wiped it off and threw it on

the ground of the Acropolis, from which sprang a monster, half man and half snake. Athene raised this creature as her son, and he became Erichthonius, the first King of Athens.

Then Proclus would take his students to the western pediment, where a man and a woman stood in opposition, their antagonism frozen in marble. Once upon a time, he would say, Athene was in dispute with her uncle Poseidon, the god of the sea, since both of them claimed the Acropolis for their own. The wise people who lived there suggested to the gods that the dispute could be settled quite simply. 'Give us gifts,' they said, 'and the one whose gift we accept shall be our god.'

Poseidon roared his assent, and he plunged his trident into the Acropolis. The earth shook, and a spring of seawater issued forth from the rock. Athene was quiet. She bent over the ground and planted a seedling. 'Wait,' she said. And from that seedling, which was the first olive tree, issued forth oil, and food, and timber, and tinder, and all manner of useful things.

And the people of the Acropolis, being wise, chose the gift of Athene, and dedicated their city to her. Under Athene, the Athenians developed a passion for wisdom. Philosophers disputed and taught in an unbroken chain from Socrates, Plato, Aristotle, and Zeno all the way down to Proclus himself; and the grove of the Academy and the *stoai* of the market place gave their very names to concepts of learning and conduct. Sophocles, Euripides, and Aeschylus wrote their sublime tragedies for the theatre of Athens, while Aristides and Demosthenes perfected the art of rhetoric in her assembly, and Thucydides recorded their acts in his immortal history of the Peloponnesian Wars. In the bright morning of civilization, the Athenians both invented and perfected all the arts: rhetoric, politics, philosophy, drama, history, sculpture, painting, and architecture, and in doing so made their city 'the school of all Hellas'.

It was their leader, Pericles, who persuaded the Athenians to set their achievements in marble and to build a magnificent temple to Athene, so that her holy wisdom might be apprehended by the eye as well as the soul, the mind, and the ear. The temple was, like any other shrine, just a darkened chamber surrounded by a colonnade; but it possessed a splendour that set it apart from its rivals and predecessors. This splendour had nothing to do with size or expense. Rather, it resided in the proportion and the refinement of the architecture of the building, whose stones possessed the same undying youth and strength as the carved bodies that adorned it. There was not a single straight line in the temple of Wisdom. The platform upon which it stood was built very slightly convex, so that it seemed to push upwards from the earth. The columns of the peristyle were not simple cylinders, but were wider at the bottom than at the top, and subtly curved, as if they were flexing to support the architrave and the roof above them. They also lean in towards one another, so that if each column were extended upwards it would meet all the others several miles above the centre of the temple. The building was not even symmetrical, but tilted slightly towards the south, so that it might appear more imposing from the plain below the ramparts of the Acropolis.

The temple of Wisdom was no mere building. The columns that surrounded the inner sanctum were as vigorous and as beautifully proportioned as gods or heroes. Arranged in a phalanx guarding the goddess within, they were in such perfect harmony with one another that it might be said that they were themselves one body: that of the virgin Athene herself. And because the temple was the body of a divine virgin, it never aged. Plutarch saw it some five hundred years after it had been built, yet even then he was moved to write: 'There is a sort of bloom of newness upon these works ... preserving them from the touch of time, as if they had some perennial spirit and undying vitality mingled in the composition of them.'

After he had shown his students the outside of the building, Proclus would lead them into the interior, which was known as the *hekatompedon*: the

'Hundred Footer' shrine. Therein stood an image of Athene, over eighteen feet tall, made of gold and ivory. She wore a helmet, and brandished a shield and a spear, and held a winged figure of Victory in her hands.

This image of Athene, Proclus would say, was wrought by the sculptor Phidias, who was the friend of Pericles. One might imagine that, when he had finished it, he would have been honoured by the Athenians for his artistry. But instead they accused him of stealing gold from the statue. He was flung into prison, where not even his friendship with Pericles could save him, and there he died. And so Athene was ravished a second time by the very man who had made her.

After he had taken them inside the temple, Proclus would bring his students outside again, and show them the sculpted frieze that ran around the outer walls of the inner sanctum. This frieze depicted a procession of horsemen, and officials with their staffs, and women bearing jars of water and oil. At the head of this procession was a child holding up a folded gown.

Once upon a time, Proclus said, a Macedonian warlord named Demetrius Poliorcetes – 'the besieger of cities' – became the King of Athens. In order to honour him, the Athenians wove a great gown and embroidered it with scenes of all his victories. In accordance with annual custom, this gown was ceremonially carried in a procession to the Athene of Phidias. It was woven, like all the other gowns before it, by a group of young virgin women – the *parthenoi* – who inhabited their own space in the rear of the temple, a room that was named after them and the goddess they served. Now, since they had no royal palace to give him, the Athenians invited Demetrius to take up residence in this *parthenon*, the room of the virgins, so that he could be close to the goddess who now wore the gown decorated with his triumphs.

But Demetrius was a barbarian despot who had at least four wives, countless mistresses, and a sexual appetite so voracious that it was said that one young man jumped to his death in a cauldron of boiling water in order to escape his advances. And Demetrius's gown, embroidered with his own image, turned out to be a dubious gift with a blasphemous price. You can imagine the way he had with the weaving virgins and their unfortunate goddess. Demetrius didn't last long. His rival Lachares seized Athens from him, and also took up residence in the sanctuary of Athene; he stripped her image of its gold, and cut it up in order to pay his barbarous soldiers.

Athene had been ravished many times, said Proclus, but somehow she remained the virgin goddess, enshrined in her virgin temple, perfect, beautiful, and unchanging. In the nine hundred years since it had first been built, the temple itself had acquired the name of her virginity: the Parthenon. The Romans, the Herulians, and the Visigoths had done many terrible things, Proclus said. They had reduced Athens to ashes, had enslaved her citizens, and had carried off many treasures; but they had left the Parthenon intact. Nero was so captivated by the beauty of the temple that he adorned it with his name in bronze letters, and Alexander gave the temple 300 Persian shields in recompense for the 300 Hellenes who had fallen at Thermopylae. 'May it ever remain so,' Proclus would say; and he would conclude his lesson and return to his little house on the southern slope of the Acropolis, where he would meditate on the inviolate wisdom of Athene.

Then, in the year of Our Lord 391, Theodosius, the Emperor of Constantinople, sent a proclamation throughout his empire: 'No-one is to go to the sanctuaries, walk through the temples, or raise his eyes to statues created by the labour of man.' And then he had the festival days of the old pagan gods declared as work days, and the doors of the temples closed.

The Christians took possession of the temple of Wisdom, and they turned it into a church. The *parthenon*, the room of the virgins at the back of the building, became the front porch, and the *hekatompedon* the nave of the church. They blocked up the door to the *hekatompedon* and placed their altar there, and they opened a new door where Phidias's image of Athene had been, so that the faithful who entered the church now shook the dust off their sandals onto the pavement where the goddess had stood. The temple, whose doors had opened to the east so that the light of the rising sun would come through its doors, now faced in the opposite direction, so that the altar of the Christians faced the dawn. In a final irony, the Christians named their new church 'Hagia Sophia': Holy Wisdom.

Some fifty years later, the goddess of Wisdom completed the Christians' work for them. Athene appeared to Proclus in his dream and whispered an order into his ear. 'Make your house ready,' she said. 'They have turned me out of my temple, so now I come to live with you.' Proclus wept, and then he prepared himself. The goddess, it is said, went to live with him in his little house on the southern slopes of the Acropolis, and she was never seen again. Her empty image was removed from its sanctuary and shipped away to Constantinople by the emperor's agents. And so the Parthenon, whose virgin goddess had been cast out of her own sanctuary, was ruined for the first time.

Eight hundred years later, the Christian rabble of Constantinople would tear an ancient statue to pieces because they were convinced it was the habitation of a demon. It was said that this statue stood over eighteen feet tall. She wore a helmet and held a shield and spear, and a winged figure of Victory fluttered in her hands.

1687

When it was some twenty-one centuries old, the Parthenon was ruined a second time. A Holy League of Christians descended on Athens, now a city in the Ottoman Empire, and laid siege to the Acropolis. Cannonballs rained onto the marble, and smoke blackened the sky and choked the air. Terrified, the harem of the Ottoman garrison, who were trapped on the rock, gathered their children about them, and took refuge in what was now their mosque. Holed up in the shadows as the cannonade rumbled and cracked outside, the women told their children stories to reassure them.

One woman recounted tales from the Turkish traveller Evliya Çelebi. This mosque had been built as a *madrassa* by the wise man Plato many thousands of years ago, she said, and he had delivered his lectures from the throne now used by the imam at prayer time. He had dwelt here with the goddess Athene, to whom he used to pray for wisdom. The mosque had been standing here for many thousands of years, the woman told her children, and it was not about to fall down now.

This Plato had constructed the *mihrab*, the niche pointing towards Mecca, in sheets of alabaster which glowed even now in the darkness of the bombardment. The women pointed at the niche: 'See, it glows still: Allah has not deserted us yet.' Plato had taken the bronze gates of Troy, and had made them into the doors of his Academy. 'The gates of Troy, which were never breached except by treachery, will keep us safe and sound,' said the women.

A Christian woman of the harem recounted tales from another traveller, the Italian Niccolo Martoni. Plato had lived long before the time of Jesus, let alone the Prophet Muhammad, she said, and in those days many came to study the arts of wisdom in this building. One day, a young student called Dionysius was standing in the porch when the sky went dark and the earth began to tremble. This young Dionysius felt that some event of great significance was happening. Something moved him, and he turned to the mighty column next to which he was standing. With his knife, he carved an emblem on to the marble: a cross. And the day on which he carved it, the Christian woman of the harem said, was the very day on which Jesus Christ was crucified for all our sins; and she crossed herself.

Later, when the Christians came and converted the building into a church, they repeated the little vandalism of Dionysius again and again. They worked their way round the friezes of sculpture, and they hacked off the heads and faces of the horsemen, the officials, the women bearing jars of oil and water, and the small child who carried the sacred gown: these were pagan idols, and the habitation of demons. Just one sculpture – a pair of robed women, one seated and one standing – was left alone by the Christians, because they imagined that it represented the Annunciation. Centuries passed, and every passing archbishop cut his name into the marble walls, just as Dionysius had once carved a cross. In those days, the woman said, this darkened hall had been gorgeous with golden mosaic, clouded with incense, ringing with bells and chanting. There had been an ikon of Our Lady that had been painted from life by St Luke himself, a copy of the gospels that had been transcribed by St Helena, the head of St Makarios, the arms of St Dionysios, St Cyprian, and St Justin, and the elbow of St Maccabeus.

When the Christian woman had finished speaking, her Muslim sister picked up the story. Not so very long ago, she said, when the Roman Empire of the Christians finally fell to the forces of the Prophet, the church had been turned into a mosque. The Sultan Mehmet had come to see the place, and had marvelled at its beauty. As the Christians had done before them, the people of the Prophet excised from their temple the idolatrous images they found, and the gruesome frescoes of the Last Judgement disappeared under whitewash. There was one image that they did not dare to remove, a mosaic of the Virgin Mary in the vault of the *mihrab*. Once upon a time a soldier had taken a shot at it, and the Virgin Mary had withered his arm away in punishment; so despite the disapproval of the authorities, the ikon was allowed to remain.

Even though the virgin goddess of wisdom who held a winged Victory in her hand had been cast out of the Parthenon many centuries before, something of her spirit remained in the mosque on the Acropolis with its ikon of the Virgin, once the church of Holy Wisdom. Because this was so, the women and children thought the spirit of the Parthenon would protect them, and they stayed in the shadows, telling their stories. And because he listened to their stories, the commander of the garrison decided to store not only his wives and his children in the building, but also a great magazine of gunpowder.

The forces of the Holy League shelled the Ottoman position for three days, but the Acropolis held out; it seemed to be as invulnerable as the women and the children and the commander had imagined. Then, on the third day, an Ottoman deserter told the gunners that there was a store of gunpowder hidden inside the ancient mosque.

They took aim.

The explosion shook the earth. The middle of the mosque blew apart, and the columns of the northern and southern colonnades were flattened. Sharp shards of white marble fell on the hills a mile away from the Acropolis. A fire raged for two days, and nearly all the people who had taken refuge in the building perished.

The general commander of the Holy League, Francesco Morosini, sent a terse report back to the Senate in Venice. 'A fortunate shot reached a depot containing a considerable quantity of powder,' he wrote. 'It was impossible to extinguish the flames.'

The Ottoman forces surrendered, and Morosini made his way up to the smoking ruin of which he was now the master. His men set up ropes and pulleys and they climbed up the face of the building towards the pediment, where the images of Athene and Poseidon were locked in their ancient contest for the suzerainity of Athens. The soldiers were going to do what the Venetians always did: take the statues down and bring them back to Venice, to adorn the piazzas and palaces of their robber republic. But the pulleys came free of their housings and the ropes snapped, and Athene and Poseidon crashed to the ground and smashed to pieces. Morosini walked away from the ruin, and it was returned to the Ottomans about a year later. Other things were more important to the Holy League than a derelict mosque.

And so the Parthenon, whose virgin goddess had been cast out and whose usefulness as a building had come to an abrupt end, was ruined a second time. There was one survivor. It is said that when the troops of the Holy League walked up to the remains of the Parthenon, a young virgin girl walked out of the ruins. It is not recorded what they did with her.

1816

When the Parthenon was in the twenty-third century of its existence, it was ruined a third time. The House of Lords sat in Parliament in the Palace of Westminster in London, and before them lay the *Petition of the Earl of Elgin, Respecting his Collection of Marbles*. Before them, indeed, stood the Earl of Elgin himself.

In his garden shed in London's Park Lane was a jumbled heap of broken images. Once upon a time they had been beautiful and perfect and whole, but now their noses (and their heads and their hands and their feet) were missing. They were cracked and scarred and worn down by time, and so was Lord Elgin. He stood before his peers and told them his story.

Once upon a time, he said, he had been young, and – as all young *milordi* should – he thirsted for improvement and politeness, beauty and truth. To learn the art of warfare he studied his Herodotus and his Thucydides, for statesmanship he read his Plutarch, for wisdom his Plato and his Aristotle, and for feeling his Euripides and his Aeschylus.

Lord Elgin knew all about the Parthenon. The modern publications that made their way to his library showed him just how perfect the Parthenon actually was. Stuart and Revett's *Antiquities of Athens*, the result of much scholarly measuring and excavation, illustrated the temple in a state of completeness. Pale aquatints showed the severe colonnade of eight Doric columns at each end, surmounted by an architrave and a pediment filled with the magnificent marble bodies of the ancient Athenians frozen in time. Stuart and Revett's seductive topographical views of Athens recalled to his mind the pleasing prospect of Edinburgh Castle viewed over the Firth of Forth at sunset.

Just as Thucydides had once predicted, Lord Elgin was convinced that Athens had been mistress of a greater empire than it ever had been; and he hoped that one day his own nation would come to equal, if not surpass, the greatness of that empire. He dreamt of Scotland – North Britain, he called it – as a new Hellas, and of Edinburgh as a new Athens of the North. When he was made ambassador to the court of the sultan in Constantinople he saw himself as a modern Alcibiades, called to foreign climes in the service of a country about to taste greatness.

On his way to Constantinople, Lord Elgin collected an entourage. There was Giambattista Lusieri, a landscape painter; Feodor Ivanovitch, a Tartar freedman whose talent for figure drawing had much distinguished him at Baden Baden; and two architectural draftsmen and two moulders of casts. He engaged these artificers to measure, to draw, and to make plaster copies of the antiquities of Athens, with a view to assembling a collection of sculptures, drawings, and casts that would be beneficial to the fine arts of Great Britain.

Lord Elgin and his entourage disembarked in 1800, but the Athens they found was not the imperial capital for which they had hoped. The decrepit market town was ruled over by a provincial governor of the Ottoman sultan. The Parthenon, meanwhile, lay under the jurisdiction of the commandant of the Acropolis, which was then a fortress no less barbarous than those of Lord Elgin's homeland.

These Turks did not appreciate the significance of the ruins which lay all around them. They treated the Parthenon more like a quarry than a building, collecting the fragments of marble and grinding them down into a dust which they used to make lime mortar. They broke the stones into small pieces for the maze of garden walls and cottages that covered the Acropolis.

But to Lord Elgin's horror, the British dilettanti resident in Athens were no more reverent in their attitude towards the Parthenon than their Ottoman hosts. One of them, John Bacon Sawry Morritt, wryly observed:

> It is very pleasant to walk the streets here. Over almost every door is an antique statue or basso-relievo, more or less good though all much broken, so that you are in a perfect gallery of marbles in these lands. Some we steal, some we buy ... We have just breakfasted, and are meditating a walk to the citadel, where our Greek attendant is gone to meet the workmen, and is, I hope, hammering down the Centaurs and Lapiths [from the frieze of the Parthenon] ... Nothing like making hay when the sun shines, and when the commandant has felt the pleasure of having our sequins for a few days, I think we shall bargain for a good deal of the old temple.

He wasn't the only one thus occupied. Just as Morritt was filching what he could, Louis Fauvel, the agent of the French ambassador to the Ottoman court, received his instructions: 'Take away everything that you can. Do not neglect any opportunity to remove everything in Athens and its neighbourhood that is removable.'

If Elgin was to 'improve the arts of Great Britain', speed was of the utmost necessity, since Napoleon's agents had exactly the same idea in respect of their own nation. Lord Elgin left his entourage behind in Athens and sailed on to Constantinople, hoping that he could persuade the sultan and the grand vizier to stop the French in their tracks.

He didn't have to wait long. Napoleon was roundly defeated by the British in Egypt, and the grand vizier saw which way history was turning. On 22 July

1801 a directive from the court of the sultan appeared in Athens. The vizier's letter ordered the commandant of the Acropolis to allow Elgin's men:

1. To enter freely within the walls of the citadel, and to draw and model with plaster the ancient temples there.
2. To erect scaffolding and to dig where they may wish to discover the ancient foundations.
3. Liberty to take away any sculpture or inscriptions which do not interfere with the works or walls of the citadel.

Fourteen years later, some several hundred pieces of the Parthenon – the frieze of the procession of the gown, the pedimental sculptures of Athene and Poseidon and all the gods, the Lapiths and the Centaurs, and even a capital of the colonnade – were safe in London, rescued from the Turks, the dilettanti, and the French.

These sculptures had been prised off what was left of the Parthenon, dug up from the ground about it, and extracted from the cottages of the feckless peasants who still inhabited the site. They had been packed into crates and loaded onto ships. Some of the ships were captured in war, and the sculptures had to be recovered from the enemy; others of them sank, and the sculptures were salvaged from the bottom of the sea. On their journey, these marbles attracted wonder, veneration, and envy. In Rome, Lord Elgin asked the sculptor Canova to restore the statues, but the artist refused, saying that it would be blasphemy to take his chisel to that which the hand of Phidias had touched.

Now the Parthenon lay in a shed in a back garden in Park Lane, and presiding over it was a man as broken as the marbles he possessed. Lord Elgin's term as ambassador was over. He had barely made it home: he had been taken prisoner while travelling in France, and had languished there for three years before being allowed to return to Britain. His coffers were empty. His very body had come to resemble the violated perfection of his marbles, since he had contracted an infection in Constantinople and, like a classical statue, had lost his nose. Elgin had only one hope of restoring his lost fortunes: he would have to sell his marbles. But he was keen to stress to his peers that this was not for wanton gain, and he concluded his petition *Respecting his Collection of Marbles* with a noble if self-serving statement:

> In amassing these remains of antiquity for the benefit of my Country; and in rescuing them from the imminent and unavoidable destruction with which they were threatened, had they been left many years longer the prey of mischievous Turks, who mutilated them for wanton amusement, or for the purpose of selling them piecemeal to passing travellers; I have been actuated by no motives of private emolument.

The Lords and their advisors were not impressed. Richard Payne Knight, a connoisseur of the Society of Dilettanti and founder of the British Museum, listened to his story and replied: 'You have lost your labour, my Lord Elgin. Your marbles are overrated: they are not Greek, they are Roman, of the time of Hadrian.' The refined *milordi* and the dilettanti of Great Britain were not used to gazing upon broken fragments of marble, pitted with shrapnel wounds and worn away by the wind and the rain. This heap of stones represented not an improvement of the arts of Great Britain to them, but a fool's errand.

There were some who were horrified by the way in which Elgin's men had destroyed what was left of the unity of the Parthenon to amass this pile of stones. His peer Lord Byron included a devastating attack on Lord Elgin in his poem *Childe Harold*:

> *Cold is the heart, fair Greece! that looks on thee,*
> *Nor feels as lovers o'er the dust they lov'd;*

Dull is the eye that will not weep to see

Thy walls defac'd, thy mouldering shrines remov'd

By British hands, which it had best behov'd

To guard those relics ne'er to be restor'd.

Curst be the hour when from their isle they rov'd,

And once again thy hopeless bosom gor'd,

And snatch'd thy shrinking Gods to northern climes abhorr'd.

And he argued that the Parthenon should be allowed to crumble away in the place where it had always stood.

When Lord Elgin went before the House of Lords, he offered his marbles to the nation for the sum of £62,440. The Lords laughed in his face, and proposed to give him less than half that sum. Lord Elgin appeared before them a second time, and then the House of Lords ordered that he be paid £35,000 for his trouble. Elgin, deeply disappointed, had no choice but to accept.

In that year of 1816, the Elgin marbles were moved into the British Museum, and there they remain. They are now entombed in the Duveen gallery, built especially for them in the 1930s. The gallery inverts the original arrangement of the sculptures, so that the frieze and the pedimental statuary face inwards towards a toplit room, rather than outwards towards the dazzling marble plateau of the Acropolis. Mutilated, perching on plinths in the gloomy London light, the Elgin marbles confront us at eye height, simultaneously impressive and tragic.

Other pieces of the Parthenon were scattered all over Europe. There are two heads in Copenhagen that fit onto bodies that are now in the British Museum, and there is another one in Würzburg, in Germany. There are pieces in the Vatican, in Vienna, Munich, and Palermo. There are fragments in the Louvre, collected by the defeated and disgraced French from Lord Elgin's leavings. There are, of course, a few pieces left in Athens, not many of those actually fixed to what had once been the Parthenon.

Six years after he had sold his collection, the noseless Lord Elgin was once again in Athens, facing the Parthenon. Or, rather, he was in Edinburgh, the Athens of the North, facing what he hoped would become the Parthenon. A monument to the fallen of the Napoleonic wars had been proposed several years before, and this monument was, at the behest of Lord Elgin and his friends, to take the exact form of the Parthenon. The whole thing was to be constructed for £42,000 – only £7000 more than the House of Lords had paid for the sculptures that had adorned the original. Even so, the committee managed to raise only £16,000 for the project, and so the ten columns of the partially constructed Edinburgh Parthenon stand like a ruin in anticipation. Ever since work stopped in 1830 they have been known as 'Edinburgh's Disgrace'.

So Lord Elgin, the man who had pulled apart the original Parthenon, now presided over the broken ruin of a replica. His disgrace was complete. He retired to his estates with a substantial collection of plaster casts, and what had once been the temple of Wisdom he pondered in its fragmented, chalky derivative. The Parthenon, whose virgin goddess had been cast out, which had ceased to be useful as a building, and whose very stones had been scattered to the ends of the earth, had been ruined a third time.

1834

When the Parthenon was 2267 years old, it was ruined for a fourth time. The new king of a new nation ascended the Acropolis to survey the treasures of which he was now the master. Otto Von Wittelsbach was the ruler of a country which had never existed before. It had taken fourteen years of war for Greece to come into being, and in that war the ruins of the Parthenon had acquired the status of a talisman for a nation born of ancient nostalgia. The Acropolis was besieged twice during those fourteen years; and it is said that during one siege the Turks, searching for iron to make bullets, started to break open the remaining marbles of the temple, hoping to find the metal cramps with which ancients had bound the stones of the building together. The Greeks were so horrified at this violation that they sent their enemies a consignment of ammunition, so that they could continue the battle without despoiling the building.

Once the country was free, the Greeks cast around them for a king. They found one in a younger son of the house of Bavaria, and a queen in his wife, the Princess Amalia. Since there was no royal palace in Athens, many debates were held about how King Otto and Queen Amalia might live in the state befitting crowned heads of Europe. Perhaps inevitably, they cast their eyes up to the ruined Parthenon; and, perhaps inevitably, the German king turned to an architect of his own race to provide him with all the comforts of home.

Karl Friedrich Schinkel was the court architect of Prussia. He did not visit the Parthenon before designing his palace. He had already seen the stones of the Parthenon in London, and he had seen that aborted reconstruction in Edinburgh. He had studied his Stuart and Revett, and he had read his classics. He knew all about the Parthenon. Indeed, Schinkel had already built a Parthenon or two at home in Prussia: a guardhouse on Unter den Linden in Berlin, the tomb of a Hohenzollern princess at Charlottenburg, a royal retreat for the Crown Prince of Prussia at Sans Souci. All of them were built in the Doric order of the temple of Wisdom.

Schinkel's design for the Acropolis was to transform the decrepit remnants of the Ottoman garrison into a grandiose palace. The ancient gateway was to be restored; just as it had done once upon a time, it was to lead to a gigantic statue of Athene. Next there would be a forecourt in the form of a hippodrome, and then the palace itself would unfold: a filigree Alhambra of courtyards and colonnades and fountains, where the king and his Queen

Amalia, who loved roses, could walk in the shade and look out over the ramparts at the barren plains of their alien kingdom. Schinkel's palace was a bold appropriation of a remnant of ancient Greece in the service of the modern nation. Still, just as his contemporary, the great Canova, had refused to raise his chisel against the marble that Phidias had touched, Schinkel's design left the stones of the Parthenon itself untouched: an ancient jewel in a modern setting.

But Schinkel was not the only German architect with an interest in the Parthenon. The court architect of Bavaria, like Schinkel, had built a few himself. When, after the defeat of Napoleon, the King of Bavaria wanted to honour the fallen heroes of his country with a monument, he commissioned Leo von Klenze; and von Klenze, like the citizens of Edinburgh, knew exactly where to turn for a model. His Parthenon, the Valhalla, was set on a series of terraces above the river Danube at Regensburg. Within it, the heroes of the Bavarian – and then the German – nation are immortalized in marble. (A committee still sits to decide who will join the exalted ranks in the Valhalla; one of the latest additions was Sophie Scholl, the young woman who resisted Hitler and paid for it with her life.)

Because of his Bavarian connections, von Klenze had access to the court of King Otto, and he dismissed Schinkel's proposed palace with faint praise as 'a charming midsummer night's dream'. So in 1834, when Otto ascended the Acropolis, it was not to lay the cornerstone of a new *Residenz* or, indeed, to do anything new at all. Unlike Demetrius Poliorcetes, the Emperor Theodosius, the Holy League, or the armies of Sultan Mehmet II, King Otto came to bring the repeated violations of the Parthenon to an end.

The whole event had been designed by von Klenze. The king was, naturally, trussed up in all the uncomfortable corsetry and frogging of his rank; but his people, the maidens and the youths of Athens, were dressed in the simple robes of their ancestors and carried branches of myrtle. The king sat in front of the Parthenon in all his finery, and Leo von Klenze ascended a rostrum. He spoke in German:

> Your majesty stepped today, after so many centuries of barbarism, for the first time on this celebrated Acropolis, proceeding on the road of civilization and glory, on the road passed upon by the like of Themistocles, Aristides, Cimon and Pericles, and this is, and should be, in the eyes of your people, the symbol of your glorious reign ... All the remains of barbarity will be removed ... and the remains of the glorious past will be revealed in a new light, as the foundations of a glorious present and future.

Ever since, the Acropolis has been the ground upon which the consequences of von Klenze's plan have been played out – in constructions, reconstructions, demolitions, legal cases, learned papers, and diplomatic missions. Generation by generation, on behalf of the modern nation of Greece and in memory of the Athens of Athene, people have attempted to put the Parthenon back together again: to make it whole and perfect, like a virgin.

The first fifty years of this process involved the eradication of all of those 'remains of barbarity' that had sullied the Parthenon since classical times. The guards were expelled from the little building that stood on the marble pavement of the Parthenon, and the cottages and gardens and the harem of the Turks were all demolished. When these were gone, the remains of more ancient violations were also removed. The ruins of the minaret of the Ottoman mosque, which had once been the bell tower of the church of Holy Wisdom, were taken down; and with them went the apse of the church, which had once been imagined to be the ancient throne of Plato.

Then the very ground itself was excavated. Until the 1830s the Acropolis was covered in gardens, though now it is almost impossible to imagine anything growing on the bare rock scattered with broken columns and pieces of cornice. Underneath the Turkish village the Byzantine citadel was brought to light, and under that the Roman sanctuary, and under that the pavement once trod by Pericles and Phidias. By removing her history from her, the archaeologists attempted to restore the virginity of the Parthenon.

In 1894, when they had barely finished, there was a terrible earthquake, and the marble columns of the Parthenon were thrown to the ground. And when they had surveyed the ruins of the ruins, the archaeologists started to restore the virginity of the Parthenon all over again. They collected the pieces of architrave, the fluted column drums, and the capitals that lay around the remains of the Parthenon – those stones that had survived barbarian sack, Christian and Muslim iconoclasm, explosion, the lime kiln, and expropriation to the museum halls of northern Europe; and with this jumbled heap of broken fragments they set to work. Column drum was placed upon column drum, and then capital, architrave, metope, triglyph, and cornice.

By the end of the 1920s the peristyle of the Parthenon was almost complete. What was more, this had largely been achieved without resorting to adding new building material. The stones of the Parthenon were, it could truly be said, the same ones that had been touched by the hand of Phidias and gazed upon by the eye of Pericles. Nikolaos Balanos, the Director of Antiquities, could justifiably claim to have restored the Parthenon to a state of integrity that it had not enjoyed since the explosion of 1687.

But when the workmen undertook the restoration of the building, they forgot, or ignored, quite how perfect it had been, once upon a time. The Parthenon in her virginity had never been a mere building, but a body as refined, as whole, as strong, and as flexible as the bodies of the heroes whose divine struggle once ornamented her skin. Her refinements were almost imperceptible to the naked eye, but their consequence is that each and every stone in the Parthenon could have only one home: no stone will fit precisely into any place other than that which had been intended for it by Phidias himself.

As they laboured over their heap of broken fragments in the heat of the day, the restorers of the Parthenon had forgotten these things. Their rebuilt Parthenon might have looked very like the original Parthenon, but it was not perfect; and because it was not perfect, it was not the Parthenon.

The Present

In 1975, a group of archaeologists, conservationists, and technologists met in Athens. Above their seminar room the remains of the Parthenon were crumbling as fast as the meeting could deliberate. There was not much time.

Lord Byron had wished that Lord Elgin would leave the Parthenon alone and allow it to dissolve into the rain and the air. His wish was coming true. Athens, which was once a village on the Acropolis, now stretched from Pentelikon, where the marble that built the Parthenon had been quarried, to Piraeus, from which its sculptures had been shipped to London. Traffic fumes choked the vast city and poisoned the rain that fell on the temple. The fragments of the restored Parthenon were held together by iron clamps that had been inserted into the columns. Before long, the iron began to rust in the poisoned air; and as it did so, it expanded. As it expanded it cracked the white marble that contained it, and shards fell away from the substance of the building. Dark red stains dribbled down a surface that had once dazzled in the antique air. The restoration of the Parthenon threatened, quite literally, to tear the building apart. Furthermore, the marble was being turned by the rain into gypsum, molecule by molecule. The ruins of the Parthenon were turning into the same plaster in which it had been cast by its eighteenth-century admirers; and then was quite simply being washed away.

The committee listened to proposals to remove the remains altogether and replace them with a fibreglass replica. They discussed banning traffic around the ancient site, and heard arguments for encasing the whole building in a gigantic bubble. They debated doing nothing and letting the Parthenon dissolve into the air. They argued over the possibility of rebuilding it from scratch.

But after eleven years of deliberation, they decided to ruin the Parthenon – at least temporarily, and very, very carefully. Work is expected to be complete in 2010, 24 years after it began, and 2443 years after the Parthenon had first been brought into being. Each and every block of marble is being removed from its location. The iron clamps are being extracted from each one; and they are being replaced, appropriately for a virgin temple, with titanium, a metal known for its incorruptibility. Then each and every block is being measured and analysed, in order to uncover, if possible, the secret of its original location. Very slowly, this puzzle is being resolved, and where it is possible these stones are being returned to the places intended for them by their creators.

But at the same time all the sculptures that remain on the Parthenon have been removed to a new purpose-built museum at the foot of the Acropolis, a tomb where age and air shall not wither them. At the heart of the museum, the celebrated French architect Bernard Tschumi has designed a great glass atrium whose size and proportions exactly match those of the virgin temple. This phantom Parthenon remains empty, for it has been designed to receive all those sculptures in foreign captivity – in London, Paris, Palermo, Würzburg, Vienna – should they ever return to the city that made them. Then, perhaps, Holy Wisdom will herself return to her house.

Every time the Parthenon is ruined, it takes a little longer to rebuild it, and the task becomes a little more difficult. This time it will have taken twice as long to ruin and rebuild the Parthenon as did to build it in the first place.

One day, all that will be left of the Parthenon will be fragments imprisoned in museums; copies by the banks of the Mississippi, the Kelaniya, the Thames, the Spree, the Forth, or the Danube; the drawings of Stuart and Revett; millions of fading photographs; and hundreds of written eulogies, from Thucydides's to this one.

Then, liberated from physical being, the Parthenon will have become nothing but an idea, and at last it will be perfect.

THE BASILICA OF SAN MARCO, VENICE

In Which a Prince Steals Four Horses and an Empire

A STAGING POST FOR FOUR HORSES.
The Hippodrome in Constantinople.

Theft

*T*he Parthenon is a ruin because pieces of it were removed, leaving nothing behind them but a fading dream of perfection. Liberated from the building for which they had been made, these fragments of the Parthenon were set to purposes for which they had never been designed. They became building materials for peasants, booty for soldiers, and art for dilettanti; but at the same time, they still carried something of the aura of their sacred origin. That was why they had been stolen in the first place.

The 'Dark Ages' – the centuries between the end of antiquity and the resurgence of Western Europe in the Renaissance – have often been imagined as an era of ignorance and vandalism. Their darkness is depicted in the silhouette of cathedral and forest that separates the architect from his vision of classical perfection in The Architect's Dream.

But the Dark Ages form our only link with classical antiquity. What their inhabitants chose to preserve (and what to destroy) of their own inheritance has determined ours, centuries later. The 'barbarians' of the Dark Ages were the capricious curators of a museum whose meaning we shall never fully understand.

The theft and reuse of antique fragments was a common practice in an age littered *with the remains of a culture that it lacked the capability to imitate or surpass. The people of the Dark Ages imagined that the buildings of antiquity had been built by giants, and that the bronze images of gods and emperors that adorned them were the habitation of demons. They believed that the fragments they stole would lend the creations to which they fixed them something of the authority of a lost past.*

So while the barbarians vandalized a great many antique buildings, they also created wonderful creatures out of their transfigured remains. Of nowhere is this truer than Venice, which, floating on water, had no architecture to call its own. In order to acquire one, the Venetians stole those of others, in particular the architecture of Constantinople.

Venice is a transfigured Constantinople; but Constantinople was a transfigured Rome once upon a time, and Rome was a transfigured Greece before that. The cycle of theft and the chain of borrowed authority goes back to a time of myth, from which, perhaps, all civilizations seek their ultimate source of authority.

IN THE SEVENTH YEAR OF THE REVOLUTION, THERE WAS A TRIUMPH IN the capital of the republic. The procession wound its way through the streets from the city gate to the Field of Mars, where the spoils of victory were dedicated in the temple of the Fatherland.

This was no ordinary triumph. There were no slaves, no barbarian chieftains, no cartloads of bronze armour or weaponry. Instead, the crowd was treated to the spectacle of camels, lions, and giraffes in cages, palm trees and other exotic plants in pots, and a collection of strangely shaped packing cases shrouded in dust sheets. There were few soldiers in evidence, and no laurelled general led the procession standing in his chariot. Instead, his place was taken by a magnificent group of four horses.

Their manes and their tails were stiffly combed, their legs were raised in the posture of a dignified walk, and their heads were turned towards one another as if they were engaged in noble equestrian discourse. But their attitudes were fixed and their skin flashed gold and green in the sun: they were not living horses, but statues cast in bronze. After their dedication, the bronze horses, the lions, the camels and the giraffes, the potted palms and the packing cases shrouded in dust sheets were taken to the treasure house of the republic.

As the procession passed them by, the mob shouted out the paean they had been taught to cry: 'Rome is no longer in Rome. It is all in Paris!' For in 1798 Rome was no longer the seat of triumph, nor had it been for very many centuries; and the treasure house to which the spoils of triumph were taken was the national museum of the republic, the Louvre. The spoils of triumph rolled into the courtyard; the packing crates were carried up the grand stairs and deposited in the Grande Galerie, where they were unwrapped in front of the impatient deputies of the people. From one crate, a clawing marble hand emerged, then an arm, and then a bearded face contorted with pain. As the boards fell away, Laocöon burst into view, knotted together with his sons in the fatal embrace of a serpent. The rough timbers of another crate were cracked open to reveal the smooth arrogance of the Apollo Belvedere. A dust sheet withdrawn unveiled the simple modesty of Raphael's Sistine Madonna, whose bored attendant cherubs gazed dispassionately at their new owners. A vast cloth fell to the floor at the foot of a sumptuous banqueting table at which, painted by the hand of Paolo Veronese, Christ attended the Marriage of Cana. One chest concealed the golden hoard of Bellini's Madonna di San Zaccaria, attended by solemn saints in her niche of gilded mosaic, while another was smashed open to reveal an enormous winged lion of bronze, holding a book in his outstretched paw.

Gathered in the grand gallery of the Louvre were the treasures of Roman and Venetian art. The bronze lion was the Lion of St Mark, the paintings the finest ornaments of the monasteries, the churches, and even the main council chamber of Venice. The Sistine Madonna had lately hung in the chapel of the Pope in Rome, while Laocöon and Apollo had stood in the endless galleries of the Vatican. In the republic whose motto was 'Liberty, Equality, Fraternity', the emblems of triumph were not slaves, nor piles of gold, nor martial trophies, but works of art, placed on display in a museum for the admiration of the people.

An arch was erected opposite the Louvre in the Place du Carousel. The four bronze horses who had led the triumph were provided with a bronze chariot, and then they were placed on top of the arch, in memory of the occasion.

✳ ✳ ✳

It had all happened before: as the triumphant French well knew, the bronze horses had presided over triumphs in the capital city of another republic for nearly six hundred years. Every year on Ascension Day the Doge would go from his palace to the basilica of San Marco, which was his chapel and the treasure house of his republic, to celebrate the triumph of Venice. He would kneel before the Pala d'Oro, an altarpiece studded with gems and glistering with gold, beneath which were buried the wonder-working relics of St Mark the Evangelist himself. Above the Doge's head hung five domes arranged in a Greek cross. They were covered in mosaics that, sparkling in the twilight, narrated the story of the republic and the saints and the angels that guarded it.

Then the trumpets would sound, and the Doge would emerge from the darkness of San Marco into the sunlit piazza outside. He would process down to the water between two granite columns, on top of which were mounted the two patron saints of Venice: St Theodore standing on his crocodile, and St Mark represented in the form of a winged lion. The Doge would board his ceremonial barge, the *Bucintoro*; and he would sail through the lagoon and out to the open sea, where he would cast a golden ring into the water to reconsecrate the marriage of Venice to that element.

Having consummated the union, the Doge would return to San Marco and stand on a balcony over the basilica's west doors. Above him were gilded kiosks crowded with countless carved saints; beneath, an arcade lined with sheets of precious green and red marble, set here and there with sculptures of Hercules and the Caesars of old. And from the very heart of this façade, below the saints and above the basilica's central door, rode forth the four bronze horses. Standing between them as if he were driving their chariot, the Doge would review his citizens as they processed round and round the piazza below him. Dressed in a golden mantle and holding the insignia of his office, he was frozen in an attitude as rigid and regal as that of an oriental emperor.

✶ ✶ ✶

It had all happened before, of course, or at least that's what the Venetians told their new French masters in 1798. The four bronze horses – and the gem-studded ikons of the Pala d'Oro, and the winged lion – had presided over triumphs in the capital city of yet another republic for eight hundred years. On the anniversary of the foundation of that city, the emperor would open a door between the Sacred Palace and the Hippodrome; and with his train of *magistri*, proconsuls, senators, priests, and relics, he would appear in gorgeous array in the imperial box before the citizens of Constantinople.

The Hippodrome was some 1500 feet long, an elongated bowl of stone seats that, on those days, might be filled with 100,000 people. A raised barrier, the *spina*, ran down the middle of the Hippodrome, dividing it into two tracks. At one end the starting gates resembled a triumphal arch, while at the other end the track was curved to allow racing chariots to wheel round an obelisk.

The primary purpose of the Hippodrome was chariot racing, but it was more than a mere sporting arena. The Blues and Greens, which had started out as two different racing teams, had over time become powerful political factions that could bring the whole empire to its knees. The *Milion*, the pavilion from which all distances in the empire were measured, stood right by the gates where the chariots started their races.

The Hippodrome was also the treasure house of the empire. The *spina* and the starting gates were mounted with two obelisks and a whole menagerie of statuary: sphinxes, a column of brazen snakes twisted round one another, a colossal Hercules in bronze, an elephant wrought in the same material, a Nile horse with a scaly tail, a beautiful Helen of Troy, a she-wolf suckling Romulus and Remus, and many more besides. Among them were at least three – and perhaps more – *quadrigae* of bronze horses, with another coupled to a gilded chariot that was kept inside the *Milion*.

On the day of triumph this gilded chariot would be coupled to a foursome of live horses, and a golden statue would be placed inside. This statue showed Constantine, the founder of the city, dressed as Apollo the Sun God and holding in his hand a little angel: the guardian spirit of the city. The divine founder was carried around the Hippodrome in his chariot, while the reigning emperor, dressed in gold and standing perfectly still, watched the ritual from his royal box. His attendant priests clouded him in incense and bells as if he were Jupiter the Best and Greatest himself.

* * *

It had all happened before, for the *quadrigae* of the Hippodrome – and the bronze Hercules, and Romulus and Remus, and many other creatures of the Hippodrome's menagerie – had presided over triumphs in the capital of still another republic for four hundred years. That's what the citizens of Constantinople said, anyway, and the Venetians were only too willing to believe them.

Whenever a general – an *imperator* – achieved a particularly important victory against the barbarians, the Senate and the People would grant him a triumph, and at the head of his army he would enter the city of Rome. All of these triumphs followed the route of the *Via Sacra*, the holy way that led into the city from the south: past the Colosseum, along the foot of the Palatine Hill, through the Forum, and up under the Tarpeian rock to the Capitoline

Hill, which was crowned with the temple of Jupiter Optimus Maximus, the Best and Greatest. It was to Jupiter that the shackled barbarians would be brought, so that the proper sacrifices might be made: of their treasures in the temple, their families in the slave market, and their lives in the circus. Jupiter's temple was hung with the chains of captives, the broken gates of cities, and the truncated deities of defeated republics.

After they had celebrated each triumph, the *imperatores* of Rome would erect an arch over the *Via Sacra* so that their victories might be remembered. The arches looked like gaudy city gates, framed with Corinthian columns, bedecked with winged victories, and carved with reliefs and inscriptions depicting the exploits of the generals. (Some of those memorials still stand in Rome to this day: the Arch of Constantine records his victory at the Battle of the Milvian Bridge, while the Arch of Titus depicts with casual pride the sack of the Temple of Jerusalem.) Because the generals had entered the city in chariots, each of their arches was surmounted by a sculpture of horses drawing just such a vehicle. There must have been hundreds of these *quadrigae*.

Then the *imperatores* of Rome had their images stamped on coins and carved in marble. They had the sculptors twist their bull necks into the postures of Grecian heroes, lift their dull eyes as if in divine contemplation, and cover their shaven heads in curly wigs – tousled, they hoped, by the winds of history.

✳ ✳ ✳

It had all happened before. The Venetians, the Constantinopolitans, and the Romans all used to tell a story about the origin of their *quadriga*; or, at least, they dimly remembered the last time these horses had run with heroes.

When he was young, and before all his triumphs, Alexander loved horses. Indeed, he came of a royal line that loved them. One day, his father Philip showed Alexander a horse running wild on the plain.

'No-one can tame this horse,' said the king to his son.

'I shall,' said Alexander.

'Well, if you can, you can keep him,' his father replied.

And so Alexander went out into the field. He walked up to the horse, and whispered in its ear, and stroked its neck; and to the amazement of the royal court, Alexander mounted the steed, and rode up to his father as if it were the most natural thing in the world. Alexander named the horse Bucephalus, and the steed became his constant companion, down through the narrow mountain passes into Greece, through the plains of Asia Minor, the deserts of Syria and Egypt, the marshes of Mesopotamia, and the hills of Persia, all the way to the jungles of India.

When Alexander had conquered the world, he had his portrait taken by the sculptor Lysippus. This Lysippus was skilled in marble and in bronze, and was commissioned to undertake many works, including several *quadrigae*. The Venetians said – and they must have heard it from the Constantinopolitans, and they from the Romans – that their *quadriga* was among them.

Lysippus was skilled in bronze, but more skilled still in transforming the likeness of the barbarian prince into something transcendent and beautiful. Upon seeing his work, Alexander refused to have his portrait made by any other. United in Lysippus's image of Alexander were both the wild youth, who had conquered Bucephalus and then the world, and the philosopher king, the pupil of Aristotle and the sages of India. Alexander's head twisting in warlike action called to mind Achilles as he dragged the body of Hector around the walls of Troy; and his thoughtful eyes were those of Apollo as he rode through the sky in the chariot of the sun, heading to his home with the muses on Mount Parnassus.

Apollo's home – the sanctuary at Delphi on Mount Parnassus – housed both the oracle of the god and a bewildering array of votive gifts that had been given to him in gratitude, supplication, or fear. Before Apollo's temple stood a column of three twisted snakes, given to him by all the Greeks in thanksgiving for their victory over the Persians at the Battle of Plataea; it had been cast from the armour and weapons stripped from that vanquished Asiatic horde. Beneath the temple was a mysterious cave that spewed forth noxious vapours, under whose influence the priestesses of the sanctuary spoke with the voice of the god. The cave had been stolen, the legend ran, by Apollo from a serpent who had dwelt there since the beginning of the world. It is in such dark caves, filled with poisonous smoke, that myths and legends find their origin.

There were also games held at the sanctuary of Delphi; and just as cities victorious in war gave images to Apollo, so did the athletes and the charioteers who competed in the stadium. There is only one of these images left: a tall, slim charioteer cast in bronze, who stands with his hands outstretched and his reins in his hands. His horses have disappeared. It would be tempting to imagine that two millennia later they ended up in Paris.

Not that there is any surviving evidence for such a claim. The starting point of the journey of the *quadriga* – from Greece, to Rome, to Constantinople, to Venice, and to Paris – is unknown for a simple reason: they have always been stolen goods. Their presence at all the triumphs from Rome to Paris was invariably under duress. They were not the victors, but the vanquished; and history is only ever written by the victors. All we know about the four horses are the stories their rustlers used to tell about them.

✳ ✳ ✳

Some say the horses were taken by the consul Sulla when he ravaged Greece in the days of the Roman Republic; others say that the *quadriga* was taken by Augustus, the first Roman emperor, when he did the same. They say he placed them atop his mausoleum in the Field of Mars, associating himself in death with Alexander, and decorated his tomb with paintings of the hero.

But of all the Roman emperors who were enslaved by the legacy of

Alexander, none was more egregious than the Emperor Nero. After he had murdered his own natural mother, and after fire had reduced Rome and its treasures to ashes, Nero decided to improve himself by tasting the refined arts of Greece. He played his lyre and enacted Greek tragedies in the theatres. He competed in the arena and the stadium and, needless to say, he won the victor's laurel every time. So impressed was Nero by the culture of Greece that he stripped her of her works of art. From the sanctuary of Delphi alone he removed some five hundred bronze statues, and carried them back to Rome. Perhaps the bronze charioteer and his horses were separated in this act of theft.

Nero's Grecian antics did not impress his subjects, who expected their *imperator* to wage war rather than play the lyre; and he realized that he would have to improve his reputation the old Roman way. As it happened, at this time the Romans were engaged in an interminable conflict against the Parthians. Nero seized upon a minor victory in this war, and made the Senate grant him a triumph. He was a new Alexander, he said, who, like the ancient hero, had vanquished the Eastern barbarians.

A triumph was contrived in the capital city of the republic: a procession wound its way from the city gate to the Field of Mars, and the spoils of victory were dedicated in the temple of Jupiter. An arch was hastily erected on the Capitoline Hill, and the four horses, recently stolen from Greece, or perhaps from the mausoleum of Augustus, were placed on top of it. The arch didn't last long: Nero's fantasies soon evaporated. He killed himself less than a year after his triumph, and the whole pageant was quietly dismantled.

* * *

Nearly three centuries later, the Emperor Constantine decided to move his court from Rome to Byzantium, giving that city a new name: *Nova Roma*. In his new capital Constantine established a palace, a hippodrome, and a forum with a senate house; and in that forum he set up a column topped by a bronze image of Apollo, whose head he removed and replaced with his own. On his deathbed, Constantine was baptized into the Christian faith, and declared himself the fourth member of the Trinity.

Fifty-six years later, the Emperor Theodosius finished what Constantine had started; for while Constantine had allowed the worship of the old gods to continue, his successor proclaimed himself their enemy. In AD 393, Theodosius attended the chariot races at the Olympic Games, declared himself the victor, and then abolished the games altogether; they would not be convened for another fifteen centuries. Theodosius cast down the altar of Victory in the Senate House in Rome, and extinguished the eternal flame in the temple of Vesta. The Delphic oracle was silenced; the Parthenon was vandalized; and in Alexandria the emperor's agents split open the head of the god Serapis, revealing not the residence of a divinity but a secret hoard of jewels jealously guarded by avaricious priests.

Having demonstrated the empty vanity of the pagan idols, Theodosius had them all brought to the Hippodrome of New Rome. On the raised *spina* that ran down the middle of the racetrack he erected an obelisk from Luxor, made two thousand years before by the Pharaoh Thutmosis. It was joined by the column of brazen serpents from Delphi, made by the Greeks in the dawn of classical antiquity, and by the statue of Athene Parthenos captured in Athens. Among all these treasures was a bronze *quadriga* that, some said, had been taken from Nero's arch, or from Augustus's mausoleum in Rome.

Trapped on the *spina*, an island surrounded by a sea of sand and careering charioteers, these obsolete idols were captives on display: the booty of an old order that had been looted by a new one. But although the empire and the emperor were Christian, and laughed in face of idolatry, they were a little frightened of their art collection. It represented the civilization that had mothered them; and over time, as that civilization disappeared from view, they came to regard their statues as the dwellings of demons, possessed of magical powers. The hoof of the bronze horse that supported the classical hero Bellerophon concealed, they said, the image of the future destroyer of Constantinople, while the colossal statue of Justinian hid a hoard of priceless jewels which would only be discovered on the day the city fell. There was a bronze snake whose magical power, they said, had cast out all the serpents of Constantinople, and a nymph atop a pyramid who answered to the call of the winds. These things were wonders; but they were also evidence that, in their fallen state, the Romans of Constantinople could no longer conjure the magic of their forefathers.

∗ ∗ ∗

Four hundred and fifty years after the great iconoclasm of Theodosius, when Constantinople was a great and thriving city, Venice was as yet merely a marsh inhabited by humble fishermen. Humble they might have been, but every evening, as they watched the sun set over the world's flat edge, they dimly remembered that once upon a time they too had been Romans, and nobles at that. The Venetians had escaped to this lagoon when Huns had attacked their ancient city of Aquileia. It is said that they gathered together the carved stones of their temples and rowed out with them into the water to evade barbarian capture. (Take a boat today to the quiet island of Torcello and you can still see these carvings, built into crumbling cathedrals of a much later date.) Hidden amid the shallows and the reeds, they remained inviolate, beyond the reach of siege engines, archers, and cavalry. Floating on the surface of the waters, suspended between the horizons of the orient and occident, the Venetians answered to no-one. Their dwellings were made of the clay they dug up from their muddy islets and baked into bricks; when these buildings fell into ruin they dissolved back into the slime from which they had come, and disappeared.

Every morning, as they watched the sun rise over the sea in the east, the Venetians dreamed of a destiny consonant with the greatness of their lost heritage. And so it was that the people of Venice decided to steal themselves a past, in order to conjure themselves a future. They decided first of all to steal a patron saint, who would give them a pedigree, protect them from evil, and bring good fortune upon their enterprises; and they sent their boatmen out over the waters to find one.

At that time Alexandria was in the sway of the Fatimid caliphate; but two merchants of Venice, by the name of Buono da Malamocco and Rustico da Torcello, went to the city and found an old church dedicated to St Mark the Evangelist. St Mark had been martyred in Alexandria, and his remains had been kept in this church ever since. The two merchants spoke with the guardians of the saint. They were in danger, these priests said, for the governor of Alexandria intended to demolish their church and send its marbles and columns to the caliph's new palace in Babylon. The two merchants of Venice offered to conceal the body of the saint until the peril had passed, and the holy fathers agreed with gratitude.

One night, under the cover of darkness, the priests let them into the church. Torcello and Malamocco took the body of St Mark and substituted it with the body of another, less exalted martyr, St Claudia – although legend does not relate how her body had been acquired. They put the relics of the more venerable saint into a wicker basket, and they covered them with joints of pork, so that the Muslim soldiers who guarded the city would not investigate what was apparently a container of defiled meat.

But the merchants had no intention of returning the body of St Mark once the danger had passed. Instead they made their way to the docks, and loaded the wicker basket with its sacred contents onto their galley. As they cast off, it is said, a sweet smell started to emanate from the shrine of St Mark. The people of Alexandria ran to the shrine to see – or smell – what was going on;

but they were fooled by the bones of St Claudia. The priests' lips were sealed, and everyone went back to their homes, while the Venetians slipped away to sea. Thus did Buono da Malamocco and Rustico da Torcello steal the body of St Mark from under the noses of the Alexandrians.

A modest church was built in Venice to house the remains of the saint, the stolen patron of a city that had been stolen from the sea; but when this first church burned down in 976, the Venetians decided to replace it with something altogether more ambitious, and once again they looked east for inspiration. The new basilica of San Marco was built in imitation of the church of the Holy Apostles, which stood next to the Hippodrome in Constantinople. This church was known as the *Heröon*, because it had been built by Constantine, the founding hero of the city.

The *Heröon* that the Venetians made for their stolen founder followed precisely the form of the original. It was fashioned in the form of a Greek cross surmounted by five graceful domes. The domes were supported on heavy brick arches and piers that were themselves pierced by smaller domes and arches, as if the church were a series of microcosms nestled inside one another at ever-decreasing scales. It was surrounded by arcades that opened onto the muddy space outside, facing the castle of the Doge.

This church took some fifty years to build, and when it was finished the Doge and the Patriarch and the people marvelled at the lofty vaults and fine pavements. They sensed, though, that there was something missing. Then they realized that they had forgotten where they had stored the body of St Mark.

The people wailed out loud at their loss, and they demanded a miracle from their forgetful masters. The Doge Vitale Falier and the Patriarch Domenico Contarini gathered them all together in the new basilica, and they began to pray. For hours their chant and their incense rose into the domes, and nothing happened. Then, after a while, a sweet smell began to pervade the church. Suddenly one of the piers to the right of the altar began to shake, and the masonry began to buckle. With a crash and a roar an arm appeared, then a shoulder, a torso, and a head; and then the whole body of St Mark fell lifeless onto the pavement of the sanctuary. The Doge Falier placed this body in a marble sarcophagus in the crypt, and the *Heröon* of the Venetians received its patron saint.

The basilica of San Marco was now complete, but it was a bare sort of building, lacking in the ornaments that were surely proper to the shrine of the patron saint of a great republic. The Venetians knew what they had to do: just as they had sailed east and had stolen the body of St Mark from Alexandria, just as they had looked east and copied the design of his shrine from Constantinople, so they would sail east again to find the gold and the marble, the ikons and the relics and the ornaments that would adorn their church.

Now at this time there lived in Venice a blind man by the name of Enrico Dandolo. Once upon a time Dandolo had been a merchant in Constantinople, but he had caused so much trouble there that he had been expelled from the city. Dandolo returned to Venice, having been blinded, he claimed, by the Byzantine Imperial Guard; and he nursed hatred and bitterness in his heart against Constantinople. From year to year Dandolo plotted how he might avenge himself on the city that had cast him out. His cunning and his determination raised him through the ranks of the state until he became the Doge himself. Still he waited, and then one day an opportunity presented itself.

In 1201 the Pope had declared a crusade to reclaim Jerusalem for the faith. The Venetians, living as they did on the water, were unable to contribute knights or infantry, but they did offer to provide the fleet that would carry the crusading army to the Holy Land. 'Give us 85,000 silver marks,' they declared, 'and we will take the crusaders from Venice to certain glory.' The Pope agreed, the Venetians started building their ships, and the knights of Europe left their northern manors behind and began making their way to Venice. By 1202 the ships were nearly built, but only a third of the 33,000 promised knights had turned up. A savage rabble they were, and the Venetians did not permit them to enter the city but kept them encamped by the surf of the Lido until their group might reach the promised number.

It never did, and the few knights who had come did not have enough money to pay the full 85,000 marks that the Venetians required. Things began to turn nasty, and it was at this point that Enrico Dandolo saw his chance. He made a proposal to the barbarians gathered on the beach. 'You can purchase your fare to the Holy Land,' he suggested, 'by acting as our agents along the way. You can fight our wars for us, providing us with the booty we require, until the 85,000 marks we need has been collected. Then we will take you to Jerusalem.' The crusaders readily agreed, and then they asked which infidel they would be sent to fight against. Dandolo licked his lips and told them: 'The Emperor of Constantinople.' Their faces fell. They had not come all this way to murder other Christians.

The Emperor of Constantinople at the time was named Alexius III, and he had risen to the purple by imprisoning and blinding the emperor before him, Isaac III. Dandolo, who knew what it was like to be blinded and cast down by the Byzantines, told the crusaders that they could attain merit in Heaven by restoring Isaac to his rightful throne. They would gain additional merit, he said, if they were also able to place Isaac's son on the throne with him, a different Alexius. This other Alexius, he said, would bring Constantinople into the fold of the Catholic Church, from which it had long been separated by doctrinal schism. And by this specious argument, Dandolo refashioned a crusade against the Muslim unbelievers in the Holy Land into a war of vengeance against his old enemy. The reluctant crusaders, stuck as they were on the windy sands of the Lido, unacquainted with the intrigues of the Levant, had no choice. They set forth in their ships, not for Palestine, but for Constantinople.

The people of that city heard of the Venetian plan, and they were terrified, Though their city was surrounded by gigantic walls and filled with priceless bronze statues, gorgeous sanctuaries, and gigantic palaces, their empire was not what it once had been, and their legions were small compared with the barbarian horde that was on its way to meet them. Riots and commotions disturbed the city, and it is said that a mob fell upon a statue of Athene and tore it to pieces because her arm and her gaze were outstretched to the west – the direction from which, any day now, the Constantinopolitans expected their nemesis to arrive.

Then arrive it did. After nine months of byzantine politicking, awful cannonade, siege, parley, ecclesiastical council, and the deposition and murder of three emperors, including the very Isaac and Alexius they had come to restore, the crusaders took possession of the city in April 1204. The first to the walls was Dandolo himself. He and his soldiers fanned out through the city, spreading terror wherever they went. Nuns were dragged from their abbeys and raped, children taken into slavery, monks and bishops alike executed. The crusaders ran to the *Heröon*, the model for San Marco itself, and they tore it to pieces, despoiling the bodies of the emperors within. They broke into the church of Holy Wisdom, stripped its interior of its astonishing ornaments and relics, and set a whore on the throne of the emperor. They went to the church of St Polyeuktos and ripped pilasters, architraves, and sheets of marble from the building, leaving a denuded shell behind them.

The crusaders came in the end to the Hippodrome. The classical scholar Nicetas Choniates, who witnessed the scene, later recalled how

> these barbarians, haters of the beautiful, did not pass over the destruction of the statues standing in the Hippodrome and other marvellous work. They cut these into coinage, exhanging great things for small ones and things laboured over at great expense for worthless small

change … For a few staters, and what is more, copper, they consigned these ancient and revered objects of the nation to the smelting furnace.

And he composed a lament for the lost creatures of the Hippodrome, enumerating their wonderful artistry, the miracles they had performed, and their mythical antecedents.

What the soldiers did not destroy, the Venetians loaded onto their galleys and shipped away, leaving the crusaders behind to rule the city and the empire they had wrecked. Some of the treasures were lost at sea, some were sold along the way, but a great many made it to Venice intact. The booty was unloaded into the Arsenale of Venice, and unpacked in front of the impatient deputies of the people. Fragments of architecture were lifted onto the wharf: capitals, architraves, and pediments of white marble, columns of red Numidian granite, and green onyx ripped from the shrines and palaces of Constantinople. There was a block of porphyry carved with the crude likenesses of the Emperor Diocletian and his deputy Caesars, and there were strange and wonderful fragments of bronze sculpture: a lion, a pair of angel's wings, the cuirass of some ancient general, a crocodile, a disembodied head. Crates were prised open, and a rainbow shower of mosaic chips scattered across the pavement. Other chests revealed grisly relics: the head of St John the Baptist, drops of Christ's blood in a vial, a nail of the Cross, pieces of St Lucia, St Agatha, St Helena, St Symeon, St Anastasius, St Paul the Martyr. There were ikons, in which the solemn faces of saints peered through windows of gem-studded incrustation; and, of course, there was a *quadriga* of bronze horses.

Over the ensuing years all of these things made their way onto the basilica of San Marco, so that what had been an austere brick structure soon shone, and sparkled, and flashed in the sun. The sheets of marble, onyx, and granite from the churches of Constantinople adorned the outside of the building, so that the nakedness of San Marco was clothed in the borrowed raiment of vanished sanctuaries. The porphyry Caesars were set into the corner of the basilica; beside them, two beautiful pilasters from St Polyeuktos acted as plinths for the heads of decapitated criminals. The façade of the church was set with reliefs of Hercules, and a head of the Emperor Justinian was placed on one pinnacle on the southwest corner. The gilded ikons were bolted together to make magnificent altarpieces, set with gems ripped from the bodies of the emperors who had lain in the *Heröon*. The saints' relics were stored in the crypt, to be brought out on festival days. The brazen wings and lion were welded together to make the emblem of St Mark, while the centurion's cuirass, the crocodile, and the disembodied head became the body of St Theodore; and these two patrons of Venice were placed on top of two colossal columns of Numidian granite, raised by the waterside to receive them. The bronze horses, of course, were placed high on the balcony over the main entrance to the church, as if they surmounted a triumphal arch surrounded by a great heap of precious spoils.

* * *

In 1789, time began all over again. The people of France deposed and executed their monarch and his nobles and declared a republic, in which all the former subjects of the king became free and equal brotherly citizens; and in the year of Our Lord 1789 they renamed the Year Zero. And then, having created the best of all possible worlds, they went out to bring their message to the less enlightened nations of Europe: the ramshackle duchies, republics, counties, and prince bishoprics of the old Holy Roman Empire.

Of the republic's free, equal, and brotherly citizens, none were more zealous in the service of his country than Napoleon Bonaparte. An Alexander, an Achilles – an Apollo, to be sure, in his own estimation, and a Nero in that of his enemies – Napoleon crossed the Alps and descended into Italy with dreams of glory. Genoa, Tuscany, Rome, and Naples fell before the revolutionary conqueror, but the Republic of Venice ignored the signs of their approaching doom. They even allowed Napoleon's armies to cross their territory as they wrecked the ancient order of Italy. 'Venice has always been here,' they said to themselves. 'Venice answers to no-one. Venice is a free city, suspended on the face of the water, floating between orient and occident.'

Then on 20 April 1798 a warship entered the lagoon of Venice unannounced, a French vessel named the *Libérateur*. The Venetian government, not in the mood for Napoleon's brand of liberation, ordered their guns to fire on the ship, and they killed her captain. Napoleon was incandescent: 'the murder of the commander of the *Libérateur*,' he declaimed, 'is without parallel in the annals of the nations of our time'. He set out to avenge it. Within two weeks his forces were at the shores of the Venetian lagoon. Napoleon sent the Venetians an ultimatum: surrender their republic to the revolution or see it demolished by modern artillery, against which the water between the city and the mainland would prove no defence.

Once upon a time the Venetians would have laughed in the face of such a provocation; but on 12 May a Great Council of the Republic was called, which all the ancient families listed in the Golden Book were invited to attend. Few bothered: many had already loaded up their boats and left for the mainland. The council was not even quorate, with only 537 members attending out of a necessary 600, and this sorry rump of an assembly voted by 512 to 20 to accede to Napoleon's demands. Five members abstained.

So ended the Most Serene Republic of Venice. The Doge walked out of the council chamber, returned to his apartments, and handed his traditional Phrygian cap and his ancient ring of office to his manservant. 'Take them away,' he said. 'We shan't be needing these any more.' The French forces were welcomed by the Venetian mob, which was delighted to have ousted the ancient oligarchy of the Doge and the families of the Golden Book. They erected a tree of liberty in the Piazza San Marco and they danced around it, singing revolutionary songs of freedom. They congratulated themselves that the old order was past.

Travelling with the French forces on their campaign was the man who had become known as the 'Eyes of Napoleon'. Baron Dominique-Vivant Denon was a connoisseur, and a good friend of Napoleon's wife Josephine. At the triumphant entries into ancient cities, at peace conferences and the signing of treaties, he was always there, telling his master what to plunder, what to steal, what to demand, and what to extort. Denon made sure that a demand for works of art – twenty paintings, in total – was included in the terms of surrender dictated to the Venetians. It was these paintings that were unwrapped in the Louvre on the day of the triumph of Year Seven.

But the French liberators of Venice went much further than collecting pictures, for Napoleon was no mere connoisseur. The *Bucintoro* of the Doge was burnt and sunk, the winged lion of St Mark and St Theodore's crocodile were removed from their eminences. And then Napoleon sent his troops to the triumphal arch of the Venetian Republic, the façade of San Marco, and removed the bronze *quadriga* that surmounted it. Denon had told him that these horses had once pulled the chariots of the Emperors of Constantinople, of Nero, and of Augustus; even, perhaps, the chariot of Apollo himself.

✳ ✳ ✳

Less than two decades later Napoleon had been deposed, and by 1814 his empire and its treasures were being carved up between the powers that had defeated him. Denon, by now the director of the Louvre, fought tenaciously for his collection. The treasures of the Louvre belonged to France by right of conquest, he said. The treasures of the Louvre had been the property of states that no longer existed, he said, and therefore there was no rightful owner to which they might be returned. The treasures of the Louvre were and always had been the property of the once deposed, now restored, monarchy of France; they had been in the Louvre since time immemorial, he said. No-one believed him, and the troops of the allies who had defeated Napoleon came to repossess what belonged to their masters.

But to whom might the *quadriga* be returned? Not only had it been stolen many times over, but it had belonged to states that no longer existed. Macedon, Rome, Constantinople, and even the Republic of Venice were no more.

Still, to the city of Venice the bronze horses were returned. Their new overlord, the Emperor of Austria, was good enough to be present at their restitution on the façade of San Marco, even though Venice was now but a provincial port in his vast empire. Soon enough, they were put out to pasture, as it were, in the diocesan museum. There, stabled inside, they are protected by a sophisticated security system, so that no-one can ever steal them again.

AYASOFYA, ISTANBUL

*In Which a Sultan Casts a Spell
and Moves the Centre of the World*

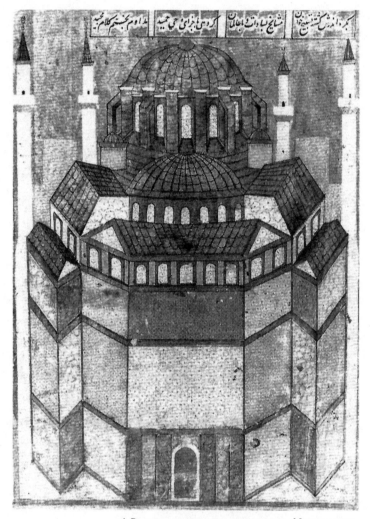

A ROMAN BUILDING SEEN THROUGH MUSLIM EYES.
Miniature commemorating Selim II's renovation
of Ayasofya and his burial there in 1581.

Appropriation

*T*he Parthenon might have passed into the insubstantial realm of dreams altogether had it not been turned into a church and then into a mosque. Each time the function of the Parthenon was changed the building was converted: the front door was blocked up with an altar, and the altar removed to make way for a new front door. But as each successive conversion was laid over the last one the hold of Athene over the Parthenon was enriched, for she was the virgin goddess of wisdom with a winged Victory in her hand.

The people of the Dark Ages did not just vandalize the architecture of antiquity; they also turned it to new uses. When the barbarians came to Rome, they did not simply sack it: indeed, the buildings they encountered were often too solidly built to demolish. But having no use for theatres, temples, and fora, they turned them into fortresses for their warriors, prisons for their captives, and enclosures for their cattle.

These were often brutal conversions, but it is thanks to them that any theatres, bathhouses, or fora have survived at all. We have inherited hybrid buildings, double-coded with both their original and their subsequent purposes. The Theatre of Marcellus in Rome, for instance, is both a theatre and a palace; the Forum of Trajan both a market place and a fortress.

Ayasofya in Istanbul was once Hagia Sophia, the great church of the Roman Empire, and the place where that empire made its last stand. Its conversion into a mosque is a late example of the appropriation of an antique building. The terms of that approriation were particularly controversial, and still are, since it involved nothing less than moving the centre of the world.

The Ayasofya we possess today is both church and mosque, both an antiquity and a very modern problem. It stands as a testament to the simultaneous reverence and scorn with which the inhabitants of the Dark Ages treated the buildings they had inherited from their classical forebears.

ONCE UPON A TIME THE CENTRE OF THE WORLD WAS CONSTANTINOPLE, mistress of Europe and Asia and the Middle and the Euxine seas; and at the centre of Constantinople stood the church of Hagia Sophia, which means, in Greek, Holy Wisdom; at the centre of Hagia Sophia, which was the centre of Constantinople, which was the centre of the world, there was a purple stone called the Omphalos, which was the navel of them all.

On 28 May 1453 the Emperor of the Romans, who was called Constantine, was standing on the Navel of the World. He raised his eyes to the mosaic of Christ Pantocrator, the Last Judge, in holy and hopeful pleadings. This mighty judge resided at the apex of a dome some 100 feet in diameter and some 185 feet high, which was pierced with countless windows and set with thousands of oil lamps. This dome was supported on four gigantic arches, the junctions between which were inhabited by six-winged seraphs. To the east and west these arches were supported on semidomes as wide as the dome itself. These were also pierced with windows, and were themselves supported on three smaller semidomes — a cascade of vaults so breathtaking that people told one another that it must be hung from Heaven on a golden chain. These vaults were filled with a mosaic pantheon of the angels, the prophets, prelates of the Orthodox Church, and the families of the emperors; and above the altar, in the most holy vault of them all, was depicted the Virgin Mary accompanied by two angels.

Now, as the Emperor Constantine stood on the Omphalos, the open space beneath the image of the Virgin was filled with clergy: so many of them that their jewelled robes seemed to be nothing more or less than the mosaics of the walls set into motion. Before these priests stood the altar, and in front of the altar there was a silver screen set with ikons. From time to time one of the priests would appear in the door of this ikonostasis in a cloud of incense. Bells would shake, and the people gathered on the other side of the screen would prostrate themselves before him. The rest of the time they stroked and kissed the solemn faces of the saints, encrusted with silver and blackened by centuries of adoration.

And the priests and the congregation used the words they always used at the acclamation of emperors:

> *For the glory and elevation of the Romans*
> *Hearken, O God, to your people*
> *Many, many, many,*
> *Many years upon many,*
> *Many years for you, Constantine, Emperor of the Romans.*

And Constantine imagined, for a moment, that he was the first Constantine, whose Christian empire had stretched from Caledonia to Arabia, Mauretania to Armenia, who had founded Constantinople, and who had built the original Hagia Sophia in the year of Our Lord 360.

* * *

That first church had been shaken to its foundations by an earthquake fifty years after it had been built, and it had then been rebuilt by the Emperor Theodosius; but the Hagia Sophia in which this last Constantine stood had been born in another tremor, of a political nature. In January 532, five years after the Emperor Justinian had taken the purple, a riot between the Blues and the Greens in the Hippodrome spilled out onto the streets of Constantinople. For a week the emperor was confined to his Sacred Palace as the mob rampaged through the city. On the night of 12 January, they burned Hagia Sophia to the ground.

Justinian was in despair, and he had boats made ready to take him away; but his empress was made of sterner stuff. Theodora's father had been a bear-baiter for the Greens, her mother had been a prostitute, and so had the empress, some said. She was used to the hurly-burly of the Hippodrome, and the crowds did not terrify her. 'Purple makes a fine shroud,' she snorted, and she counselled the emperor to stay and die if necessary. Justinian, more afraid of his wife than of the mob, sent his general Belisarius to the Hippodrome. Trapped between the banks of seats, some 35,000 rioters were slaughtered there on 18 January; and order was restored.

Then Justinian called Isodore, a mathematician of Miletus, and Anthemius, an architect of Tralles and had them devise a new Hagia Sophia to replace the one that had been burned down in the riots. Only a month later, on 23 February, the foundation stone for the new church was laid, and from then on work on the basilica proceeded with an unnatural speed. Some whispered that Justinian was a devil; others said that angels were helping the workmen, watching over the building site and ensuring that their tools were not stolen. It was said later that Justinian tricked one of these angels to stay and watch over the church once it was finished.

Two days after Christmas 537, the emperor went in procession to Hagia Sophia. When he entered the new building, Justinian stepped out in front of all of his court; he stood under the magnificent dome, hung from Heaven on its golden chain, guarded by the angel he had bewitched, and he cried out: 'Solomon, I have outdone thee!' It was an hubristic moment: as Procopius, the secret historian of Justinian's reign, observed at the time, the dome 'seems somehow to float in the air on no firm basis, but to be poised aloft to the peril of those inside it'. Nemesis was duly served: twenty years later there was an earthquake, and that magical floating dome, its heavenly chain momentarily severed, collapsed in a heap of brick and a cloud of dust.

Justinian was not one to be discouraged. He summoned the son of the mathematician of Miletus, also called Isodore, and within three years the church was complete again. This time the dome was even taller than it had been before. At its reconsecration, Paul, the Silentiary of the court, stood beneath it and declaimed, 'Wondrous it is to see how the dome ... is like the firmament which rests on air,' wisely and quickly adding, 'though the dome is fixed on the strong backs of the arches.'

Hagia Sophia was subsequently subjected to numerous tremblings of the earth, shaken in 896, and 1317, and 1346; but she always withstood the shocks, and became even more magnificent than before. After each earthquake emperors, architects, and engineers added more masonry to the building, so that the dome would remain standing; and while the interior retained its celestial splendour, the outside of the church came to resemble a labyrinthine Babel that never quite reached the Heaven to which it aspired.

In the iconoclastic fury of the eighth and ninth centuries the church was stripped of its images, but in the tenth century they were returned from banishment even more beautiful than they had been in the first place: Christ Pantocrator, Mary, the saints, the angels, and the emperors were woven into embroideries of mosaic on dome and vault and wall. The emissaries of Prince

Vladimir of Kiev visited the restored church and reported that they 'knew not whether we were in Heaven or earth. For on earth there is no such splendour or beauty, and we are at a loss how to describe it. We know only that God dwells there among men, and their service is fairer than the ceremonies of other nations.'

In 1206, when the Venetians sacked Constantinople and carried off the bronze horses and the treasures of the Hippodrome, they also attacked Hagia Sophia. They broke into the church, murdered the people they found taking sanctuary inside, and set a prostitute on the imperial throne. In a final insult, they buried Enrico Dandolo, the Doge of Venice who had contrived Constantinople's misfortune, in an aisle of the church. (His tombstone is still there.) But in 1261 the Romans returned to Constantinople, and the Emperor Michael Palaiologos proceeded directly to Hagia Sophia to be ceremonially acclaimed like all the emperors before him – above the Omphalos, the Navel of the World, under the dome that was suspended from Heaven by a golden chain.

* * *

In 1453, standing in the same place as all his predecessors, surrounded by his people and his priests, enveloped in a cloud of incense, the last emperor Constantine forgot, for a moment, that he was a petty despot whose empire extended no further than the walls of his city. He forgot that the jewels in his crown were made of glass, and that there was no more money. He forgot that the Patriarch of the Orthodox Church had fled into exile, disgusted by Constantine's alliance with the Pope; and he forgot that the aid promised from Italy in return for that alliance had never arrived. He forgot that, until this night, his subjects had shunned him and his church of Hagia Sophia because he had sold their souls to the western barbarians who had been the downfall of the city so many times before.

He forgot, for a moment, that Constantinople had been under siege for nearly two months; and he forgot that in the previous three days there had been three terrible portents. The first sign was an eclipse of the full moon that sent everyone to their beds in terror. When they awoke in the morning, the emperor attempted to rally the people by carrying the *Hodegetria* in procession. This ikon of the Virgin possessed magical powers: it directed processions of its own accord, and was said to strike terror into the hearts of the enemies of Constantinople. Constantine hoped it would do the same this time. But as the acolytes carried the *Hodegetria* out into the street it fell to the ground, and when the people ran forward to pick it up the ikon stuck fast. As they attempted to lift it, rain began to pour, and the procession had to be abandoned. The Virgin of the *Hodegetria*, it seemed, had deserted her people. This was the second sign, and the people went to their beds in redoubled terror.

The first to see the third sign were out at sea, because when the citizens of Constantinople awoke the on the third day they found their city swaddled in a fog so thick that the dome of Hagia Sophia could only dimly be seen. For centuries, ships had used the dome to guide them into the city, for at night the thousands of oil lamps guttering within it shone out over the water; and the sailor, in the words of Paul the Silentiary, would not 'guide his laden vessel by the light of Cynosure, or the circling Bear, but by the divine light of the church itself.'

That night the lights of the dome of Hagia Sophia were lit as usual, and shone out over the waters; but soon they began to behave very strangely. The monk Nestor Iskander later recalled seeing

> a large flame of fire issuing forth; it encircled the entire neck of the church for a very long time. The flame gathered into one; its flame altered, and there was an indescribable light. At once it took to the sky. Those who had seen it were benumbed; they began to wail and cry out in Greek: Lord have Mercy! The light itself has gone up to Heaven.

Everyone knew that the golden chain was broken, the angel was departed, and that the next day would be the last day of the Roman Empire. It was too late for sectarian divisions, too late to blame the emperor for having asked the Italians for aid, too late to shun the Omphalos. And so on 28 May 1453 they gathered together in Hagia Sophia to pray one last time. When the service was over, the emperor gathered his senate and his generals around him and, weeping, he made one last desperate plea: 'Hurl your javelins and your arrows against them, so that they know that they are fighting with the descendants of the Greeks and the Romans.' Then he went out to defend the city. The people raised their voices to Heaven in desperate prayer; but Heaven no longer heard them.

* * *

On the other side of the city walls the armies of Islam had also seen the signs, and they were ready. They had been waiting for them for some time.

In 628, the Emperor Heraclius had received a letter from an unknown desert tribesman. It read:

> In the name of Allah the most Beneficent, the most Merciful: this letter is from Muhammad, the slave of Allah and his apostle, to Heraclius … Peace be upon the followers of guidance. I invite you to surrender to Allah. Embrace Islam and Allah will bestow upon you a double reward. But if you reject this invitation you will be misguid-ing your people.

The emperor laughed. He had just defeated the King of Persia in battle, and he had no intention of surrendering to anyone, or embracing Islam, or Allah, whatever they might be. But within eight years half his empire had fallen to the unknown tribesmen, and within another thirty the armies of Islam were encamped by the walls of the city whose name they mispronounced as Istanbul. It took four years to drive them off. They returned four decades later, and they even started to till the soil around the city as if it were their own, until the Rumi – the Romans – of Istanbul drove them away again.

Since Muhammad had written his letter to Heraclius, the armies of Islam had spread their faith as far west as Spain, as far east as India, as far north as the walls of Vienna, and as far south as the deep Sahara; but there was one city that resisted their advance. Istanbul was, they said, the 'bone in the throat of Allah'.

A bone in the throat of Allah it might have been, but the armies of Islam knew that Allah would swallow Istanbul one day. They told one another a story about the dome they saw from the sea, riding over the city like a ship in full sail. Ayasofya had been built in time out of mind, they said, by one of the emperors of the Rumi, or by Solomon himself; but on the night of the birth of the Prophet Muhammad, the dome of the great church had collapsed. Attempts to rebuild it were unsuccessful until the Rumi sent emissaries to see the Prophet, and he gave his consent to the reconstruction. He told the emissaries to rebuild the dome with a mortar composed of sand from Mecca, water from the sacred well of Zem Zem, and his own spittle. They returned to Istanbul with this miraculous mixture, and ever since the dome of Ayasofya had held firm, waiting for the day that the armies of Islam would take possession.

In January 1453, Mehmet of the tribe of Osman raised a horsetail on a lance in the courtyard of his palace in Erdine, and in so doing called the people of his empire to arms. On 23 March they set out, and at the beginning of April they made their camp before the walls of Istanbul. They had been waiting ever since. Now Mehmet the Sultan saw the darkened moon and the flame ascending from the great dome, and he remembered the prophecies; and he knew that the time for waiting was over. At half past one in the morning he gave the order to attack. By sunrise his troops had planted the standard of the Prophet Muhammad on the walls of Istanbul.

Constantine, the last Emperor of Constantinople, had disappeared; his body was found later, identifiable only by his crimson shoes embroidered with the imperial eagle. Those of his subjects who could neither escape nor hide raced to the great church, where, amid tinkling bells and clouds of incense and a chanted drone, they reminded one another of prophecies of their own. The armies of Islam will be turned back at the Column of Constantine in the forum, they said, and then an avenging angel will drive them out of the city all the way to Persia. The emperor, resurrected, will ride up to Jerusalem, and the empire, restored, will be taken up to Heaven.

But none of these prophecies came to pass. Instead the people heard the crash of weaponry on the Beautiful Doors of Hagia Sophia, which once upon a time had been the doors of the temple of Zeus at Pergamon. As the soldiers burst in, the priests picked up the sacred vessels and the sacraments they were using. The eastern wall of the apse opened up and they disappeared into it, never to be seen again until the emperor rides once more to Jerusalem and the empire is restored.

Anyone who resisted was slaughtered on the spot, and the rest were herded together and led out of the church like cattle to market. The soldiers of the armies of Islam fanned out across the church, ripping out lamps and furnishings. They took sacred vestments for saddle cloths, and they cut up ikons for the gold and the gems that covered them. All good Muslims abhor images of living things, for, as they say, Allah is the only creator: it is blasphemy to usurp his creative will, even if only in the service of art. The mosaics and the ikons of Hagia Sophia had presumed to depict angels and prophets, the living and the dead, and so they were all abhorrent blasphemies and superstitious idols. They deserved the indignities that were heaped upon them.

By the time the Sultan Mehmet arrived in the middle of the afternoon, the building had been cleared of almost everything that had adorned it. As he entered, he came across a soldier who was trying to prise a sheet of marble from the wall. The sultan flew into a rage, shouting: 'The gold is thine, the marble, mine!' And he beat the man about the head, and cast him out of his service.

When he had spent his fury, having achieved everything that the armies of Islam had hoped to do for eight hundred years, the sultan cast a spell. He commanded a muezzin to mount the pulpit and to make the call to prayer. Then he walked into the sanctuary of Hagia Sophia, climbed on the altar table, and bowed down and prostrated himself in the direction of the centre of the world.

But the centre of the world was no longer the porphyry Omphalos upon which the last Constantine had stood the day before. This was a stone of quite a different sort, which had fallen from a cloudless sky to an empty desert in time out of mind. The Bedouin, who from time to time passed by that way, saw the stone; and they worshipped it, because it had fallen from Heaven to Earth. They built a temple of timber around it, carved with the beasts of the desert and the birds of the air, and over the years a city grew up around this temple.

One day, a merchant walked up into the stony hills around that city. The angel Gabriel appeared to him, and spoke, and commanded him to write down what he heard. Three years later, Muhammad began preaching. 'God is One,' he said, 'and Muhammad is his Prophet.' But the people of Mecca, who had worshipped many gods – and a large black stone – for time out of mind, were enraged, and they drove Muhammad out of their city. Muhammad fled to the city of Medina, and he continued to tell people about what the angel had said. Eventually he returned with a band of followers, and this time the people of Mecca listened to him.

To this day, once in a lifetime, all Muslims must dress themselves in white cotton and make a journey to the city where the angel Gabriel first spoke to Muhammad. When they arrive there, they walk to the black stone which the pagan ancestors of Muhammad worshipped long ago, and they prostrate themselves before it, and they pray.

And every day, five times a day, all Muslims – wherever they are – must prostrate themselves on the ground in the direction of the black stone, which they call the *Ka'aba*, and pray. Every mosque is nothing more or less than a device that shows all good Muslims, wherever they may be, the *Qibla*, the direction in which the *Ka'aba* might be found. Every mosque is defined by nothing more or less than a niche – the *mihrab* – that points to the black stone that fell from Heaven to earth.

* * *

The effects of the sultan's spell were slow, for it took many years for the Roman to become the Ottoman Empire, Constantinople to become Istanbul, and the church of Hagia Sophia to become the Ayasofya Mosque.

Mehmet had a wooden minaret erected in front of the great church, so that the muezzin could climb it and sing out the call to prayer. His son Beyazit replaced this minaret with a tower in stone. Over the next two centuries this tower was joined by three more, which, with the first, described a cube of song around the dome. Inside, wherever they could reach them, Ottoman craftsmen covered the mosaics of emperors and saints with whitewash; and to hide the six-winged seraphs that supported the dome they hung huge roundels, on which were written suras of the Holy Koran in letters larger than a man.

At the end of the sixteenth century, two fountains were erected at the western end of the building, for all Muslims must wash themselves before performing their prayers. Water tinkled from two ancient alabaster urns, which the Sultan Murat had brought from Pergamon, and around them the faithful sat on the carved Ionic capitals of some long-vanished pagan shrine, washing their feet.

A woven garden of carpet spread out over the white marble floor so that the faithful could prostrate themselves in prayer. Timber pews were erected here and there in the nave, like kiosks in a field of tulips. The most prominent of them all belonged to the sultan himself: it was raised on marble columns, and concealed the ruler in a latticed cage of gold. In the 1590s the Sultan Murat had the *minbar* or pulpit placed against the southern pier of the apse, a little kiosk with a conical hat at the top of a steep stair; and in the apse itself he placed the *mihrab*. To either side of it he placed two gigantic candles which the Sultan Suleyman had captured from a monastery in Hungary.

Every single element of the Ayasofya Mosque was oriented to the black stone in Mecca. Every single element, that is, except the building itself. When Hagia Sophia was built, it was oriented, like all Christian churches, between the rising and the setting sun. To the west was the world of death and suffering; in the direction of the rising sun was the altar, where the rising of the Son was celebrated. But the *Ka'aba* lies not due east from Istanbul, but southeast, and therefore the orientation of Hagia Sophia and of Ayasofya did not align. The *mihrab* of Ayasofya sat some ten degrees off the centre line of the apse of Hagia Sophia; the steep stairs of the *minbar* were not perpendicular to the wall against which they stood; and so was it also with the pews. Even the carpets were oriented towards the *mihrab* of Ayasofya, so that they lay diagonally across the floor of Hagia Sophia; and when the mosque was filled with the rows of the faithful they formed another carpet – as magnificently embroidered, to be sure, as the first – that extended outwards from the *mihrab*, and thus from Mecca itself. Inch by inch, degree by degree, year by year, detail by detail, the descendants of Sultan Mehmet oriented Hagia Sophia towards the black stone. In an echo of what the Christians themselves had done to the Parthenon, the Muslims had literally turned the church into their mosque.

* * *

Seventy years after Mehmet's spell had been cast, the court poet Saduddin described Ayasofya as 'this ancient building ... lit with the rays of true belief and filled with the sweet smelling breath of the Law'; and he described how, after nearly a century of Islamic worship, 'the rapture reflecting interior, illuminate with the proclamation of unity, began to flash like a polished mirror'. His words echoed nothing so much as the classical hexameters that Paul the Silentiary had declaimed eight hundred years earlier, for while the people of Islam and the sons of Osman had cast a spell upon Hagia Sophia, Hagia Sophia had also cast a spell on them. By the early sixteenth century, the court poet Idris-i Bidlisi could claim that Ayasofya was equal in sanctity to the *Ka'aba* itself, and the writer Cafer Çelebi called it 'the victorious Shah of them all', in which prayer was a hundred times more valuable than in any other mosque.

Sultan Selim II addressed himself to the repair of the building in 1572. He completed the set of four minarets around the dome and demolished many of the humble outbuildings that crowded the site. He also issued a *fatwa* in which he stated that anyone who opposed the repair of Ayasofya on the grounds that it had been a church would be executed as an infidel. In the end he had himself buried in the precincts of the great mosque, inspiring many of his successors to do the same. In 1595, Murad III had a domed tomb built in the garden, and soon afterwards Muhammed III added another one. In 1622, Mustapha I had the old Christian baptistery converted into his final resting place, and a few decades later the mortal remains of the Sultan Ibrahim joined him there under its ancient dome. Today, the great dome of Ayasofya rises above a veritable town of its smaller imitators.

And as Constantinople turned into Istanbul, and Hagia Sophia into Ayasofya, so also the tribe of Osman resembled less and less the wild horsemen from whom they were descended, and became more and more like the Romans whose empire they had appropriated. Before the conquest of Constantinople, the mosques of the Turks had been central Asian in character. A typical prayer hall in these mosques was no more elaborate than the open courtyard of a caravanserai, and it was entered through a high tiled door flanked by minarets, which resembled nothing so much as a beautiful carpet slung between two lances. These buildings were designed to recall the simple house of mud and timber in Medina where Muhammad had preached while he was in exile. But the prayer hall of the Fatih Mosque – the Mosque of Victory – that Mehmet constructed in Istanbul after his conquest was not a courtyard but a gigantic interior. In it, four colossal piers supported four arches which supported a magnificent dome pierced with windows and bathed in light, and the building resembled nothing so much as the great church of the Romans.

It was a soldier in the service of the Sultan Suleyman who brought this new architecture, appropriated from the ancient splendours of Constantinople, to perfection. Sinan was a Janissary, one of the murderous personal guard of the sultan, but his superiors took notice of his great talent for all forms of drawing, building, and engineering. After his military service was over Sinan entered the ministry of works, and in 1538 he was made chief architect to the sultan himself.

Sinan's endless ingenuity was applied to bridges and aqueducts, fortifications and theology schools, tombs and gardens. Most beautifully of all, Sinan designed mosques; and most magnificent of these was the one he built for the Sultan Suleyman. The Suleymaniye Mosque was built, like Hagia Sophia, at tremendous speed: it took just seven years between the laying out of the foundations to the topping out of the dome in 1557. (St Peter's Basilica in Rome, begun at around the same time, took some two centuries to complete.) To build his mosque, Sinan ransacked the antiquities of Istanbul: supporting the aisles of its interior are columns from the old Imperial Box in the Hippodrome, from the temple of Bacchus in Baalbek, and from a monument to the Emperor Arcadius in the ancient forum.

But Sinan appropriated more than antique fragments, for the very form of the Suleymaniye Mosque stole away and transmogrified the form of Ayasofya. Its vast interior is sheltered by a dome some eighty feet in diameter, and as in Ayasofya this dome is supported on four arches. As they are in Ayasofya, the side arches are closed with ranks of arched windows and marble colonnades, while the two end arches are closed with semidomes that are supported on three more semidomes themselves.

But the Suleymaniye Mosque differed from Ayasofya in one crucial respect: its *mihrab* lay in the dead centre of the easternmost apse, precisely on the line of symmetry of the whole building. Unlike in Ayasofya, all the parts of the Suleymaniye Mosque – and the gardens all around it, and the colleges and pilgrims' rests that surrounded the gardens, and the tomb of Suleyman himself – were oriented to the black stone in Mecca.

In his later years, Sinan dismissed the Suleymaniye as an 'apprentice work'; and while it was vast and beautiful, it was merely the overture to a long and prolific career. Istanbul is studded with the mosques of Sinan, from the Rustem Pasha Mosque in the Bazaar, dazzling blue with Iznik tiles, to the pale radiance of the Mihrimah Mosque by the city's ancient walls. All of them are variations on the themes of Ayasofya: a dome that glows with light, supported on a cascade of vaults, as the circle of Heaven negotiates its way to the square of the Earth. Isodore of Miletus and Anthemius of Tralles would have understood – and would have envied – the mosques of Sinan.

In the centuries after Mehmet cast his spell, Hagia Sophia became a mosque, and every mosque became a Hagia Sophia. The skyline of Istanbul is the masterpiece of Sinan, but also the last testament of Justinian and his wife Theodora, who told him not to leave the city.

* * *

In 1922, in the Ottoman Empire's last days, a new potentate was anointed in the courtyard of the Imperial Palace, next door to Ayasofya. It was a quiet affair. 'What a travesty it is!' one traveller wrote. 'Instead of the solemn ritual in the Mosque of Eyoub and a Sultan girded with the sword ... here is a delegation of ... deputies notifying an elderly dilettante that he has been elected by majority vote like any other leader.' The ceremony wasn't much to see: 'A little ring of curious sightseers and correspondents crowds around, there is a short prayer, and a comic Palace dwarf, with some eunuchs, give a note of local colour.'

Local colour was all it was: the last sultan had fled to exile in Malta, and his successor was not even allowed to take the sultan's title. He was restricted to using the title of *caliph*, leader of the faithful. He wrote to the real ruler of his country, Mustapha Kemal, asking for an increase in his meagre allowance, and received a curt reply: 'The Caliphate, your office, is no more than an historical relic. It has no justification for existence. It is a piece of impertinence that you should dare to write to one of my secretaries.' Soon enough the caliph was sent into exile like his predecessor. Mustapha Kemal, once an obscure officer of middling rank, was given the title 'Gazi', or warrior, as Mehmet had once been given it; and eventually 'Ataturk', which means 'Father of the Turks'. But he did not take the title of sultan or caliph. These he regarded with scorn as decadent anachronisms in a modern, progressive age.

In 1925, in a move controversial even to this day, Ataturk abolished Islamic rules for headgear: no longer would women have to wear the veil, nor would the status of a man be defined by the shape and colour of his fez. Ataturk preferred a panama hat and a linen suit, himself. At the same time he closed all the imperial mausolea, to which the faithful had long gone to pray, and all the dervish lodges, in which mystics had danced themselves into distinctly

unmodern trances. In 1928 he abolished the use of the Arabic alphabet, ordering his officials to concoct a version of the Latin one, and not long after that,
the last practices of sharia law were brought to an end. In short, Mustapha
Kemal did everything in his power to break the hold of Islam over his people;
and he moved the centre of the Turkish world away from Istanbul to a new
capital in Ankara, in the heart of Anatolia.

And having done so, he went to the National Assembly in Ankara and
addressed himself to the largest, most visible, and perhaps most inconvenient
relic of the past: the Ayasofya Mosque. In 1920, the European victors of the
First World War, in a vengeful mood, had demanded that the spell of Sultan
Mehmet be reversed, and that Ayasofya should become Hagia Sophia once
again. In other words, the terms of the humiliating Treaty of Sèvres demanded
that the greatest mosque of the greatest city of the nation of Turkey become
a church.

Everybody knew that Ayasofya had not always been a mosque. Everybody
knew that under the whitewash and the carpets, behind the *mihrab* and the
minbar and the minarets, there was another building that, some five hundred
years ago, had been placed under the spell of Islam. But surely the tribe of
Osman had undergone enough in their painful rebirth as the nation of Turkey?
Surely it was enough that the sultan had been sent into exile, and that the
caliphate had been abolished? What further humiliations prompted by the
European enemy would the Father of the Nation heap upon his people?

Ataturk may have been a radical secularist, but he was nothing if not a
canny politician. His clear blue eyes twinkled as he announced: 'We have
invited the Byzantine Society of the United States to begin excavations at
Ayasofya. Ayasofya will become a museum.' The vaunting powers of Europe,
who preached to others about modernity and liberal democracy, could hardly
object to something so modern, so liberal, as a museum. And the people of
Turkey, who could surely be forgiven a little nostalgia for their old customs,

could be spared the humiliation of the conversion of Ayasofya into Hagia Sophia.

And nothing would give Ataturk greater pleasure than to exorcise such a pile of the superstitious spell that had afflicted it for centuries. A museum it would be, a historical document, a memento of yesteryear, connected to no one religion, the international patrimony of a disinterested modern mankind. Just as the golden chain that connected the dome of Hagia Sophia to Heaven had been broken in a vision of moving flame on the night of 25 May 1453, so the invisible line that had connected the Ayasofya Mosque to the *Ka'aba* in Mecca was now also severed. In 1929, some fourteen hundred years after it had been built, Ayasofya became a building, no more, nor less. It pointed nowhere in particular, and was the centre of nowhere.

The archaeologists of the Byzantine Society dug beneath the pavement in front of the building and found the remains of the basilica of Theodosius, burned down by the Blues and the Greens in the Nika riots of 532. They scraped away the whitewash that covered the walls and found the glittering mosaics of Constantine and Justinian, of the Virgin Mary and Christ himself. They took away the carpets, and underneath them they found a purple stone: the Omphalos, which had once been the Navel of the World. But because Hagia Sophia had also been Ayasofya, the archaeologists did not take away the minarets, or the fountains, or the pews, or the *minbar*, or the *mihrab* itself. They all remain, the fragments of the spell that was cast when Mehmet the Conqueror climbed on the altar table, turned his face to Mecca, and said his prayers.

Petitions and campaigns to return the building to both Christian and Islamic use still abound, each citing the custom of centuries to justify their cause; while others propose the use of Ayasofya as a memorial to the victims of the great clash of cultures that the building embodies, from the Crusades to the War On Terrorism. All sides agree that the Turkish government and

UNESCO do not adequately fund the work required to keep the building stand-ing, and all see political motivation – secularist, Islamist, Christian – in this parsimony.

In 2006, Pope Benedict went to Ayasofya. He stood in front of the *mihrab* and said his *Ave Maria*s, while at the same time Islamist protestors prostrated themselves before the mosaics of Roman emperors and called out to Allah. No spells were cast that day, or if there were neither Maria nor Allah seems to have heard them. The babble of the crowd echoed against a dark and empty dome, and their aimless feet trampled the stone that had once been the navel of the world.

THE SANTA CASA OF LORETO

The Wondrous Flitting of the Holy House

THE HOLY HOUSE OF LORETO CARRIED BY ANGELS.
Nineteenth-century devotional engraving.

Reproduction

*T*he *Parthenon was a church for a millen-
nium, longer by far than it had ever been a temple to Athene, and its transformation from
one to the other took more than a single act of vandalism or conversion. For a thousand
years every bishop of Athens would carve his name into the marble of the old temple to
make it his own, in a rite common to all his predecessors and his successors. Visiting digni-
taries would donate relics and treasures to the building, to sustain what they hoped would
be an endless cycle of prayer.*

*If the architectural transformations of the Dark Ages were characterized by
brutal shocks of theft and appropriation, those of the later Middle Ages were characterized by endless repetition. Medieval lives were lived within the enclosed worlds of the
monastery and the village, the fixed social hierarchy of aristocrat, priest, and peasant.
They were governed by the repeated rituals of the church year and the monastic hours,
the routine of the seasons, and the inexorable cycles of birth, inheritance, reproduction,
and death.*

*This repetitious stability was an astonishing achievement for the societies that emerged
from the catastrophes of imperial collapse and barbarian invasion. All those familiar*

prayers and curses, all that monastic copying of antique texts, all those seasonal songs and dances suffused the medieval world with a sense of divinely ordained order.

The Holy House possesses nothing of the unique perfection of the Parthenon, the stolen splendour of San Marco, or the layered complexity of Hagia Sophia. It would never have qualified as a member of the elite band of buildings that inhabit the architect's dream. It is distinguished not by its originality, but by its ubiquity: it can be found around the world in any number of outlandish places. And the building of the Holy House — the very process by which it appears — was a ritual repeated again and again, as the joys and sorrows of the Virgin are told again and again on the beads of the rosary. For the story of the Holy House, like the story of the Virgin herself, is a tale of miraculous reproduction.

THE HOLY HOUSE CONTAINS ONE ROOM, THIRTEEN FEET WIDE AND THIRTY feet long. At the west end of the Holy House there is a square window; and there are two doors, one to each side. The inside of the Holy House is dark, and it smells of candle wax. The walls have a greasy dampness to them, and they are bare, save for the fragments of a fresco that once adorned them.

The Holy House is everywhere. There is a Holy House above a meadow in the village of Walsingham in Norfolk. There is a Holy House on the hill of Acireale in Sicily, where holy men used to take refuge from brigands; and there is a Holy House in the high valleys of the Valtelline, where it rests under the dome of the church of Tresivio, overlooking steep vineyards and snowy hills. In San Miguel de Allende in Mexico there is a Holy House that dates back to 1735; it is enshrined in the church of San Felipe Neri, blazing with Aztec gold.

There are some fifty Holy Houses in the Czech Republic alone. In Prague it resides in the cloister of a nunnery whose rococo ornamentation is as sensuous and joyful as the lives of its inmates were ascetic and contemplative. In Slany it is hidden in a church on the edge of a dusty municipal park, where somnolent Romanies doze and argue with one another on benches under the lime trees. In Rumburk, a dusty truck stop between Prague and Dresden, it is guarded by a young girl; while in Českâ Lipa the Holy House is found in the town museum, at the end of corridors inhabited by stuffed animals, geological specimens, defunct agricultural machinery, and Nazi memorabilia. In Kosmonosy you must ask for the Holy House at the psychiatric hospital, while another Holy House perches on a crag in a forest outside Poděbrady. In the shabby village of Zětenice the Holy House is found at the end of a long walk up a wooded hill, so altered by time that only tiny cracks in the stucco reveal where its doors and windows once opened.

There are also places from which the Holy House has already flitted away. Ancienne Lorette, now a suburb at the end of Quebec airport, is a place of Travelodges and Comfort Inns, temporary storage containers and taxis into town. Its tourist literature advertises just one historic attraction: 'The Church of the Annunciation,' boasts the brochure, 'dates all the way back to 1907.' But the tradition of reverence for Our Lady in this place is much older than that, and this story is older still.

1674

Once upon a time, a tribe appeared with their sorcerer in a clearing by a great river. The tribe was the Huron, and they called the great river Kaniatarowanenneh; but the old sorcerer's name was Father Marie-Joseph Chaumonot, and he insisted on naming the river for St Lawrence, whoever he might have been. Chaumonot and the Huron had wandered together for many years through the wilderness, and they had endured terrible hardships. They were tired and ill, and they needed to rest, so they laid down their burdens and they built a village in the clearing in the forest by the river.

The sorcerer named the village Lorette, and in the middle of it he built a Holy House. There was one room, thirteen feet wide and thirty feet long. At the west end of the Holy House there was a square window, and there were doors on the northern and southern sides. The house was dark and the walls were bare, save for frescoes that adorned them in crooked patches. At the east end of the house, on a simple table, the sorcerer placed an image of a little baby and his mother.

And when the Holy House was finished, Father Chaumonot went into it and uttered his magic in a language that the Huron could not understand.

> *Hail Mary, full of Grace,*
> *The Lord is with thee.*
> *Blessed art thou among women,*
> *And blessed is the fruit of thy womb, Jesus.*

The Huron elders waited outside. When he had finished, Father Chaumonot came to them, and told them his story in their own language.

1631

Once upon a time there was a naughty little boy called Joseph, whose parents were very poor. This naughty boy stole 100 sous from his uncle, and he ran away from home and wandered for many years. He grew up on the road, and lived on his wits. He learnt the smooth manners of a valet, the spurious authority of a tutor, and the ardour of a lady's lover; but ultimately he fell on hard times. He found himself begging on the streets of Ancona in Italy, covered in sores, wearing only filthy rags, unshaven, unkempt, unloved.

He had heard about a shrine nearby that was frequented by many pilgrims. Not, of course, that he was interested in pilgrimages: he had seen enough of the world to sneer at superstition. 'Let them keep their eyes on Heaven and their hands clasped in prayer,' he thought, 'while I relieve them of their worldly goods!' So Joseph followed the pilgrims on the day's walk to the sanctuary. They could see it for miles before they got there: a dome atop a fortified hill on the horizon.

The walls of the sanctuary enclosed a magnificent piazza. A fountain played in the centre, and colossal colonnades shaded the thirsty, the sick, and the hopeful. At the end of the piazza the doors of the church were open, and Joseph entered the sacred gloom. A queue of pilgrims led to a shrine under the great dome he had seen from afar.

Directly under the dome, right at the heart of the church, was a small structure entirely encased in marble. Between Corinthian columns as slim and as beautiful as a young virgin, bas-reliefs told the story of the life of Our Lady. There was Mary at her birth, with her mother St Anne lying in bed and her father St Joachim poking his nose round the door. There was Mary taken to the Temple. There was Mary betrothed to Joseph. There was Mary receiving the visitation of the Angel Gabriel; and there was Mary coddling the infant Jesus in the stable in Bethlehem. There was Mary at the empty tomb, grieving for her lost son. The prophets and sibyls who had foretold all these things were also there, seated in niches.

Joseph followed the pilgrims into the marble structure. Inside, there was one simple dark room. The walls had a greasy dampness to them and they were bare, save for scraps of painting and graffiti in a language that Joseph could not understand. At the east end of the house, in a mandorla, an aura of gilded flame, resided a magnificent idol: a little baby with his mother, Our Lady. The beggar forgot for a moment why he was there. He knelt with the other pilgrims at the altar and said his *Ave Marias*.

And when he emerged into the sunshine, he realized that something had changed. His lice and his sores and his filth had left him, and he had been made clean. He ran back into the basilica, and accosted the nearest priest he could find. He told him, breathlessly, of the miracle that had occurred.

The priest expressed no surprise whatsoever. He led the young man back into the church, sat him down in front of a stone plaque fixed to the wall, and pointed to the words carved upon it: 'The Wondrous Flitting of the Kerk of Our Blest Lady of Laureto'.

1294

Once upon a time, the priest said, there was a virtuous matron called Laureta who lived in a grove of laurel trees. She had spent many years secluded there, praying to Our Lady amid the beasts of the forest and the wilderness.

One night Laureta had a vision. Her grove was filled with light, and a small building descended from the heavens. As it touched down, the laurels of the grove bowed to the ground. Laureta did not move; but the next morning she found that a clearing had appeared in her grove, and in the middle of that clearing there was now a small shrine. She entered it. At the east end of a dark room, thirty feet by thirteen, scrawled with foreign graffiti, she saw the little baby and his mother at the heart of a flaming golden mandorla.

Laureta knelt down and said her *Ave Marias*. She valued her solitude, and for several days she kept the Holy House secret among the laurels; but it was not to remain hidden for long. First came the curious, who had heard the commotion and wanted to see what had happened. Then came the devout, who made their way to the little house to honour Our Lady in prayer. And then came thieves and bandits, who hid amid the dark laurel trees and stole the offerings that the pilgrims brought to the shrine. What had once been a quiet retreat had become a seething mass of people, and Laureta prayed to Our Lady for deliverance.

Her prayer was answered. The Holy House flitted away as quickly as it had appeared, and it reappeared moments later in a meadow outside Laureta's grove which belonged to two brothers. There the pilgrims could approach the sacred structure on open ground, and the thieves could not come close to them without being seen. So many people flocked to the Holy House with offerings that the small building was soon piled high with gifts. The two brothers who now owned the shrine looked at their newfound wealth, and they looked at one another; and they licked their lips, and rubbed their hands, and laughed.

But it was not long before they laughed a little less, and rubbed their hands a little less, and looked at one another sideways. It was not long before they started to suspect each other of filching gifts from the shrine. And it was not long before the two brothers, who had once loved one another, began fighting amongst themselves; and as they fought over the gifts it had brought them, the Holy House flitted away once more.

It reappeared moments later on a nearby hill. There, only the most devoted could reach it. There guards could guard it; and there it stayed. The guards and the priests lashed the Holy House to the ground with ropes and pegs so that it would not flit away again, and they built a wall around it so that no-one could steal its treasures.

Everyone knew the house was holy, but they had no idea where it had come from or what it was. Then, a couple of years later, a hermit came to the authorities with a dream. The Blessed Virgin had appeared to him, he told them, and revealed to him the true nature of the Holy House and the source of its flitting. The authorities passed the information to their masters, and they to theirs, until eventually it reached the ears of the Pope, who – not being the type to believe such stories too readily – gathered together some sixteen men of credit to verify the tale.

He gave them the measurements of the Holy House as he had been told them, and sent them on a journey to the place from which the building had supposedly flitted. The Pope's emissaries crossed the Adriatic Sea, and arrived at the Croatian port of Fiume. They were directed up to the fortress above the town; and there they were introduced to an old priest, Father Alexander Georgevich, who told them his story.

1291

Once upon a time there were some shepherds abiding in the fields, keeping watch over their flock by night. The angel of the Lord came upon them, and the glory of the Lord shone round about them, and they were sore afraid. And the angel said unto them: 'Fear not: for, behold, I bring you good tidings of great joy, which shall be to all people.' But the shepherds were still sore afraid, and they ran back to the fortress, which was called Tersatto.

The next day the shepherds went out again into the fields. In place of the heavenly host, they found a little house sitting on the grass. But the shepherds did not dare to enter the building, and they returned to the fortress a second time.

The third time they brought the castle guard and old Father Georgevich out into the fields with them. They helped him down the hill, since at his age his limbs were painful and stiff, and now they ventured into the little building. The bare walls were streaked with grease and soot, under which could be discerned graffiti in a language that not even learned Father Georgevich could understand. At the east end of the house, mounted on a high table, stood an image of a little baby in his mother's arms.

The shepherds and the guards and old Father Georgevich left the shrine, and Father Georgevich hobbled home to pray to Our Lady for guidance. He fell asleep at his kneeler. The Virgin Mary appeared to him and told him all about the Holy House, and then she said: 'In order that you may bear testimony of all these things, be healed. Your unexpected and sudden recovery shall confirm the truth of what I have declared to you.' Father Georgevich sprung up from his kneeler without a twinge of pain, and he did what Our Lady told him to do. He went to the governor of the fortress and told him the story the Virgin Mary had imparted to him.

The governor reported it to his master, the Ban of Croatia, who sent artificers to examine the building. They told him that its dimensions were thirty feet in length, and thirteen in breadth; and that the golden stone of which it was constructed was a certain type of limestone, and the sweet smelling timber of its roof was cedar, neither of which was then obtainable in Croatia. Then the Ban sent the clerics of his court to their archives, and they told him that such limestone and cedar could be obtained from Palestine alone. They also told him that the dimensions of the house matched those of only one other, in Nazareth, in Palestine, in the basilica of the Annunciation.

And so the Ban sent deputies to distant Nazareth to see this Holy House of Mary of which his clerics had spoken. The deputies travelled over sea and mountain, suffering many dangers, until they arrived in Nazareth. The Christian crusaders had only just been expelled from the Holy Land, which was now firmly under the sway of Islam. Churches had been demolished or made over into mosques, and Christians everywhere were converting in droves to the religion of their new rulers. The Croatian deputies found Nazareth desolate and the basilica of the Annunciation in ruins. They picked their way through the rubble, until at last they found a makeshift shrine on the spot where their guide had told them the Holy House would be. There was one old priest at the door. They went in, and he told them his story.

328

Once upon a time there was an innkeeper's daughter who married a soldier. Some say it happened in Nicomedia, others in York, but at any rate, her name was Helena, and her son – who also became a soldier – she named Constantine. He became the Emperor of Rome, moved its capital to Constantinople, converted his empire to Christianity, and declared himself as the fourth member of the Holy Trinity, joining the Father, the Son, and the Holy Ghost on his deathbed. And so Helena, whose beginnings were humble, ended up as the mother of a god.

Helena was a Christian at least as enthusiastic as her son, and when he had pacified the eastern parts of his empire she undertook a pilgrimage to the Holy Land. Three hundred and twenty-eight years after Jesus had been born, Helena went to see the places where he, the co-divinity with her son, had lived and died and risen again.

Helena travelled all over Palestine, doing good works, endowing churches, and discovering miraculous relics. She founded the Church of the Nativity in Bethlehem and the Church of the Ascension in Jerusalem. Helena discovered the True Cross, upon which Christ had hung for our sins, hidden in a cistern on Golgotha. In the governor's palace in Jerusalem she located the staircase down which Pontius Pilate had walked after condemning Jesus to death. Among the ruins on Mount Moriah, Helena had her men excavate columns from the very Temple of Solomon. All of these things she ordered to be labelled, packed, and shipped back to her son in Rome. They are all still there.

Nazareth had always been a small village, and hard to find, but Helena found it. She swept into the hamlet with her imperial entourage and began to seek out the childhood haunts of Our Lord. She found the well from which Mary used to draw water, and the carpentry shop used by St Joseph. She also found a little house with just one room, thirteen feet wide and thirty feet long, lit by a single square window high on the western wall. On a shelf of living rock at the east end perched a statue of a mother and child.

'What is this shrine, and what is that image?' demanded Helena. 'Is it Cybele, or Juno? Or some other pagan idol?'

The attendant of the shrine shrugged his shoulders, and told her.

O

Once upon a time, in an obscure village, there was a little house. In this house there was but one bare room, about thirty feet long and thirteen feet wide; and in this little room there dwelt a mother and her child. The name of the village was Nazareth. The name of the child, who was a girl, was Mary.

As Mary sat in her house, to her great surprise, an angel flew in through the window on the western wall and spoke to her. 'Hail Mary, full of grace,' he said, 'the Lord is with thee. Blessed art thou among women, and blessed is the fruit of thy womb, Jesus.'

'Behold the handmaid of the Lord,' said he.

'Be it unto me according to thy word,' said she.

So in the house the Word was made Flesh and dwelt among us. Many years passed; and Mary's son, Our Lord Jesus Christ, died, was buried, and rose again, in accordance with the scriptures. So now, when we think of Mary, it is difficult for us to imagine the little girl and her surprise. Instead we say:

> *Pray for us O Holy Mother of God*
> *That we may be made worthy of the promises of Christ.*

Holy Mary, Mother of God,
Pray for us sinners
Now, and at the hour of our death.

Amen.

328

The dowager Empress Helena, who was herself the mother of a god, knelt in front of the humble image in the lowly shrine and said her *Ave Maria*s. And in order to venerate the holy spot, she commanded that the house should itself be housed: that the sacred vessel that was the house (that had contained the sacred vessel that was Mary that had once contained Our Lord) be placed in a sacred vessel. A small church was built around the little building, and a convent of nuns established to tend the shrine.

1291

And that shrine, the old priest told the deputies of the Ban of Croatia, was the one in which they now stood. Here was the site of the Holy House, the place where the Word had been made Flesh, the home of Our Lady and Our Lord, the spot blessed by the presence of St Helena.

There was nothing there. Helena's church was gone. The mighty basilica raised in its place by the crusaders was gone. There was only a little shed built over the spot where the Holy House would be; and the Holy House itself had disappeared.

And then the old priest told them when it had disappeared. The day upon which the Holy House had flitted away from Nazareth, they realized, was the very day upon which it had appeared at Tersatto. The deputies of the Ban of Croatia did not speak, but left Nazareth, and went on their way, pondering what they had seen and heard.

1294

The Ban's deputies were glad to be on home shores again, and they were glad to be able to bring good tidings to their master. Their ship docked at Fiume, and they were led up the hill to the fortress of Tersatto. The Ban of Croatia met them with a grim face. They began to tell him their news, but he stopped them short. In silence, they were led to the field of the Holy House outside Tersatto. There was nothing there. The Holy House had disappeared.

Old Father Georgevich told the emissaries of Pope Boniface just when the Holy House had disappeared; and they realized that the night upon which the Holy House had flitted away from Tersatto was the very night upon which it had appeared in the laurel grove over the sea. What's more, Father Georgevich said that the shepherds who were in the fields that night had seen a multitude of the heavenly host appear in the sky. The angels lifted the house off the ground and bore it away into the darkness. The emissaries of Pope Boniface did not speak, but left Tersatto, and went home to tell their master of all the things they had heard.

1631

The priest took Joseph Chaumonot by the hand and he led the beggar back towards the Holy House of Loreto, encrusted in marble, thronged with pilgrims, shaded by a gigantic dome. They went in together. There was the small room where Mary had once sat. There was the window through which the angel Gabriel had flown in order to bring the good news to her. The walls were bare, save for the fragments of an ancient fresco. There had been a fire in the Holy House, the priest told the beggar, and the paintings had been damaged by the flames – except, he pointed out, for those parts that showed the face of Mary. The strange graffiti scratched on the walls, the priest explained, were messages written by the faithful, in Greek and Aramaic and Hebrew and the other languages of the Holy Land, when the Holy House had been at home in Nazareth.

Then the priest walked Joseph Chaumonot around the outside of the Holy House. It was encased in a gorgeous marble reliquary, made, the priest said, at the behest of Pope Julius II by his master artificer, Donato Bramante. On its sides, bas-reliefs told the story of the life of Our Lady: her birth, her presentation in the Temple, the Annunciation, the Crucifixion, and the Assumption. There was one scene carved there that Chaumonot did not recognize from the Bible. A battle was taking place as the armies of Muhammad overran the Holy Land. Above the battle there was the Holy House, resting on a cloud that was borne aloft by angels. It was flying over the sea and the land, flitting over mountains to the fortress of Tersatto, and then onwards, until at last it came to rest on top of a dark grove of laurel trees. On the steep roof of the little house sat Our Lady and her child, her veil fluttering in the wind. It was all exactly as the priest had said.

Young Chaumonot turned to his companion. 'The Holy House of Our Lady, in which God and Man were joined, which flew through the air, and before which I stand today, has saved me,' he said. 'I was a beggar, filthy, covered in sores, sunk in error, and now I am made clean. What can I do to repay the debt I owe the Holy House?'

The priest answered him with another story, a poem about another Holy House. In a soft voice, he began to sing 'The Ballade of Walsingham'.

1061

Beholde and se, ye goostly folkes all,
Which to this place have devocyon
When ye to Our Lady askynge socoure call
Desyrynge here hir helpe in your trybulacyon:
Of this hir chapell ye may se the fundacyon.
If ye wyll this table overse and rede
Howe by myracle it was founded indede.

Once upon a time, the priest sang, when King Edward the Confessor ruled England, a noblewoman had a dream. Her name was Richeldis de Faverches, and she was the lady of the Manor of Walsingham in Norfolk. Her husband had recently died, leaving her with a small baby boy and a large country estate. Richeldis was a busy woman, with many responsibilities and much to worry her.

Each night her peasants corralled the livestock, her servants cleared the hall, and her workmen laid their tools aside, but Richeldis did not rest. Each night she placed her baby son in a basket next to her on the floor, knelt down, and turned to Our Lady. She prayed for the opportunity to honour her in devotion. She often fell asleep at her kneeler.

One night as she slept the angel of the Lord appeared and took the dreaming Richeldis to faraway Palestine. He showed her the church that St Helena had built over Mary's little house and led her in. You will know by now what she saw.

Our Lady, seated with her child at the east end of the house, spoke to Richeldis and said:

O doughter, consider ...

Of thys place take thou surely the mette,

Another lyke thys at Walsyngham thou sette

Unto my laude and synguler honoure;

All that me seche there shall fynde socoure

Where shall be hadde in a memoryall

The great ioy of my salutacyon.

Fyrste of my ioys grounde and orygynall

Rote of mankyndes gracious redempcyon,

Whan Gabryell gaue to me relacyon

To be a moder through humylyte,

And goddys sonne conceyue in virgynyte.

'Be it unto me according to thy word,' said Richeldis, and in her dream she set about measuring the Holy House.

In the morning Richeldis rose from her kneeler and walked out of her house, out through her garden, to the meadow by the village. There she gathered her people about her, and she chose craftsmen from among them to carry out the work that Our Lady had set her. She explained her intention: they were to build a replica of the Holy House of Nazareth, in which Our Lady had received the Annunciation and had raised Our Lord. As the men set to work preparing materials, Richeldis looked about the village for the right spot to build their Holy House, but none presented itself: the ground was riddled with springs and too boggy to build on.

At the end of the first day the workmen laid their tools aside, but Richeldis did not rest. She knelt down and turned to Our Lady, praying for guidance as to the location of her Holy House. Again she fell asleep at her prayers, but this time she spent a dreamless night, for no sign came to help her.

On the second day Richeldis rose from her kneeler and walked out of her house, through her garden, to the meadow by the village. She found it covered with a sparkling celestial dew. Our Lady had sent a sign to help her, for there were two plots in the meadow that the dew had not touched, each identical in size with the Holy House in Nazareth itself. Richeldis had asked for an answer, but she had been given a choice.

She chose the first site, and set her men to work at once. They laid the necessary foundations and began to build the walls of the house on top of them. But somehow stone would not rest above stone, nor mortar set, nor timber align; and the Holy House was no closer to completion by evening than it had been in the morning. At the end of the second day the workmen laid their tools aside, but Richeldis did not rest. She knelt down and turned to Our Lady, praying for a solution to a devotion that seemed to have gone hopelessly awry. She fell asleep at her kneeler.

The next day was the third day. Richeldis rose from her kneeler and walked out of her house, through her garden, to the meadow by the village. Once more it was covered in a celestial dew. Where the workmen had left a hole in the ground with piles of building materials, there was now nothing at all. It seemed as if Our Lady had not answered the prayers of Richeldis de Faverches this time.

But then a sensation of being watched made Richeldis turn. She glanced towards the other spot that the miraculous dewfall had made the day before. There, steaming slightly in the early morning damp, stood her Holy House, so perfect, so immaculate, so beautiful, that it might have been made by the hands of Our Lady herself.

A prayer rose to the lips of Richeldis de Faverches:

> *O gracyous Lady, glory of Jerusalem,*
> *Cypresse of Syon and Joye of Israel,*

Rose of Jeryco and Sterre of Bethleem,
O gloryous Lady, our askynge nat repell,
In mercy all wymen ever thou doste excell,
Therfore, blissed Lady, graunt thou thy great grace
To all that the devoutly visyte in this place.

And it was surely granted, for soon enough

Many seke ben here cured by Our Ladyes myghte
Dede agayne revyved, of this is no dought,
Lame made hole and blynde restored to syghte,
Maryners vexed with tempest safe to porte brought
Defe, wounded and lunatyke that hyder have sought
And also lepers here recovered have be
By Oure Ladyes grace of their infyrmyte.

Young Chaumonot interrupted the song. 'So there is a Holy House in Walsingham, then, that's a miraculous copy of the very Holy House before which we stand, made by the hands of angels at the behest of the Virgin Mary? If it is so great and efficacious a shrine, why have I not heard of it?'

The priest answered him with another story, but this time poetry died upon his lips and he reverted to bitter prose. Many years after Richeldis de Faverches had died, he said, King Henry VIII visited the shrine of Walsingham. He walked barefoot into the village, as all pilgrims must, with his lady, Queen Katherine, at his side. Like all pilgrims, he stopped close by the entrance to the shrine to kiss a gigantic bone that came, he was told, from the finger of St Peter. He saw the breast milk of Our Lady, preserved in a crystal phial. He drank from the holy well that was claimed to cure diseases of the head. He placed a gold circlet around the neck of Our Lady in the shrine.

Twenty years later he wanted it back. In 1534, a letter was delivered to the priory in Walsingham demanding that the canons acknowledge that King Henry – rather than the corrupt and distant Pope of Rome – was the head of the Church in England. The prior agreed. He had heard about King Henry and, more importantly, he had heard about what happened to those who crossed him. Besides, Rome was very far away. This was surely just an administrative change. Nothing would happen, he assured his canons.

Nothing did happen for a while, but then one day the king's agents arrived and began to interfere in the priory's affairs. Those few who objected did not last long: the subprior and his lay assistant were soon swinging on gibbets outside the priory walls, and within a year the place was closed. The king's agents took the image of Our Lady that resided within the Holy House, and the milk of the Blessed Virgin in its crystal phial, and the fingerbone of St Peter; and they carried these to London, where they were publicly burnt along with thousands of other idolatrous trinkets.

The priory was demolished, its chapels turned into byres and barns, and the Holy House itself was destroyed. The prior received a handsome pension of £100 a year for his assistance, and the ruins of the abbey were sold to Sir Philip Sidney for £90. All that survives of the dream of Richeldis de Faverches is one broken arch standing in a meadow outside the village, which on the days of Our Lady sometimes sparkles with a celestial dew.

1631

'But what can the pious actions of a lady who died centuries ago have to do with me?' asked Chaumonot. 'The Holy House of Walsingham is gone, but the Holy House of Loreto – the one true house, surely – is still here. Is that not enough?'

The priest answered the young man with a final story. Not so long ago, he said, in Prague, a Bohemian noblewoman had a dream. Her name was Baroness Beligna Katherina von Lobkowicz. The baroness supported the Emperor Ferdinand in the Wars of Religion that ravaged her country, and she feared and despised the reformed faith of his enemies. She had heard stories of the atrocities committed by the reformers in England, of shrines desecrated and ikons destroyed, and she had seen the Protestants of her own land do the same. She had prayed long and often that the emperor would vanquish the heretic armies, and at the Battle of the White Mountain her prayers were answered: the Protestant forces were defeated. Now the baroness prayed to Our Lady for an opportunity to honour her, in thanks for the restoration of Bohemia to the Roman Catholic faith.

You will know what she was asked to do – an angel, some said, told her to do it in a dream. She sent to Vienna, where the Empress Eleanora had just dedicated a new chapel in the Augustinerkirche to Our Lady of Loreto. This chapel, indeed, had been built in exact imitation of Our Lady's dwelling; for the empress, who was herself an Italian, had sent her artificers to Loreto to study the Holy House. The chapel they constructed for her in Vienna was so detailed a copy that it even reproduced the cracks and irregularities in the brickwork of the original, and was decorated with feigned fragments of a fresco damaged by fire. The same artificers now came to Prague, and they built for the Baroness Lobkowicz an exact copy of the Holy House of Vienna, which was an exact copy of the Holy House of Loreto, perfect in every detail.

The Baroness Lobkowicz is not alone, the priest told Chaumonot. All over Bohemia and the other lands engulfed in religious war the pious and the faithful are building copies of the Holy House. They are at work in palace chapels and remote abbeys, on hilltops and in villages, striving to honour Our Lady. They are building to restore the shrines that were desecrated and images that were destroyed; and they are building because, in their devotions, their actions mean more than their words – the things they make more than the things they say.

1674

Joseph Chaumonot knew what he had to do. Made clean by the miraculous intervention of a building, he vowed to repay his debt to the Holy House by making another copy of it and by devoting his life to its occupant, Our Lady of Loreto. He went to Rome, where he presented himself to the Jesuit fathers, the knights of the Virgin Mary; and he ceased to be Joseph the beggar, and became Father Marie-Joseph Chaumonot, Jesuit missionary to the heathen of Canada.

And the little shrine behind him now, far away from Loreto, or Palestine, or Bohemia – this little house in the forest clearing by the banks of the river Kaniatarowanenneh – was his Holy House and the payment of his pledge.

When Father Chaumonot had finished his story, the Huron elders sat on the ground around the Holy House he had made, and they sang in their own language the story of Mary that their sorcerer had taught them:

> 'Twas in the moon of wintertime when all the birds had fled
> That mighty Gitchi Manitou sent angel choirs instead;
> Before their light the stars grew dim and wondering hunters heard the hymn,
> Jesus your King is born, Jesus is born, in excelsis gloria.

> Within a lodge of broken bark the tender babe was found;
> A ragged robe of rabbit skin enwrapped his beauty round.
> But as the hunter braves drew nigh the angel song rang loud and high,
> Jesus your King is born, Jesus is born, in excelsis gloria.

The earliest moon of wintertime is not so round and fair
As was the ring of glory on the helpless infant there.
The chiefs from far before him knelt with gifts of fox and beaver pelt.
Jesus your King is born, Jesus is born, in excelsis gloria.

O children of the forest free, O seed of Manitou,
The holy Child of Earth and Heaven is born today for you.
Come kneel before the radiant boy who brings you beauty, peace, and joy.
Jesus your King is born, Jesus is born, in excelsis gloria.

It is said that the word of the Lord is like seed: some falls on good soil and brings forth crops, but some falls on stony ground and it withers. Father Chaumonot was old when he told his story, and it fell on stony ground. After he died the Huron drifted back to hunting on the prairie and to tracking animals in the forest, and their Holy House disappeared. All that remains of the miraculous tale of Joseph the beggar is the name of his settlement, Ancienne Lorette, and the dedication of the church there to the Annunciation; and the fact that, nearby, large structures full of people take to the air and fly to other places. Our Lady of Loreto is, after all, the patron saint of air travel.

But old Father Chaumonot need not have been disappointed. Uncountable others have heard the message of the Holy House, and followed the example of Richeldis de Faverches: in Italy, in Mexico, in Holland, and in Scotland. The Holy House looks like a simple building, but it is in fact a complex and subtle prayer. Building it is an act of devotion; and like all devotions, it must be repeated again and again. The Holy House is a prayer that exists in time. It abides only for a while before it flits away on a cloud, suffers iconoclastic desecration, dissolves back into the forest, or slides into neglectful ruin. Then it must be made again, as all prayers must be made again.

1931

And like all answers to prayer, the Holy House appears when least expected. Once upon a time in England, not so long ago, in the reign of King George V, a new vicar was appointed to the country parish of Walsingham, in Norfolk. One morning, Father Patten walked to the meadow beside the village, which was covered in a sparkling dew. He picked up a small metal disc lying in the grass and held it in his hand, and he had an idea.

Farmers were always ploughing up old medals that depicted Our Lady of Walsingham. Father Patten had a local craftsman make a statue out of the image on the medal, and he set it up in his parish church. Soon enough, people started to visit the church to pray to Our Lady of Walsingham to intercede for them. At first just a few showed up from the village itself; then the news spread, and more and more people came to the modest shrine, and regular pilgrimages began.

A decade after Father Patten had established the statue in his parish church, the sacred image was moved through the narrow streets of the village to a new home. On a knoll overlooking the meadow where Richeldis de Faverches had built her shrine nearly a thousand years before, the mother and her child were carried into a new church, taken round the aisles, and borne down the nave to a little house thirty feet long and thirteen feet wide. There they were installed, back at home, as if nothing had ever happened.

Every year in May Our Lady of Walsingham is carried in procession around her village. In a floral litter, she is preceded by acolytes, crucifers, thurifers, priests, bishops, Monsignors of the Roman Catholic Church, friars, penitents, choirs, and soldiers. Umbrellini, barques of flowers, and congeries of plaster saints crowd the narrow streets of the village, and high gilded crosses peer into the bedroom windows of the low cottages. Because this is not the fifteenth century, the route of the procession is lined with reformers and the reformed, their placards denouncing superstition and idolatry, the corruption of the Church, and the sheer vulgarity of the scene; and because this is England, everyone pretends not to notice.

At the end of the procession Our Lady is carried back to her home, with its one small room and its square window. There she waits, until she is called forth the next time.

GLOUCESTER CATHEDRAL

In Which a Dead Body Brings a Building to Life

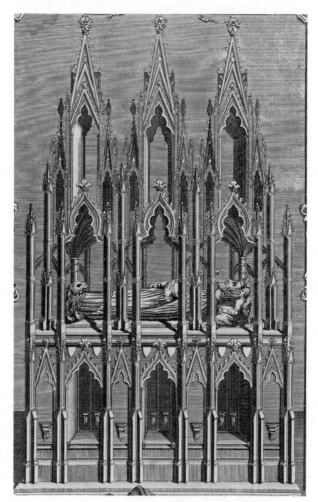

THE GERM OF A CATHEDRAL.

The monument of Edward II (1284–1327) in Gloucester Cathedral.

Evolution

*W*hen the women and the children of the Turkish garrison hid in the Parthenon in 1687, they repeated stories about their place of refuge to reassure themselves; but the stories they told had been repeated so many times that they had long departed from the original script. The doors of the temple had become the gates of Troy, and the Christian apse the throne of Plato. There is no such thing as a perfect copy, and stories and buildings are transformed quite as much as they are preserved in the process of repetition.

The rituals of the Middle Ages sustained a seemingly stable world, but they were also the agents of transformation. The long construction and reconstruction of Gothic cathedrals was a process of copying: each generation of apprentices learned at the feet of the master mason, became master masons themselves, and passed their wisdom on to their own apprentices. But this process was also one of evolution: each generation, in learning from its predecessors, altered what it found, and passed its altered learning on to successors who did the same. The architecture of the earliest cathedrals was an austere, simple affair, but over several centuries it grew into something of wondrous sophistication and complexity.

Because cathedrals took such a long time to build, this evolution manifested itself not only in the construction of new buildings but in the refurbishment of existing ones. Gloucester Cathedral in England provides one of the strangest examples of this process. The original building was a stern Norman basilica, but that church is now festooned with the more florid architecture of later centuries. Each generation of architecture at Gloucester is an increment of refinement laid over its predecessor, and carries tics and quirks derived from its own genealogy.

The origin of the transformations of Gloucester is found in a royal tomb. The architectural development of the cathedral is like the cult of the body that lies within it: an affair of repeated rumours, grown ever wilder with each retelling.

IN 1327, A CART RUMBLED OUT OF THE GATE OF BERKELEY CASTLE, AND its wooden wheels bumped down the track into the grey floodplain of the River Severn. When the cart reached the edge of a forest, two white harts emerged from the trees to meet it. Tall, luminous, and still, they allowed the carters to harness them to the vehicle, and then they bore its burden all the way to Gloucester.

The monks at the abbey in Gloucester were waiting for them. They were fearful; and well might they have been afraid, for the cart that had left Berkeley Castle that morning carried the body of none other than King Edward II. It had been three months since the king had died, and the stories that had spread about his demise were colourful and horrifying. He had been deposed by his faithless wife Isabella, they said, and her lover Roger Mortimer; and the monks whispered a poem that the king had supposedly written:

> *In winter woe befell me,*
> *By cruel Fortune threatened.*

My life now lies a ruin.

Once I was feared and dreaded,

But now all men despise me

And call me a crownless king,

A laughing stock to all.

Edward had been imprisoned at Berkeley Castle for five months, murmured the monks, suspended above a cesspit filled with corpses. He had refused to die, and so, tired of waiting, his keepers had murdered him. He had been a sodomite, the story ran, and his executioners had shoved a red hot poker up his arse. You could hear the screams for miles around, but there were no wounds visible upon the king's body.

Well might the monks of the abbey have been afraid. The other priories in the shire had refused to take the body, so frightened were they of Isabella and Mortimer; but Abbot John Thokey reassured his charges. He had been a friend to the murdered king, and he reminded the monks of the time the two had dined together. It was right there, in the *Historia* of the abbey. 'Sitting at the table in the abbot's hall and seeing there paintings of the kings, his predecessors', Edward II had jokingly asked the abbot whether there was a painting of himself among them. 'The abbot replied, prophesying, rather than making it up, that he hoped he would have him a more honourable place than there.' And so he would: Abbot Thokey had plans for King Edward II. The king had suffered an ignominious end, the abbot told his monks, but now it was time to accord him the honours he had forfeited in life.

On 20 December the king's body, being in no fit state to be seen, was hidden under a wooden effigy, and it was paraded through the streets of Gloucester on a catafalque carved with gilded lions. Behind the hearse walked the people who had most benefited from Edward's demise: his wife, Queen Isabella; her lover, Mortimer; and her son, the young King Edward III. A silver vessel containing the heart of the dead king was held aloft for all the crowds to see, and then Edward II was laid to rest.

No sooner had it been planted in the abbey church than the royal corpse began to generate activity. The masons of the abbey were called to make a sarcophagus of Purbeck marble around the body of Edward II, and on the top of this sarcophagus they placed another image of the king, carved from alabaster. The longing eyes and petulant lower lip of this effigy recalled Edward to those who had known him. The pillow upon which his head lay was supported by angels, as if they were lifting him up to spy the celestial realm, and at his feet lay two lions, marks of his royal rank.

Above the sarcophagus and the effigy floated the very Heaven to which the stone king's sightless eyes aspired. The masons had constructed around the tomb a miniature cathedral too delicate to be inhabited by rude man in this life, a habitation only for the dead and the sanctified. The arches of its vaulted aisle seemed to flicker with holy flame, and it was crowned with three miniature shrines, which were themselves crowned with openwork spires bristling with crockets and finials.

It was just the sort of building that caused one to wonder how many angels could dance on the head of a pin. It was a minor miracle; but, at the time, it occurred to no one to write the names of the men who had wrought it in the *Historia* of the abbey.

* * *

Gloucester Abbey had been founded by Osric, prince of the Hwicce tribe, in 680. But the building in which Edward was laid dated from 1089, when, after a fire had swept through the abbey, Abbot Serlo commanded that a new church be built in the form of a cross. On 15 July 1100 the head of the cross was completed, and this choir was consecrated for service. Over the high altar was a semicircular apse, and the heavy vault of the choir was supported by thick walls, which the masons had pierced with round arches resting on squat columns.

Four years after the consecration of the choir Abbot Serlo passed away, and was succeeded by Abbot Peter and then by Abbot William. It was under the abbacy of this William that the nave – the foot of the cross – was completed, so that the congregation might have somewhere to stand as they listened to the chanting of the monks in the choir. Stretching away towards the west, it was as dark as the sanctuary of Abbot Serlo, and they ornamented its massive arcades with chevrons of a savage simplicity.

And then Abbot William passed away, and was succeeded by Abbot De Lacey and Abbot Hameline. In the Year of Our Lord 1179, Abbot Hameline passed on, and was succeeded by Abbot Carbonel, and then Abbot Blunt; and then Abbot Blunt died, and was succeeded by Abbot Foliot.

It was in the time of Abbot Foliot that a tower was raised above the crossing, where the nave and the choir, the foot and head of the cross, met the transepts – the cross's arms. It was also at this time that the nave was given a new vault, whose pointed arches, slender ribs, and high clerestories relieved some of the heaviness of the ancient architecture.

And when the new vaulting of the nave was complete (but before work could begin on the rest of the abbey) Abbot Foliot died, and was succeeded by Abbot John de Felda, and then Abbot de Gamages; and when Abbot de Gamages died in 1306, he was succeeded by Abbot Thokey, who received the body of the murdered King Edward II and laid him to rest in the abbey. Soon afterwards, Abbot Thokey resigned the abbacy, and was succeeded by Abbot Wigmore; who, it is said in the *Historia* of the abbey, 'took much delight in working with his own hands, both in mechanical arts as well as in embroidery'.

It was not long before the wonderful tomb of Edward II erected in the time of Abbot Thokey began to perform wonders, and it was not long before people came to see it in hope of cure and aid. The Purbeck marble of the sarcophagus and even the alabaster face of the king himself are still marked with crosses the pilgrims carved there. Soon, the monks recorded, 'the offerings of the faithful and the devotion which the people showed for King Edward who had been buried in the church were such that the city of Gloucester could scarcely hold the multitude of people flowing together there from the cities, towns, and villages and hamlets of England'. The shrine of Edward II glowed and hummed with prayer, a tiny seed germinating in the dark choir of the abbey.

And in the time of Abbot Wigmore, who loved embroidery, the delicate tomb of Edward II spawned the first of its offspring. Soon, the pilgrims who came to gaze upon the tiny shrine of Edward II found themselves inside its progeny: a gigantic reproduction of the original. The new structure was so large, in fact, that it necessitated the partial demolition of the southern transept of the church. The masons broke down the end wall of the transept and replaced it with a huge tapestry of stone and coloured glass, through which light flooded into an interior that had hitherto been dark. They replaced the original vault that had covered the transept with a complex triangular mesh of ribs; and then they added new clerestory windows, whose four-centred arches and stiff grid of traceries were ornamented with delicate trefoils. Finally, they embroidered the blank walls of the transept with the same grid of tracery as the windows, so that from some angles it was impossible to tell where the windows ended and the walls began.

It was a complex and delicate task, and the signs of the struggle may still be seen. All that lightening of the ancient structure had reduced its ability to support what was above it. At some stage during the work the masons realized that the abbey tower was now in danger of collapsing into the transept, and they devised a huge buttress to support it. It was an emergency measure; but rather than hide it away, the masons allowed this diagonal shaft of stone to slice right through the delicate cage of traceries they had made, so that everyone would see and remember that their ingenuity had averted a disaster. Medieval building was always, to some extent, experimental, relying as it did on margins of safety and rules of thumb derived from experience rather than engineering calculation. The flying buttress that slashes through the south transept at Gloucester shows just how experimental it was.

Experimental, and dangerous: another story is told in the south transept on a tiny scale. Fixed to one of the walls is a small stone bracket made in the form of a mason's 'T' square. It is thought that it once supported an image of St Barbara, whom the masons often invoked to protect them from wind and fire. The top of the bracket is crowned with minute castellations, as if it were the roof of a great building, and its underside is carved with a miniature reproduction of ribbed vaults. A tiny figure of a beardless apprentice clings in desperation to this vault, while his master looks on in horror: it appears that the apprentice is about to fall to a certain death on the abbey floor. It happened to masons all the time, but no-one thought to record the names of their dead in the *Historia* of the abbey they had built.

* * *

When the tomb of Edward II and the southern transept of Gloucester Abbey were finished, Abbot Wigmore was laid to rest, and he was succeeded by Abbot Staunton. In the time of Abbot Staunton, Edward III came to pay his respects at the tomb of his father, and he brought his whole court with him. It was a profitable visit for the abbey. Edward donated a model ship made of gold, in thanks for a safe passage across the sea; his Queen Philippa gave a golden heart and an ear, in thanks for the cure of some malady or other; and their son Prince Edward gave the shrine a cross made of the same material. It is thought that King Edward III saw the offspring of his father's tomb in the southern transept of the abbey church, and desired that the monks and the masons transform the choir where his father was laid in a similar manner.

And so the southern transept of the abbey, which was generated from the tomb of Edward II, generated its own descendant; and the masons started work under the central tower, where all the arms of the cross met one another. Again they took away the ancient ceiling, and again they replaced it with a new vault; but they had learned some lessons from their work in the southern transept. This new vault was even more complex than the one they had made before, and its many ribs sprouted from elaborate bosses carved with angels and saints and wild men of the woods. The new ceiling appeared to be less a structure of stone, resting on heavy walls, than a canopy of creepers hanging in a luminous forest.

When the crossing was complete Abbot Staunton was taken to God, and Abbot Horton took office in his stead; and in the time of Abbot Horton the new vault was extended towards the semicircular apse of the original choir, where the high altar stood. The masons demolished the apse, replacing it with a great window, the largest in the world at the time: it was so enormous that it had to be reinforced with two tall buttresses lest the wind blast it in. At the heart of this window the glaziers put an image of the Virgin Mary receiving the crown of Heaven from her Son. Angels fluttered in the sunny panels above her, and below her the saints, the prelates of the church, and the kings of England stood in multitudinous array. Below these notables were ranked the coats of arms of the nobles and the knights who had fought for King Edward III at the Battle of Crécy.

And just as they had done in the transept, the masons now draped and embroidered the walls of the choir with the same panelling which divided the great window. A screen of narrow shafts and tiny trefoils of stone made it impossible to tell what was window, what was arcade, and what was wall. It was as if the vault above had spread its tendrils down over the heavy walls of the choir, dissolving it into a cage of thin stone ribs webbed with coloured glass and sparkling with light. The grandchild of the tomb of Edward II had learned from its predecessors, and had evolved into forms and languages of even greater elegance and elaboration.

The refurbished choir of Gloucester Abbey was descended from the heavenly mansion that floated over the body of Edward II; but its habitat was an earthly building of thick walls and heavy arcades, and the difficulties of adapting Heaven to Earth are apparent everywhere. While the body of the choir is a model of celestial order, the aisles that run on either side of it are a jumble of mismatched architectures: blocked openings, seemingly random demolitions, and improvised junctions.

Medieval building was rarely, if ever, the simple implementation of a preconceived design. Buildings were not drawn or modelled in their totality before work began on site, and much was therefore left to chance and ingenuity. At the same time, large structures took so long to build that no one generation could ever hope to see them completed in their own lifetime. As a consequence, medieval architecture is almost always the result of a slow collective process of adaptation, rather than the invention of an individual genius.

Nowhere is this more apparent than in the crossing at Gloucester, where the walls of the choir, with their narrowly spaced supporting columns, met the wider transepts. This was a structural problem born out of the misfit between the existing shell of the building and the new design evolving inside it, and it left the vaults of the crossing – and the tower above them – with nothing to rest upon but thin air. It was, perhaps, a miscalculation; but just as they had done before, the masons decided not to conceal their problem but to celebrate it. They decided to make it seem as if their vault was indeed floating on almost nothing at all. They spanned an arch of almost impossible thinness and lightness over the opening of the transept, and then they balanced a tiny pedestal at the apex of this arch. The massive load of the tower came down the ribs of the vault, through the tiny pedestal and the delicate arch, and safely to the ground; but the ribs showed no strain whatsoever, fanning out from the pedestal as if they were dancing around the head of a pin. The masons had taken an intractable problem of engineering and construction, and had conjured an illusory moment of angelic grace.

✳ ✳ ✳

When the choir of Gloucester Abbey was complete, King Edward III died, and Abbot Horton took to his bed; and he was succeeded by Abbot Boyfield. It was in the time of Abbot Boyfield that King Richard II came to stay at the abbey. He prayed at the shrine of Edward II, and embellished it with his ensign of the white hart – in memory, perhaps, of the creatures that had drawn the king's hearse from Berkeley Castle to Gloucester. He even wrote to the Pope proposing that Edward II be canonized.

When Abbot Boyfield was taken to God, he was succeeded by Abbot Froucester. And in the time of this Abbot Froucester the choir of Gloucester Abbey, which was the child of the southern transept, which was the child of the tomb of Edward II, spawned a further descendant: a cloister of four walks surrounding a central garden.

On one side of these walks, a luminous grid of windows looked into the garth; on the other, a solid stone wall hid the secular functions of the abbey. The masons covered every surface of the new cloister with the same traceries they had employed in the transformation of the choir, so that it was impossible to tell what was wall and what was window. Indeed, so elaborate was this masking that it was possible to imagine even the heavy vault above the cloister walks as a skeleton of stone ribs, webbed with a skin of glowing glass.

But there was an additional elaboration here in the cloister, a further step in the evolution of the tomb's descendants. The vaults above the tomb of Edward II, and the vaults in the new southern transept and in the refurbished choir, were all essentially just barrel-shaped tunnels intersected at right angles by other tunnels; but the masons vaulted the walks of the cloister in a completely different manner. In between each cloister window they placed a thin shaft of stone, and from this shaft emerged a conical fan of ribs which fanned out above each window. Each of these fans met its neighbour tangentially, so that the cloister walks read as an avenue of palm trees with spreading fronds rather than a crossing of tunnels. Indeed, it was almost impossible to imagine that this was the work of the same masons who had made the transepts and the choir.

The cloister was an entirely new structure, built on new ground outside the church; but it still recalled in stone the quirks and idiosyncrasies of its ancestors caused by the mismatch between them and the original abbey. There is a door on the west side of the cloister, for instance, that used to lead into the abbot's lodging. It's easy to miss. Here, the ribs of the vault fan out not from a shaft of stone between the windows, but from the apex of a slender arch placed above the door – repeating, in miniature, that angelic moment in the crossing of the church where the masons made a vault that seemed to dance on air. There, the device was an ingenious response to structural necessity, but in the cloister its presence is apparently arbitrary: an inherited tic, a family trait outlasting the original reason for its existence.

After the cloister was complete, Abbot Froucester passed away, and was succeeded by Abbot Moreton, who 'died without having done anything worthy of particular notice'. And when Abbot Moreton was taken to God, he was succeeded by Abbot Morwent, who started to rebuild the nave of the abbey church but was cut off after three arches.

When Abbot Morwent died he was succeeded by Abbot Boulers, who was made the king's ambassador to Rome and was imprisoned by the Duke of York in Ludlow Castle. He had little time for building. In 1450 Abbot Boulers was elevated to the see of Hereford, and was succeeded by Abbot Sebrok; and in the time of this abbot the descendants of the tomb of Edward II spawned yet another descendant, larger and more prominent than all its ancestors. The tomb of King Edward II, having remade the south transept and the choir, now pierced the roof, transforming the bell tower that rose above the crossing of the abbey church.

The new tower advertised the presence of that tomb to the distant fields and the flood plains that surrounded the city, all the way to the River Severn. It does not reach upwards to Heaven like a pointed spire. Rather, it seems as if a weightless shrine of traceries, cusped arches, thin buttresses, and pointed crockets has descended from above to float upon the abbey roof. The top of the tower is embroidered with castellations and corner towers, so riddled with a fretwork that they might have been embroidered in lace rather than carved from stone.

Abbot Sebrok was succeeded by Abbot Hanley, and then Abbot Farley; and in their time the ancient abbey church burst open and gave birth to another descendant of the tomb of Edward II, a new chapel extending from the east end of the church behind the altar. This Lady Chapel was not imprisoned in the earthly cave of the old building, and the sun poured in on all sides, refracted through colourful stained glass that shimmered against golden stone. Liberated from the ancient structure, the Lady Chapel had no need for any of those oddities – evolved in response to emergency and miscalculation – that disrupt the regular composition of the transept, the crossing, and the choir.

But the masons put them there all the same. Buttresses sliced diagonally through grids of tracery, vaults sprang from etiolated arches that flew through the air, and clusters of stone ribs fanned out from tall thin shafts. Redundant and diminutive as these motifs were, their presence was no arbitrary quirk. The Lady Chapel was a record in stone of all the strange and wonderful things that the masons had devised, generation after generation, in the transform-ation of Gloucester Abbey. It was their testament and their history. One can only suppose that, since the monks would not write it for them, the masons had decided to build their own *Historia* of the abbey in stone.

* * *

The identities of the masons are, in the absence of written records, a matter of rumour and speculation. Some have noted similarities in conception and detail between the south transept at Gloucester and the chapel of St Stephen at the Palace of Westminster, although that chapel burned down in 1834. On that basis, scholars argue that Edward III sent the master mason of St Stephen's, a certain Thomas of Canterbury, to dignify the resting place of his father in the manner of the court. We shall never know. Thomas of Canterbury disappears from the record in 1336, just nine years after the death of Edward II.

There are a few broken stones on display in London which are all that remain of the chapter house of the medieval cathedral of St Paul's. The mouldings carved on these stones are so similar to those in the choir at Gloucester Abbey that some believe that the same person must have made them both. That person, they argue, was the master mason William Ramsay, the chief scion of a dynasty of masons that built the cathedrals and the castles of eastern England in the middle of the fourteenth century. He had worked under the tutelage of Thomas of Canterbury at St Stephen's in Westminster, perhaps as his apprentice.

But there is no record of William Ramsay in the *Historia* of Gloucester Abbey. There is no mention of any workmen during this period at all. We do know that a certain John of Sponlee surveyed the castle of Gloucester in 1336, and was later engaged at court. Perhaps he implemented the design of William Ramsay for the abbey choir. Perhaps the great man spotted him, and made him his apprentice, and carried him off to Edward III's Court of the Round Table. We shall never know.

The fan vaults of the cloister present further mysteries. They are obviously the descendant of the vaults of the abbey interior in some respects, but they represent a radical departure from their predecessors in others, and they certainly betray the hand of a new master. Perhaps a clue lies in a seventeenth-century drawing made of the chapter house at Hereford Cathedral, near Gloucester, before it was demolished. The paper is rough, and the line uncertain, but the resemblance is unmistakable: the vault of this vanished chapter house – or at least its manuscript ghost – is so similar to the cloister vault at Gloucester that it is almost impossible to imagine that the two were not in some way related.

And we do know who designed the chapter house at Hereford: a certain Thomas of Cantebrugge, who became a freedman of that town in 1365. Now, Cantebrugge is the old name for Cambridge, a hamlet on the road between Gloucester and Bristol. Some have argued that this Thomas of Cantebrugge must have begun his career under William Ramsay or John of Sponlee, working on the choir of Gloucester, and became master mason there before moving on to Hereford. Perhaps. Maybe this Thomas of Cantebrugge was the inventor of the fan vault. We shall never know.

It is written in the *Historia* that the transformation of Gloucester's bell tower under Abbot Sebrok was designed and carried out by a canon of the abbey, a certain Robert Tully who went on to become the Bishop of St David's in the principality of Wales. There is, however, an old country rhyme that contradicts the *Historia*:

> *John Gowere,*
> *Who built Campden Church*
> *And Glo'ster towre.*

Of John Gower we know nothing more; and of those who designed and built the Lady Chapel we know nothing at all.

* * *

Perhaps it is no coincidence that the Freemasons of today – who are, of course, sworn to silence in all that they do – trace their origins back to a document produced in 1390, when the cloisters of Gloucester Abbey were under construction. This document, known as the Regius Manuscript, is written in a dialect of English associated with Gloucestershire; and in it, the masons, for the first time, wrote their history down on parchment rather than building it in stone.

The Regius Manuscript opens in grandiose Latin: 'Hic incipient constituciones artis geometriae secundum Euclydem [Here begin the constitutions of the art of geometry according to Euclid]'. For the masons of the Middle Ages were not ignorant craftsmen, as some have supposed. If they were silent, it was not because they lacked means to communicate, but because they chose not to do so. The masons were learned men of ancient lineage; what is more, they were free men, not the serfs of some lord or abbot. Master masons like Thomas of Canterbury, John of Sponlee, and Thomas of Cantebrugge were free to come and go as they pleased, following the great building programmes of cathedral and castle and abbey around the country.

These men had minds and secrets of their own, and in order that they might all share and benefit from their knowledge, the master masons agreed to a list of regulations. Foremost among these were two articles: first, that they should all assemble and meet together at regular intervals; and second, that they should all employ and train apprentices in their craft.

It is the relationship between master and apprentice that underlies the story of the many descendants of the tomb of Edward II and their successive superimposition on the old church of Abbot Serlo. For more than a century after the king was buried in the abbey, apprentices succeeded their masters in an unbroken chain. The master masons who built the Lady Chapel in the time of Abbots Hanley and Farley had been the apprentices of the masters who had built the tower in the time of Abbot Sebrok, who had been the apprentices of the masters who rebuilt the west end of the nave in the time of Abbot Morwent, who had been the apprentices of the masters who had built the cloister in the time of Abbot Froucester, who had been the apprentices of the masters who had built the choir in the time of Abbots Staunton and Horton, who had been the apprentices of the masters who had built the transept in the time of Abbot Wigmore – and so on, ultimately, to the original, unknown master who had devised the tomb of the dead king itself.

Every generation learned at the feet of the generation that preceded it, and so, in the end, did the abbey itself. The Lady Chapel is a recitation of all the lessons learned during a century and a half of construction; the bell tower is the external application of the interior architecture of the choir and the crossing; the choir and the crossing are an elegant refinement of the experimental design of the south transept; and the south transept is the reconstruction, at a vast scale, of the tomb of Edward II.

That original tiny building, an embroidery of strange oriental arches and lacy openwork spires, in which stone became angelically weightless, was the progenitor of a whole race of architecture. Generation over generation, its descendants adapted themselves to – and transformed – the primitive and sometimes hostile environment of the abbey of Serlo. Their first ancestor, the tomb, is now scarcely visible amid their crowded clamour.

✳ ✳ ✳

In 1498 Abbot Farley passed away and was succeeded by Abbot Malvern, who died within the year and was succeeded by Abbot Braunche, Abbot Newton, and Abbot Parker. Abbot Parker was succeeded by no-one, for in his time King Henry VIII dissolved the monastery, and cast out the monks from the place that they had been building for nine hundred years. But rather than destroying the abbey church of Gloucester, King Henry raised it to the status of a cathedral, because he wished to honour the resting place of one of his forefathers.

Or, at least, he believed it was the resting place of one of his forefathers. In 1337, just as the masons were beginning to transform the choir of Gloucester Abbey, King Edward III received a letter from a certain Manuele de Fieschi, a priest in Genoa:

> In the name of the Lord, Amen. Those things that I have heard from the confession of your father I have written with my own hand, and afterwards I have taken care to be made known to your highness.
>
> First, he has said that, feeling England in subversion against him after the threat from your mother, he departed from his followers ... and he was captured by Lord Henry of Lancaster. And they led him to Kenilworth Castle ... and there, many people demanding it, he lost his crown. Subsequently, you were crowned at the feast of Candlemas next following.
>
> Finally, they sent him to the castle of Berkeley. Afterwards, the servant who was guarding him, after some time, said to your father: 'Sire, Lord Thomas Gurney and Lord Simon Barford, knights, have come with the purpose of killing you. If it pleases you, I shall give you my clothes, that you may be better able to escape.' Then, wearing the said clothes, at twilight, he went out of the prison. And when he had reached the last door without resistance, because he was not recognized, he found the porter sleeping, whom he quickly killed. And, having got the keys out of the door, he opened it and went out with his keeper.
>
> The said knights who had come to kill him, seeing that he had thus fled, and fearing the indignation of the Queen, for fear of their

lives, thought to put that aforesaid porter in a chest, his heart having been extracted and maliciously presented to the Queen, as if they were the heart and body of your father; and, as the body of the King, the said porter was buried at Gloucester.

... Finally, after various deliberations, all things having been considered ... he went to Paris, and from Paris to Brabant, and from Brabant to Cologne so that, out of devotion, he might see the shrine of the three Kings. And, leaving Cologne, he crossed over Germany and headed for Milan in Lombardy.

In Milan, he entered a certain hermitage in the castle of Milasci and because war overran the said castle, he moved to the castle of Cecima in another hermitage of the dioceses of Pavia in Lombardy. And he remained in this last hermitage for two years or thereabouts, always the recluse, doing penance or praying to God for you and other sinners.

There is a simple tomb in the mountain hermitage at Cecima, a quiet place where nothing has changed for centuries. And this crude recess in the rock, so they say, is the true resting place of Edward II. Gloucester was a rumour, a cover-up, repeated and elaborated so many times that in the end everyone believed it.

THE ALHAMBRA, GRANADA

In Which Two Cousins Marry One Another

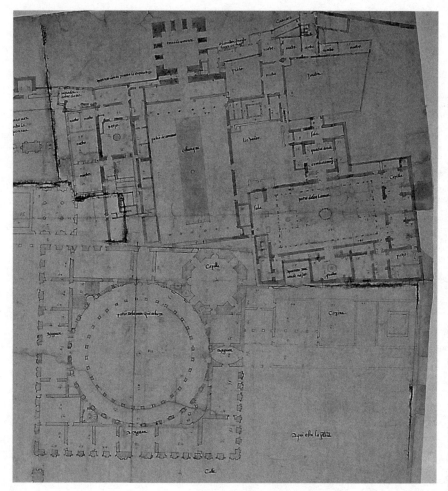

A CONTRACT OF ARCHITECTURAL MARRIAGE.
Pedro Machuca, Planta Grande de la Alhambra y Palacio de Carlos V.

Misunderstanding

T*he Ottoman mosque on the Acropolis was destroyed in 1687 by a Holy Christian League; but even before that explosion, it exemplified the uneasy three-way relationship between Islam, Christianity, and antiquity. The* mihrab *of the mosque housed both the throne of Plato and a miraculous mosaic of the Virgin Mary; the headless sculptures that freckled the exterior of the building were at once the cynosure of pagan art and testimony to monotheistic iconoclasm. It is said that Mehmet the Conqueror wept when he saw the Parthenon, so moved was he by its beauty and its spoliation.*

Islam and Christianity were both inheritors of classical culture: the Latinity of medieval monks and the Greek learning of Islamic scholars may be traced in parallel through the Middle Ages, as classical authority was handed down, preserved and transformed, from generation to generation. But though these traditions were parallel, and sometimes complementary, they were not identical. The Architect's Dream *could not have been painted in the Islamic world; even if it had, it would have had to depict different buildings, standing in very different historical relationships with one another. The classical learning of Western Christianity was twisted by centuries of barbarism, and its fragments appropriated by the very tribes who had destroyed the Roman Empire. Islam, on the other hand, engaged with the metropolitan culture of the Levant with greater ease and continuity.*

With the dawning of the Renaissance in the fifteenth century, these parallel traditions were brought into sharp contrast. Renaissance means, literally, 'rebirth'; in the eyes of Renaissance scholars, antiquity was a corpse waiting to be resurrected rather than a living body that had continued to grow. Indeed, the very notion of the Middle Ages was a Renaissance invention, shorthand for the long sleep of civilization between the ancient past and the reawakened present. There is no equivalent sense of discontinuity in the Islamic Mediterranean.

The reconquista of the Alhambra in Granada represents — like Ayasofya in Istanbul, which is its mirror narrative — a meeting of Christendom and Islam at the dawn of the Renaissance. But while Ayasofya is subtly laid over the structure of Hagia Sophia, the Palacio Real of Charles V merely stands next to the Alhambra in a shotgun marriage of sorts. Both palaces in Granada were descended from the palaces of antiquity, but by very different routes, and so they were unable to communicate with one another. The Alhambra remained barren: an exotic oddity, incomprehensible except as an object of delighted reverie.

IN JANUARY 1492, ISABELLA OF CASTILE AND FERDINAND OF ARAGON completed the *reconquista* of Spain from the Moors. They looked up from their encampment of Santa Fé in the plain; they saw the standard of the Cross raised over the Alhambra of Granada; and they set out to take possession of what God had granted them.

On their way, they met a group of Moors heading down the hill. Among them was the deposed Emir of Granada, Abu Abdallah Muhammad, whom they called Boabdil. The two parties stopped briefly, but negotiations were no longer necessary. Boabdil had already handed over the keys to his fortress. In return the Christian party now produced his young son, who had been their hostage, and they gave him back to his people. And then the two parties continued in their opposite directions.

Isabella and Ferdinand made their way up into the Alhambra. They purified the castle mosque with holy water, and proceeded into the Hall of the Kings in the Court of the Lions, where a Mass was sung to the accompaniment of a tinkling fountain. Then they donned Moorish robes and they set up their thrones in the Hall of the Ambassadors in the Court of the Myrtles. Within a month, they would send Christopher Columbus to find a western passage to the Indies that bypassed the Moorish shipping lanes. Within six, he would return to tell them that he had planted the standard of the Cross in an entirely New World.

Abu Abdallah Muhammad's train trudged on into the mountains. It is said that he looked back at the fortress that had been the seat of his ancestors and burst into tears. His mother rebuked him, saying, 'You do well to weep like a woman for what you would not defend like a man'; and having sighed the Moor's last sigh, he went on his way. The hill where it happened is still known as *El Ultimo Suspiro del Moro*.

Muhammad had been granted land in the hills above Granada, but he did not stay to witness the conversion of what had once been Moorish Al Andalus into Spanish Andalucia. Instead he crossed the sea, and went to serve the kings and chieftains of the Maghreb. It is said that the inhabitants of that part of Ifriqiya kept their keys and title deeds in expectation of the day when they would be restored to their houses and their estates in Al Andalus. They are still waiting.

* * *

In 1526, two of the grandchildren of Isabella and Ferdinand were married to one another. Keiser Karel was the Holy Roman Emperor, King of the Romans, Emperor of Constantinople, Duke of Burgundy, Brabant, Limburg, Lothier, and Luxembourg, Count of Artois, Flanders, Hainault, Holland, Namur, Zeeland, and Zutphen, King of Aragon, Majorca, Valencia, Navarre, and Sardinia, Count of Barcelona, King of Naples and Sicily, King of Castile and Leon, Archduke of Austria, Duke of Styria, Carinthia, and Carniola, and Count of Tyrol. His bride was his first cousin, Ysabel, the Infanta of Portugal, heiress to the fabulous wealth of the Portuguese empire. Since Vasco da Gama had sailed east to follow the Moors, and Columbus west to avoid them, the sun never set upon the dominions of Portugal, which stretched from Brazil to the coasts of Africa, India, Ceylon, Cathay, and Cipango.

Advantageous unions were an old tradition in Keiser Karel's family, the Habsburgs. Once upon a time they had been stewards of a small castle in a small valley in upper Austria, but they were masters of the marriage contract, and Karel's bewildering array of titles had been acquired not by conquest but by heredity. His father was Philip the Fair, whose father was the Holy Roman Emperor Maximilian, and through that line he inherited his northern titles: all those in Burgundy, Austria, and the Netherlands. His mother was Juana the Mad, whose parents had been Isabella of Castile and Ferdinand of Aragon, whose marriage and whose conquest of Granada had united all of Spain – and now the whole New World – under one family and one faith.

Keiser Karel's titles also had heredities of their own, which stretched back far beyond the beginnings of his own family. The imperial throne of Constantinople had existed in name only ever since the Muslim sack of that city in 1453 (for which the conquest of Granada may be seen as the Western counteroffensive), but it was a title that could be traced all the way back to ancient Rome. 'Holy Roman Emperor', meanwhile, was a title invented by Charlemagne in the year 800, when he extended his rule over almost all the domains of the old Roman Empire. Karel wore the laurel on his brow; and in the Netherlands his subjects called him Keiser, in Germany, Kaiser, in Italy, Cesare, in Spain, César, in emulation of the Caesars of old.

Karel had been born in the castle of Ghent, but it would be impossible to describe him as Flemish. With possessions stretching to the farthest reaches of Christendom and beyond, the Keiser belonged to no one place and to no one language. 'I speak Spanish to God, Italian to women, French to men, and German to my horse,' he once said, in which of those languages we do not know.

When his grandfather King Ferdinand died in 1516, Karel travelled south to claim the crowns of Spain. The *cortes* of Aragon and Castile were suspicious of him, and they demanded that he take up residence in their country and learn to speak the Castilian language. He complied only in part, for crisis after crisis in his unmanageable empire called him north, from Luther's proclamation of his ninety-nine theses in Wittenberg in 1516 to the 1529 Ottoman siege of Vienna and the Council of Trent in 1545.

But Keiser Karel did agree to marry an Iberian bride, and in order to confirm his grip on the recently reconquered regions of the Moors it was decided that the marriage should take place in Andalucia. On his way to the wedding, Karel visited the ancient mosque of Cordoba, in the middle of which a new cathedral had been built in his honour. He progressed to Seville, where he was married under a bell tower that had once been a minaret; and he and his new wife spent their wedding night in the palace of their ancestor Pedro the Cruel, who had taken Seville from the Moors.

And Karel and Ysabel were astonished to discover that not only had they made an advantageous match, but they actually loved one another. The ambassador of Venice, who attended the royal couple at this time, wrote that the two of them had eyes and words only for each other, and behaved as if there was no-one else in the room. The imperial couple scandalized the court by failing to get out of bed before ten or even eleven o'clock in the morning. So in love were they that when the emperor left on imperial business, the empress would refuse to rise at all. He even, it is said, gave up his many mistresses for her.

✷ ✷ ✷

After the celebrations were over, the honeymoon was due, in which an heir was to be conceived, and Karel and Ysabel came to the Alhambra of Granada. They were met at the gate by a band of Moorish musicians dressed in turbans and flowing garments, who, sitting on the floor, played for the royal couple a strange and beautiful music, and sang to them in a language they did not understand. Keiser Karel was so impressed that he invited the musicians to the palace to play for him in his private apartments. Many nights the emperor sat stiffly with his court, in their ruffs and corsets, while the Moorish musicians played their haunting melodies punctuated with wild cries.

Then Keiser Karel proceeded to explore the fantastical habitation of his honeymoon, and he fell in love all over again. The Alhambra he discovered was a castle in the air, a parade of towers and battlements perched on a wooded precipice high above the white painted city of Granada. It was said that the children of the Alhambra used to sit on these battlements with fishing lines, catching the birds that swooped and fluttered below them.

But the Alhambra was much more than a castle. Hidden behind the battlements Karel found an intricate lattice of gardens and colonnades: a patchwork of light and shade, of scents and sounds. Everywhere, water tinkled from spouts, slid over the edge of marble basins, and ran silently in carved rills. Everywhere, plants filled the small courtyards with heavy scents. Each court led to a vaulted *mirador*, a belvedere from which the view might be enjoyed through fretted screens. Everywhere, there was ornament: geometric figures, vegetal designs, and sometimes something that looked like incomprehensible writing. It covered surfaces so completely and densely that it seemed as if the walls of the palace had been spun, embroidered, and then hung out in the brilliant sunshine.

Of the many courts of the Alhambra, the largest was the Court of the Myrtles, which contained a pool of water lined with myrtle bushes. At the northern end, an arched loggia opened into a sequence of anterooms, and ultimately into a gloomy chamber – the Hall of the Ambassadors. This hall and the antechambers that led to it were covered with domes assembled from hundreds of timber facets, each cut into the shape of a star.

Next to the Court of the Myrtles Karel found a court so richly decorated that it was called by those who saw it the Court of Gold, and this is where the new empress elected to reside. One side of this court was formed by a richly ornamented colonnade; another gave access to a grand saloon whose roof was supported on four great columns and beams, intricately carved. The third wall of the Court of Gold was entirely covered with adornment, so tightly woven that it seemed as if the whole wall was a carpet – a carpet so gigantic that it had been given a roof, had grown doors and windows, and had become a building.

Keiser Karel chose the last of the three courts of the Alhambra for his own habitation. The Court of the Lions was so called because in the middle of it twelve carved beasts supported a basin, their mouths spouting water into channels that spread the cooling liquid throughout the court and into the surrounding rooms and pavilions. To the south of this court was the Hall of the Abencerrajes, stained, it was rumoured, with the blood of that overmighty family, spilt on the orders of Boabdil. On the other side there was the Hall of the Two Sisters, which had once been, it was supposed, the harem of the emir. Keiser Karel appropriated this hall as his dining room, because it contained a *mirador* of extraordinary delicacy from which he hoped to survey his new domains.

The Court of the Lions was so cunningly wrought that it appeared to reverse the very laws of gravity. The marble columns that supported the arches seemed to hang down from them like tassels, and the walls were like screens of petrified lace, through which light could be seen. The rooms that opened off the court were vaulted with domes composed of thousands of tiny stalactites that scattered the sun in constellations of light; they seemed to drip down from the heavens, rather than rest upon the walls.

Beyond these three courts, more pleasures revealed themselves to the lovers. There was a heated bath lit from above by glass stars set into the vaults.

There was a garden palace within which, legend had it, a young Moorish prince had been confined alone lest he discover the joys (and pains) of love; in the end he made his escape with the aid of a turtle dove, and found happiness with a Christian princess in a foreign land. There was a staircase whose balustrade ran with cooling water in the summer heat; and there were towers along the battlements that, military in external appearance, contained exquisite interiors like jewels in plain caskets. Keiser Karel heard the tale of three princesses who, although they were locked in one of these towers, contrived to conduct an affair with three Christian knights by singing to them and listening to their ballads. Two of them eventually eloped with their lovers over the battlements, while the third, too afraid to jump, stayed behind, and saw out her days in her luxurious prison.

* * *

The Alhambra that Keiser Karel explored was a labyrinth of exotic and incomprehensible delights, and so too was his new wife. Karel and Ysabel had never met before their marriage, and did not speak the same languages. Karel tried to address Ysabel in all the tongues of his empire: his guttural Flemish rasping through the soft z's and j's of her native Portuguese, his German grammar tripping over sentences in Latin and French, his Italian wrecked on the numerous Spanish words of Arabic derivation. But while he loved his wife, Karel missed the easy informality and familiarity of his mistresses: childhood friends or serving women, whom he could meet behind a curtain or in a garden. The imperial bride and groom were required by court etiquette to live at opposite ends of their palace, surrounded by entourages of servants and courtiers. So it was that Keiser Karel, not wishing to be unfaithful to his wife, found himself a new sort of mistress in the Alhambra herself, whose exotic charms and intimate sensuality beguiled him.

But just as the northern Caesar struggled to woo his Latin bride, so he also struggled to woo his other new love. Keiser Karel still missed many aspects of the flat, cold lands of his youth. He missed beer, which his doctors advised him not to drink in the heat of Andalucia, and he longed to sit by a fire on a cold winter's night. He yearned for fresh herring pulled from the North Sea, and milk, and butter, and soft cheese, and all of those other delights that turned and stank in the southern heat.

To the private refuge of the Alhambra, he brought with him as many northern comforts as his entourage could carry. Not only were there Flemish chamberlains, cooks, and pages of the bedchamber, but also two Flemish choirs, so that Karel could hear the music of his homeland in the chapel royal. He brought his charts of the heavens, the orreries, astrolabes, and telescopes with which he observed the wandering planets and tried to divine his fate. He brought his maps of the earth, with which he tried to understand and rule his unwieldy empire. His library was stocked with the lives of the Caesars who had gone before him and of the saints who had advised them. It contained the martial chronicles of France and the Netherlands, of the crusades and the *reconquista*.

Keiser Karel filled the halls and galleries of the Alhambra with heavy northern furniture. There were high tables and high-backed chairs, carved from oak, softened with tooled leather, and draped with thick Turkey carpet. There were tall cabinets, brass candelabra, and tapestries that depicted the virgin and the unicorn. His rooms became crowded *Wunderkammern*. Shut off from the blazing light and the scented breezes of the gardens outside, they felt more like chambers in a tower in a Teutonic forest than the pleasure dome of the Moors of Al Andalus.

Keiser Karel had inherited from his Habsburg family a protuberant lower jaw and a sharp chin. He could not close his mouth when he ate, and his food sloshed around and dribbled down the bottom of his face. For this reason, Keiser Karel preferred to eat alone. In fact, he preferred to spend as much of his time as possible cloistered in his private apartments. Dining by himself amid his clutter in the old harem of the Alhambra, Keiser Karel never did quite work out how to consummate his love for his new mistress.

✷ ✷ ✷

Karel, the shy and clumsy lover with the ugly chin who adored spending time with his new wife in their Moorish palace, was very different from the Keiser who strode the world stage. His affection for the Alhambra was balanced by a sense of divine duty that compelled him to spurn its private luxuries for the pomp of his court. While he was on his honeymoon, he was free to drift from *mirador* to *mirador* and trail his hand through trickling fountains; but if Keiser Karel ever returned to the Alhambra in the future, he would have to preside over tournaments, masques, bullfights, *autos-da-fé*, meetings of the *cortes* and the grandees, and all the other splendours of his rank. The intimate gardens of the Alhambra would be unable to house these occasions, which gathered vast numbers of men and horses in mighty array before their emperor.

So just as kings always did for their mistresses, Keiser Karel decided to make the Alhambra respectable by giving her a husband: a palace fit for Caesar. A master plan was made in preparation for the marriage, in which the Alhambra was closely surveyed and documented like a bride and her dowry. Next door to her, the lineaments of her husband, the Palacio Real, were introduced and laid down. The drawing, like a detailed marriage contract, laid out the formal joining of the two.

This design had been prepared by Pedro Machuca, a painter who had studied in Rome under Raphael; and there was everything Roman about the new palace, and nothing Spanish, let alone Moorish. The proposed Palacio Real was an austere quadrangular block of stone. Its severe geometry, thick walls, and absolute symmetry were of a very different stock to the Alhambra's airy lattice of columns and domes and pools.

The child of the latest Italian fashions, the Palacio Real was to be absolutely modern. But those latest fashions were not intended to be something new. The masonry base of the palace and the colonnades that ornamented its principal floor were based on scholarly reconstructions of the residences of ancient Rome. The circular courtyard at the heart of the palace and its mighty gates were derived from disquisitions upon the luxurious villas of Pliny and Cicero. The pediments, columns, cornices, and mythological reliefs that covered its façade were also closely modelled on the antique, in the latest Roman manner.

The architecture of Italy was described by its practitioners at the time as a Renaissance – a rebirth – of the arts of ancient Rome. This reconstructed architecture was therefore perfectly suited to the purposes of Keiser Karel, who had inherited the offices of antiquity. Just as the emperor appeared in public with the laurel on his brow, so he intended to hold court in a palace that recalled their magnificence, and thereby deserve his title of Keiser, César, Caesar. But the laurel wreath was a mask laid over the emperor's churning jaw; and the new palace was also a mask, an attempt to give the Flemish chieftain and his band of warriors the look of imperial gravitas. And like Keiser Karel himself, the Palacio Real, while it was clearly the heir of ancient Rome, had other, altogether less respectable antecedents.

The classical décor of the Palacio Real was as correct as it could be, but its layout was quite unlike the airy colonnades and gardens of the palaces of ancient Rome. The elegant principal floor rested upon a fortified base of cyclopean stone blocks with bars on their windows. The gates were large enough to take two men riding abreast, and the courtyard within them was no elegant garden cloister but a yard for the marshalling of ordnance and the reviewing of the guard. For while the mothers of the Palacio Real might have been the palaces of the Roman emperors, his fathers were the *palazzi* of the Italian cities: gloomy blocks of stone in which rival banking families shut themselves up with their money.

These intimidating fortresses were entered through strong gates, which were often closed against the rioting mob: gangs of Guelphs or Ghibellines, or the private armies of other families. Behind the gates and the guards were hard courtyards surrounded by stables, workshops, and businesses. There were hardly any external windows at street level, and those that did exist were barred against intruders. The women were kept upstairs, away from filth and away from danger, on the principal floor a level or two above the ground; above that were the attics and garrets where children, maiden aunts, and servants were barracked in cramped obscurity under gigantic cornices that darkened the narrow streets far below. These Italian palaces were vertical fortresses, heirs to the towers of Bologna and San Gimignano, from which rival clans conducted vendettas so violent that their cities were no longer theatres of civilization but arenas of strife.

And their ancestors were the castles of the Middle Ages – made of heavy stone blocks, bristling with castellations, possessing only arrow slits for windows and portcullises for gates. Their towers were not belvederes for enjoying the cooling breeze but vantage points for archers, places from which boiling oil would be poured and rocks cast down. It was in just such a castle, in Ghent, that Keiser Karel had been born. His Palacio Real, for all the studied Latinity of its décor, was a bastard, an offspring of the bourgeois townhouses and barbaric castles of the Middle Ages.

The Palacio Real towered above the Alhambra. Its high walls cast her intimate courtyards into shadow and obstructed the view of the pale mountains from her delicate *miradores*. The refined Alhambra of the Moors had been made respectable by means of an arranged marriage with an overbearing partner, and just as in most arranged marriages of the time the two communicated through no more than a chink in the wall that divided them: a darkened passage and a narrow stair.

Karel and Ysabel stayed in the Alhambra for about six months. They delighted in the Moorish palace, and indulged themselves in dreams of classical splendour; but they did not forget that the real purpose of their honeymoon was to produce a legitimate heir to the empires of the Romans and the Roman Catholics, East and West. In December 1526, it was announced that the empress was pregnant. The court doctors were impressed to calculate that she must have conceived during the siesta on a hunting trip. Their work done, the imperial couple re-entered the world of political care and intrigue, returning to the empires of which they were the master and mistress.

✳ ✳ ✳

Keiser Karel was sorry to leave the Alhambra behind him, for it had seduced him with exotic lures and promises of pleasure. He was loath to abandon building projects that were still unborn, conceived only on paper and in conversation, and he longed to see them completed. Sighing one last sigh for the Alhambra, he thought of the Moor who had done the same before him. 'Had I been he, or he been I, I would rather have made this place my sepulchre,' he murmured; and then he turned away. He told himself that he was called to greater things, that it had all been a very happy fantasy, but that it was best for it to come to an end – it would never have worked out anyway. For although Keiser Karel loved the Alhambra, he had never quite worked out how to live in it.

There was one person who could have told him, for in 1526 the man who should have made the Alhambra his sepulchre was still alive. Boabdil, Abu Abdallah Muhammad, once Emir of Granada, was by then a mercenary in northern Africa. The emir could have shown the emperor how to read the palace; for the ornament that covered the Alhambra, which was to Keiser Karel merely a gorgeous tapestry, was in fact pages and pages of instructions. To Abu Abdallah Muhammad, able to read Arabic script, the walls of the Alhambra were poetry and proclamation, warning and holy writ.

These inscriptions brought the palace into life as they were read or spoken — as if they were secret incantations that might open a door, or show the way, or explain the forgotten purpose of a court or hall. Almost lost in the fretted decoration of the south wall of the Court of Gold, for example, was an inscription which indicated the way into the palace: that wall, it said, was 'a gate where the roads bifurcate, and through which the East envies the West'. Below, a verse from the Koran indicated the location of the emir's divan:

> *His throne comprises the Heaven and Earth;*
> *The preserving of them oppresses him not;*
> *He is the all-high, the all-glorious.*

But Keiser Karel could not read the palace, and he did not know what its courts and halls had been for. He sat at his high table in the harem, chewing his food alone, while his wife made her private quarters where once stood the throne of Heaven and Earth.

These inscriptions explained how the palace had been designed and furnished, and how it might be properly inhabited. In Arabic these inscriptions were known as *tiraz*, which also refers to the embroidered hems of textiles, and indeed the Alhambra was a palace that was woven and embroidered quite as much as it was built. The antechamber to the Hall of the Ambassadors proclaimed: 'I am like a bride in her nuptial attire, endowed with beauty and perfection.' And the court poet Ibn Zamrak wrote to whoever had decorated the Court of the Lions: 'with how many fine draperies you have adorned it, whose colourful embroidery makes us forget the brocades of Yemen'.

At night the Alhambra was lit with low lamps. Koranic verses carved into the walls of the Hall of the Ambassadors contrasted its sevenfold dome with the softness of the lanterns that hung below it:

He is the all-mighty, the all-forgiving, who
Created the seven heavens above one another ...
Thou seest not in the creation
Of the all-mighty any imperfection.
Return thy gaze; seest thou any fissure?
Then return thy gaze again, and thy gaze comes
Back to thee dazzled aweary.
And we adorned the lower heavens with lamps.

For the interiors of the Alhambra were gently illuminated, shaded by brocades and padded with divans and carpets.

In the time of Abu Abdallah Muhammad, dinner in the Alhambra would have been an affair of couches on the floor furnished with silken bolsters. Reclining, rather than sitting upright, the emir would have been able to peer out through latticed casements into the gardens and the landscape below. Indeed, the verses inscribed into the *mirador* of the Hall of the Two Sisters encouraged the emir to gaze over the city of Granada laid out below him: 'In this garden I am an eye filled with delight, and the pupil of this eye is none other than Our Lord ... In me he looks out from his caliphal throne towards the capital of his entire kingdom.' But Keiser Karel could not read the palace, and he ate alone, trussed up in rough wool and linen and leather, unable enjoy the view of his kingdom out of the low windows because he was sitting bolt upright at a high table on a high chair on a royal dais.

The inscriptions that covered the Alhambra not only explained its purpose and its form, but subjected it to magical metamorphoses. The water that trickled from the fountain of the lions was transformed by the court poet Ibn Zamrak into a miraculous substance: 'a pearl which adorns the environs with the diffusion of gems; silver melting which flows between jewels one like the other in beauty, white in purity'. Verses written in the Hall of the Two Sisters transformed it into the heavens:

The hands of the Pleiades will spend the night invoking God's protection in their favour, and they will awaken to the gentle blowing of the breeze.

In here is a cupola which by its height becomes lost from sight; beauty in it appears both concealed and visible.

The constellation of Gemini extends a ready hand to help it, and the full moon of the heavens draws near to whisper secretly to it.

And the bright stars would like to establish themselves firmly in it rather than continue wandering about in the vault of the sky.

The palace spoke her meaning to those who would read it; but Keiser Karel could not read the palace, and he sat at his high table in the harem, oblivious to the magic of the heavenly vault above him and the fountain before him.

Finally, besides explaining her function, her adornment, and her meaning, the inscriptions that covered the Alhambra also told her history. The palace was inscribed everywhere with the motto of the Nasrid dynasty that had made her: 'No victor but Allah.' Their military triumphs were emblazoned on the walls of the Court of the Myrtles:

And how many infidel lands did you reach in the morning only to become the arbiter of their lives in the evening!

You put upon them the yoke of captives so that they appear at your doorstep to build palaces in servitude.

You conquered Algeciras by the sword, and opened a gate that had been denied to our victory.

The Nasrid emirs traced themselves all the way back to the adventurer Ibn al Nasr, who seized Granada in the thirteenth century; and they also claimed to be able to trace their family all the way back to the companions of the Prophet Muhammad himself. But Keiser Karel could not read the Alhambra, and he sat in solitude on his royal dais in the harem, satisfied that the palace was his birthright.

* * *

Just as Keiser Karel liked to trace his lineage and his titles back to ancient times, so did the family of Abu Abdallah Muhammad. So, indeed, did the Alhambra herself, since she was the last in a line of great palaces. Her mother was the Alcazar of Seville, where Karel and Ysabel had married one another. The Alcazar had originally been built by the dynasty that preceded the Nasrids, the Almohads; and its courtyards of hanging vaults, cusped arches, and trickling fountains were among the examples to which the builders of the daughter palace had looked for inspiration and example.

Both the Almohads of Seville and the Nasrids of Granada traced their palaces back to the Madinat al Zahara in Cordoba, which had been built by the caliphs of Al Andalus five hundred years before. Like the Alhambra, the Madinat al Zahara was an airy complex of *miradores* and gardens, with marble columns supporting cusped arches. Here, in primitive form, were to be seen the geometric and vegetal ornaments whose lacy descendants were draped over the Alhambra's walls. In the throne room of the Madinat al Zahara there was a great bowl of quicksilver, which cast scintillating reflections around the room when its surface was disturbed by the hand of the caliph. Ibn Zamrak may have had it in mind when he composed his inscriptions about the stellar vaults and the crystalline fountains of the Alhambra.

And the Madinat al Zahara herself was the magnificent daughter of magnificent mothers, for the dynasty that built it was descended from the

Umayyad caliphs of Damascus, who had established Islam in Al Andalus in the eighth century. Each one of the Umayyad princes built himself a palace more magnificent than the last, with courtyards and cloisters and fountains, domed halls and fretted screens and perfumed gardens. In veiled throne rooms suspended below the vault of Heaven the princes reclined on their royal divans, as one day Abu Abdallah Muhammad would do in the Court of Gold.

These Umayyad palaces spawned not only the Madinat al Zahara and its ultimate descendant, the Alhambra, but also the Fatimid palaces of Cairo, the caliphal palaces of Baghdad and Persia, and the Red Forts of Mogul India. 'The Tale of the King's Son and the She-Ghoul' in *The Arabian Nights* tells of a royal residence that calls to mind nothing so much as the Court of the Lions in the Alhambra:

> The palace was furnished with silk carpets and hung with drapes ...
> In the middle there stood a spacious courtyard, surrounded by four
> adjoining recessed courts facing one another. In the centre stood a
> fountain, on top of which crouched four lions in red gold, spouting
> water from their mouths in droplets that looked like gems and pearls.

But the line of descent goes back much further than that. In the days of the Prophet Muhammad himself, the ambassadors of the Arabs went to Constantinople. They brought home stories of a throne room guarded by lions and gryphons in which stood trees filled with birds, all made of gold, which all sprang to life and tweeted and roared as the ambassadors approached the imperial presence. The throne itself, they said, could be raised and lowered at will, so that the emperor seemed to appear and disappear in a cloud of smoke. His Sacred Palace was an endless labyrinth of courtyards and vaulted chambers, more of a city than a residence; and only perfumers, they said, were permitted to ply their trade in its vicinity, so that no foul smells would assault the imperial nose. In a colonnaded belvedere looking out over the palace gardens a fountain spouted fruit juices, while in another one water issued from the mouths of brass lions and filled a nymphaeum with mysterious echoes. The walls were embroidered in silk, carved in marble, and tessellated with golden mosaic that looked like sprouting, abundant vegetation.

The Sacred Palace of Constantinople, in turn, was heir to the Golden House of Nero, in which the emperor would dine with his court, reclining on couches beneath a dome, as slaves poured rose petals down upon them and perfumed air rose through hidden grilles in the floor. It was the descendant of Hadrian's villa at Tivoli, a fantastical landscape of courtyards and porticos and baths whose vaults were pierced with crystal stars; there was a vast niche where Hadrian would dine, reclining by a colonnaded lake, while food and wine were floated to him down marble rills. And it was the heir above all of the Palatine, a natural hill which, by the end of antiquity, had been carved, extended and remodelled into a marble maze of atria, belvederes, vaulted galleries, hippodromes, and swimming pools, whose full extent is still unknown.

The first emperor, Augustus, also lived on the Palatine, but as a mere *primus inter pares* he dwelt in much more modest style. The house of Augustus was entered, like the Alhambra, through a simple door in a blank wall, which led to an atrium containing a small pool of water that reflected the sky. In the morning the emperor would sit in the atrium on his low chair in order to receive his clients and suppliants. He was framed by the columns of the peristyle behind him: an enclosed garden surrounded by a cloister. In the evening Augustus would dine dressed in loose robes, reclining, like his Muslim successors, on couches and divans. Augustus's house was just one among many on the Palatine, which in those days was merely an aristocratic district of Rome, but it was the germ of its imperial successors. From the name of the hill on which it stood we derive the very name and the very idea of 'palace'.

One can still discern, in the capitals of the slim columns of the Alhambra, echoes of the Corinthian acanthus and the Ionic scroll of classical architecture, and the pleasure domes of Nero and Hadrian are still present in the crystalline vaults that hang above every room in the Court of the Lions. In the ornament that covers every surface, the memories of Byzantium linger; and, above all, the courtyards and fountains that percolate a cooling breeze through the architecture are the scions of millennia of palaces. Thus was the classical world preserved and transformed, generation after generation, as palace succeeded palace around the Mediterranean, from Rome to Constantinople, to Damascus, and to Al Andalus.

The poets and courtiers of the Muslim world had been practising the arts and the sciences of antiquity for centuries. It was in Muslim Syria and Egypt that astronomers and geometers had continued the studies begun in Alexandria long ago by Ptolemy and Euclid. Mehmet, the conqueror of Constantinople, had the exploits of Caesar and Alexander read to him every day to prepare him for the defeat of their enfeebled descendants. It was in Al Andalus that the philosophy of Aristotle was pored over by the famous Averroes of Cordoba, long before anyone in Western Europe had even read his works. The mosque of that city is a forest of classical columns taken from the Roman ruins that once covered the site, and its *mihrab* sparkles with mosaics donated by the Emperor of Constantinople.

And because the artists and scientists of Islam had continued the classical tradition, it was as flexible and expressive in their hands, as delightful and useful, as it had ever been in Hadrian's villa. It was still alive. Keiser Karel's pretensions to Roman gravitas, on the other hand, had been derived by a different route, northwards and westwards: from the Visigoths, whose chieftain Alaric sacked Rome and went on to occupy Spain; from the Franks, whose chieftain Karel became Charlemagne and revived the title of emperor; from the Italian princelings and merchants of the Middle Ages. Keiser Karel's classical palace was a theoretical exercise, self-conscious, like a bourgeois newcomer at an aristocratic party that has been going on for centuries. The construction of the Palacio Real began in 1533; and in the same year Abu Abdallah Muhammad, the last Emir of Granada, exhaled his last sigh and died.

* * *

The heir of Karel and Ysabel was named Philip, and when his father abdicated in 1555 he inherited his possessions in Spain and the Netherlands. Philip waited until Karel was dead before he called a halt to the construction of the new palace in Granada. The Palacio Real was still incomplete, a mask without a face behind it, and its vast windows and mighty gates led nowhere. The Moorish Alhambra likewise fell into decrepitude. The Court of Gold, inscribed once upon a time as the throne of Heaven, was inhabited by cattle; the *miradores* and the cloisters were walled up so that soldiers could barrack in them; the gardens became the habitation of thieves and beggars. Three hundred years later the troops of Napoleon tried to blow up the entire palace. Only in the later nineteenth century, when writers and artists were attracted by the exotic and the curious, was the palace of the Moors restored to its original splendour; but the Palacio Real of Keiser Karel remained roofless until 1967. It is now a museum.

Philip erected himself a new palace in the mountains of central Castile. The Escorial was a square block of stone, built in the form of the gridiron upon which St Lawrence had been martyred, crowned by high towers and encircled by blank walls of grey granite. From his small plain study in this austere fortress in the middle of nowhere, Philip governed the empire upon which the sun never set.

In the centre of his palace Philip built a church surmounted by a great dome. Under this dome he gathered the bodies of all of his ancestors, so that the palace would be not only a residence but the mausoleum of his dynasty and proof of his titles. They are still there today, in room after room of marble sarcophagi: the underworld of the Escorial is a palace inhabited by dead infantas and princes, kings and queens. In the very centre of them all he placed his father and his mother, Keiser Karel and Ysabel, who had conceived him in such a different place.

THE TEMPIO MALATESTIANO, RIMINI

In Which a Scholar Translates a Temple

THE EMBLEM OF *A GREAT MAN*.
*Matteo de' Pasti medal,
showing Sigismondo Malatesta and
the church of San Franceso in Rimini.*

Translation

*T*he Parthenon was ruined in the explosion of 1687. Henceforward it was no longer a temple, a church, or a mosque, but an antiquity, one of the canonic masterpieces arrayed before the architect in his dream. Liberated from immediate use, it became the abstracted object of speculation. Scholars reconstructed the Parthenon in aquatints and copied it in plaster casts. They made it into the Platonic model of what architecture is and should be; and in doing so they ruined it further, for their adoration turned the stones of the Parthenon into Art to be placed on remote pedestals in museums. The past that the learned sought to preserve and understand disappeared before their very eyes.

The Renaissance, as its name suggests, proposed the rebirth of the arts of antiquity. But a revived civilization is not the same as a living one that has continuously grown, slowly and incrementally. The resurrected Latin of the humanist scholars of the Renaissance was hedged about with rigid grammar and syntax. Its rhetoric was a studied affair of form.

The architects of the Renaissance invented an architecture equally rigidly classified and catalogued, and architects and writers alike struggled with the problem of expressing their own living culture in the terms of the dead languages they had exhumed. How *was it possible, for instance, to discuss concepts that the Greeks and Romans had never considered? How was it possible to design churches, for example, in an architectural grammar that preceded the existence of Christianity? The architects of the Renaissance were often forced to deal with the buildings of the recent past: monasteries, castles, and churches that dated from what they regretfully imagined to have been the long sleep of civilization since antiquity. Just like their humanist counterparts, they attempted to translate these recent structures into the classical language they had revived and invented.*

The 'Famous Temple of Rimini' is one of the earliest examples of such an academic approach to the architecture of antiquity. It may be viewed as the translation of a building made in one language into another. But all languages contain some ideas that cannot be fully translated, and the Famous Temple of Rimini is now neither a church nor a temple but a curious hybrid. It represents not a union of Renaissance culture and the antique, the present and the past, but the unbridgeable gap that divides the architect atop his column from the splendours he surveys.

IN 1461, POPE PIUS II CALLED HIS CARDINALS AND HIS PRINCES TO ROME for an important meeting. They assembled in Curia, the Papal Court, to try the soul of Sigismondo Pandolfo Malatesta, the tyrant of Rimini. Pius laid the accusations before his council:

Sigismondo Malatesta was an illegitimate member of the noble family of the Malatestas, and had a great spirit and a powerful body. He was an eloquent and a skilful captain. He had studied history and had more than an amateur's knowledge of philosophy. He seemed born to do whatever he put his hand to. But he was so ruled by his passions, and abandoned himself to such an uncontrollable greed for money, that he became a plunderer and a thief to boot. He was so dissolute that he raped his daughters and his sons-in-law. When a boy, he often acted the female partner in shameful loves, and later forced men to act as women. He had no respect for the sanctity of marriage. He raped virgins who had vowed themselves to God as well as Jewesses, killed young girls, and had young boys who rebelled against his will brutally whipped. He committed adultery with many women whose children he had held at baptism, and murdered their husbands. His cruelty was greater than any barbarian's, and he inflicted fearful tortures on guilty and innocent alike with his own bloody hands. He rarely told the truth, was a master of patience and dissimulation, a traitor and a perjuror who never kept his word ... When his subjects finally beseeched him to pursue a policy of peace and to have pity on a country that was constantly exposed to pillage for his sake, he replied: 'Go. Be of good cheer, for you will never have peace as long as I live.' This was Sigismondo, a restless, sensual man and a tireless warmonger, one of the worst men that have ever lived, or ever will live, the shame of Italy and the disgrace of our generation.

The Pope nursed a particular hatred for Malatesta, who had betrayed his home town of Siena while in her service; but it was not hard for him to find other witnesses and plaintiffs, for the tyrant had plenty of enemies. King Alfonso of Naples had employed Malatesta as a *condottiere*, a mercenary soldier, only to see his employee switch sides and fight against him. Federico da Montefeltro, the lord of Urbino, was an old family foe; and Francesco Sforza, himself a rival *condottiere*, was a new one.

Sforza laid the first charge before the Curia. He had given the hand of his daughter Polissena to Malatesta in 1442, but only three years later Malatesta had taken himself a mistress: the twelve-year-old Isotta degli Atti. Malatesta, then twenty-eight, had glimpsed Isotta through a window, and they fell in love at once. He pursued her with heartfelt verse:

> *Before you blooms and grass lie down,*
> *Proud to be trod by your sweet foot*

And ruffled by your azure robe.
Vain the sun in the early morn,
But when he sees you, overcome
And pale he goes away, in tears.

The obstacles to their love were either removed, or ignored, or taken care of by blind fortune. Isotta's father soon died, leaving her a large dowry. Malatesta's wife, Polissena, may have objected, but she also died conveniently quickly, after having put up with her husband's infatuation for three years. Of course, everyone – including her father – believed that she had been murdered by her husband.

But Pope Pius's princes (and many of his prelates) had all taken mistresses. They had all spawned bastards, betrayed their superiors, and indulged in family feuds. They all knew that this charge alone could not condemn the soul of Sigismondo Malatesta. So the Pope laid another allegation before the Curia that, he hoped, would seal the fate of his enemy. It was presented in the form of a medal: a small bronze disc whose face bore Malatesta's profile. Its obverse depicted a domed building under an inscription containing the words PRAECL. ARIMINI TEMPLUM: 'The Famous Temple of Rimini'.

The most heinous accusation against Sigismondo Malatesta was architectural. He had, it was alleged, built himself a blasphemous temple, 'so full of pagan images that it seems like a temple for the worshippers of demons, not for Christians'. What's more, this temple had once been a church. The poor brothers of St Francis were able to testify to that.

Once upon a time, Malatesta's ancestor Verruchio had allowed the Franciscan friars to build a chapel in Rimini close to the old Roman forum. This chapel was, in the tradition of the Franciscans, little more than a simple brick box for preaching in. There was one arched door at the western end and a plain room within, covered with a timber roof. When it was complete, Verruchio had

Giotto, the house painter of the Franciscans, make an altarpiece at the east end of the church. This altarpiece, painted in a manner as simple and direct as the message of St Francis, represented Christ on the Cross. Before him knelt Verruchio himself, in the hope that a drop of the Saviour's blood would fall upon him and wash away his sins. When he died at the grand old age of 100, the Old Mastiff, as he was known, was buried in the church of the Franciscans in Rimini; and his descendants all made sure that they were buried there as well, hoping that their souls, too, would be cleansed from sin by association with St Francis. It was this simple family shrine that Malatesta had turned into an arrogant blasphemy.

* * *

Next before the Curia were laid the depositions of two courtiers of Malatesta, who spoke of his learning and his keen intelligence. Malatesta was a bastard and a soldier of fortune, they submitted; but he had always dreamed of being a real, legitimate prince. In 1433, when he was only fifteen years old, the Emperor Sigismund passed through Rimini, and Malatesta persuaded him to confirm him in the lordship of the town, even though this title was not in the emperor's gift but in the Pope's.

Like the real, legitimate princes of his time, Malatesta strove to excel not only in the arts of war but in the arts of peace as well: in philosophy and literature, mathematics and music, astrology and history. In attendance on the Pope at the consecration of Florence Cathedral in 1436, Malatesta would have had the opportunity to meet some of the most learned men of his day. These scholars were avid collectors of ancient texts, but they also constructed new ones. They wrote histories in the manner of Livy; bawdy tales and satires like Petronius; and invectives, panegyrics, philippics, georgics, and orations in the purest Latin of Cicero, reviving the language from centuries of ecclesiastical torpor.

In the following year the Papal Court met the Emperor of Constantinople, who sought Western aid as the armies of Islam closed in around him. While the learned men of Italy represented the apogee of Latin learning, the Byzantine embassy carried with them the wisdom of the Greeks. Among them was Gemistos Plethon, a poet and philosopher who lived in the hills above ancient Sparta. Plethon was a man of radical ideas. He had been declared a heretic for his *De Differentiis*, which compared the Platonic and Aristotelian conceptions of God; and he proposed, in his *Summary of the Doctrines of Zoroaster and Plato*, a return to the paganism of his ancestors. On his way home from the council, Plethon stopped awhile in Rimini to converse with its youthful and inquisitive ruler. Then he boarded his ship and sailed back to the Byzantine Empire, which would be extinguished fifteen years later. The two men did not see one another alive again.

Malatesta, inspired by his meeting with Plethon and keen to appear as cultured as the aristocrats who paid him to fight for them, started to collect for himself a court of humanists. He summoned Basinio Basini of Parma to act as his astrologer; and Basini took the Latin name Basinius, and composed *Hesperis*, an epic that mythologized the achievements of his master as if they were those of an Achilles in courage, an Augustus in majesty, and a Plato in wisdom. Basinius even turned the illegitimate love of Malatesta and Isotta into a cycle of poems named the *Liber Isottaeus*. Malatesta also poached Roberto Valturio from the court of Pope Eugenius IV, and Valturio wrote a Latin treatise on the art of warfare for his new master. So proud was the *condottiere* of this treatise that he sent handwritten copies of it to everyone from Lorenzo the Magnificent to the King of Hungary.

* * *

One of these copies of *De Militaria*, the Papal Curia was told, had just been found in the Venetian colony of Candia in the possession of a certain Matteo de' Pasti. This man, it was scandalously revealed, had been charged by Malatesta with the task of taking it to the Sultan of Constantinople; but de' Pasti's role in the crimes of his master was much more significant than that of go-between to the infidel enemy. Now his deposition, too, was laid before the princes and the prelates of the Curia.

At a dinner in the gardens of Maecenas in Rome, Malatesta had once admired the Prince of Ferrara's antique habit of issuing medals bearing his image. De' Pasti was a medal-maker, among his other talents, and in 1446, Malatesta lured him to Rimini for a similar series of commissions. De' Pasti cast a series of medals which bore the profile of Sigismondo Malatesta on one side and various emblems on the other, lauding the princeling's noble qualities. There was one of Fortitude (for Malatesta was, after all, a soldier) holding a broken column and sitting on a pair of elephants, which were the emblem of the Malatesta family. On another medal the elephant was alone, trampling the enemies of Malatesta and trumpeting his fame, and on a third there was a suit of knightly armour. De' Pasti also illuminated the manuscripts of *Hesperis* and *De Militaria* with images of the tyrant and his works, presented as if they were inscriptions and reliefs taken from antiquity. For his labours he was made the chief artificer of the court of Rimini, honoured with the sobriquet 'noble'.

But Malatesta was not content to play with treatises and medals and emblems. With the proceeds of his military successes he started to transform the Rimini he had inherited into the Rimini he desired it to be. He built himself a magnificent fortress, the Castel Sismondo, in which he could live like the real prince he aspired to be; and then he turned his attention to the church of St Francis where the bones of his ancestors were laid, and began to consider how he might be remembered when he had joined them. In 1447, Sigismondo Malatesta laid the foundation stone of a new chapel on the southern side of this church, dedicated to the St Sigismund from whom Malatesta took his name. When it was finished, Malatesta commissioned the painter Piero della Francesca to decorate the interior walls of the new addition.

It was a modest commission, only the painting of a wall; and Piero produced what was, on the face of it, a conventional sort of painting. It showed the Sigismondo of flesh and blood kneeling before his sainted counterpart, just as his ancestor Verruchio knelt before the crucified Christ in Giotto's altarpiece. But the similarity between the two paintings ended there. It was usual to place the saint in the centre of such an image, and the donor to one side, as if to emphasize that the saint was closer to the heart of creation than the mere mortal who adored him; but it is Malatesta's eye that occupies the dead centre of Piero's's image. Depicted in profile, like an emperor on a coin, Malatesta kneels in front of a wall, framed by a pair of Corinthian pilasters that are rendered with the closest attention to the vocabulary, grammar, and syntax of classical architecture.

In front of him St Sigismund sits on a throne, bearing more than a passing resemblance to the Emperor Sigismund who had confirmed the teenage Malatesta in his lordship of Rimini. Indeed, St Sigismund was a fitting patron for the German emperor and for Malatesta himself. He had been a barbarian prince whose rages were so terrible that he had ordered his own son to be strangled. He later sought forgiveness and fled to a forest hermitage; but forgiveness was no more forthcoming among the barbarians than it was among the *condottieri* of Italy, and he was drowned at the bottom of a well.

The lesson of the painting is found in the emblems painted behind Malatesta, placed as if on the obverse of a medal. Carved in a medallion is the Castel Sismondo, the guarantee of the *condottiere*'s security. Below the medallion, two mastiffs lie on the floor, apparently at peace. One, all white, faces the saint (the emperor), and represents the loyalty that all dogs should show their masters. The other, black, faces away, and represents vigilance: the necessary suspicion that all princes must exercise in the maintenance of their power.

Piero's image represented not a simple supplicant before his divine patron but a prince at the centre of things, loyal but distrustful, strong and barbarous. As he gazed at the finished painting, Malatesta knew that he would always be a renegade *condottiere*; and he decided that the humble church of St Francis would become a temple dedicated to his fame, in the manner of those of the ancient emperors.

At the same time as the chapel of St Sigismund was under construction, other chapels were also being built under the direction of Matteo de' Pasti and the sculptor Agostino di Duccio. On the face of it, these chapels, with their pointed arches and narrow lancet windows, simply extended the architecture of the original church. In detail, however, they were as unlike the angelic confections of a gothic chantry as could be imagined, for in them Piero della Francesca's painted classical architecture was applied in marble to the structure of the building. Each of the arches was supported on a pair of Corinthian pilasters and was outlined by a moulding carved in the manner of a Roman triumphal arch, inscribed in tall Roman capitals with epigraphs glorifying Sigismondo Malatesta.

These new chapels were nominally dedicated to the saints, but the message of the decorations that covered them was anything but Christian. Rather, the ornament formed an encyclopaedia of pagan wisdom. The sacristy – the very place where the ritual objects of the Mass were stored – was dominated by Piero's subversive fresco of the two Sigismunds. The chapel closest to the altar was dedicated to the muses, their hair flowing, their robes diaphanous, their bodies scandalously revealed. On the other side of the altar was a shrine to the planets, named for the gods of antiquity: Mercury, Venus, Mars, Jove, and Saturn, which represented stages in the journey of mortals to Platonic Wisdom. The bones of Malatesta's forebears were all piled up in an 'Ark of the Ancestors'; and their chapel was watched over by the prophets and sibyls of ancient times, who had foretold the coming of Christ just as surely as Malatesta's ancestors prefigured his own rule. The altarpiece image of Verruchio, the founder of the dynasty, was hacked away from the feet of Christ at which he knelt, lest his fame obscure that of his descendant.

Yet another chapel was dominated by the sepulchre of Isotta. Malatesta had de' Pasti and di Duccio design for her a tomb even grander than the one he built for himself. It was placed high on the wall, supported by elephants and set against the embroidered cloak of a knight surmounted by a helmet. The tomb itself is emblazoned with the arms of the Malatestas, and two putti hold aloft a sheet of bronze inscribed with the name of the *condottiere*'s mistress. The chapel (and indeed the whole church) is littered with the monogram of an 'S' intertwined with an 'I' – celebrating, some say, the scandalous love of the tyrant, while his legitimate wife lies elsewhere in the church, entombed in obscurity.

As the work progressed, the interior of the Gothic church was clothed in classical ornament. Corinthian columns, rich cornices, and balustrades covered the architecture with fragments of antiquity. The acanthus and the laurel spread their foliage over the plain walls; and the old chapels and shrines of the saints were given over to exotic elephants, putti riding dolphins, and venerated courtesans.

Sigismondo's own tomb capped the whole overblown, egotistical, pagan affair. It was piled high with armour and hung with banners that displayed his bawdy motto: 'I bear the horn that all may see, so big you cannot believe.' (It is said that when they exhumed his body in the eighteenth century, Malatesta's skull was indeed disfigured by a devilish horn.) To complete the blasphemy, Malatesta placed an inscription above the door to his temple, as grandiose as if he were some deified Roman emperor:

Sigismondo Pandolfo Malatesta, the son of Pandolfo – having survived many grievous adventures in the Italic War – a bringer of victory – in

thanksgiving for the deeds he performed with valour and fortitude, to
God the everlasting and to the city has dedicated this temple – having
in his magnanimity built it at his own expense – leaving a noble, holy
monument.

* * *

It is not recorded whether he was present at the trial of the soul of Sigismondo
Malatesta, but if he was, one of the secretaries to the Papal Curia must have
been squirming. Like Sigismondo Malatesta, Leone Battista Alberti was a
bastard, born into a bastard family. He was the illegitimate son of a house that
had been banished from Florence and whose members had a price on their
heads. His father died when he was young, his family did not honour his inheritance, and he was forced to go out into the world to make a living. Alberti
chose the life of a scholar: he studied canon law in Bologna and took Holy
Orders in 1428. He distinguished himself in all manner of things. According to
his autobiographical *Vita Anonyma*, he was so strong that he could throw a coin
up into the air and bounce it off the high cathedral vault above him, and he
could jump over a man's head with his feet together.

Alberti read and wrote in the manner of the humanists, studying the literature of the ancients so that he might better understand them and create
works in their manner. In 1424 he composed *Philodoxeus*, an allegorical love
story, in a Latin so perfect that a decade later he had to add a commentary
explaining that the play had *not* been produced in antiquity. He codified a
grammar of the Tuscan language, and composed treatises on the family, medi-
tations on *De Commodia et Incommodes Litterarum*, and invectives against the
priesthood, all in the crisp Latin of Cicero or Caesar. He also confected
Intercoenales, *Theogenius* and *Momus*, dark fables in the more fantastical manner
of Lucian.

It was through such fables that Alberti liked to explain, if that is the word, the purpose of his studies. He told one such story in *Intercoenales*. He had dreamed a dream, he said. He had found himself standing on a mountain whose base was girded about with the River of Life. The river was full of people: some holding on to the inflated bladders of animals to stay afloat, others crowded together in sinking ships, and still others attempting to brave the waters unaided and alone. Most clung to rafts made of wooden boards, some rafts drifting by themselves, others crudely lashed together.

Alberti saw a host of beings flitting through the air above the waters and the people, and he wondered who they were. A shade appeared by his side, and said:

> Offer supreme honour to those you see here set apart from the multi-
> tude … Justly … are they considered divine, not only because of their
> divine endowments, but also because they were the first to construct
> the boards that you see floating in the river. Those boards, upon which
> they carved the name of the each of the Liberal Arts, are a great help
> to those that are swimming.

And then the shade pointed out another group of beings, below the gods but above the desperate castaways in the water:

> Those others are also similar to the gods, but they do not entirely
> emerge from the waters because their winged sandals are imperfect:
> these are demigods, and they are most deserving of honour and vener-
> ation … It is their merit to have enlarged the boards by adding pieces
> of flotsam to them. Further, they engage in the admirable enterprise
> of collecting the boards from the reefs and the beaches, in order to
> construct new ones and to proffer these works to those who still swim
> in the midstream.

Render, O Mortal, honour to these. Render them the thanks that they are due for having offered excellent help with these boards to those negotiating the toilsome river of life.

'This is what I saw and heard in my sleep,' Alberti recorded, 'and I seemed in a marvellous way to have somehow managed to be numbered among the winged gods.' In his dreams he was one of the divine: not a rearranger, but an inventor of the boards that assisted those who swam through the river of life. Such, at any rate, were his aspirations.

Alberti joined the Papal Curia in 1432 as an *abbreviator*: his Latinity was useful in drafting the endless pronouncements, minuting the endless meetings, and writing the endless letters that issued forth from the Papal Court. It was in the train of the Papal Court that Alberti first returned to Florence, the city from which his family had been exiled; and it was in Florence that he first encountered the Renaissance not only of letters, but of things. Inside the cathedral, Alberti would have had time to admire the vast dome of Filippo Brunelleschi, whose completion he was there to celebrate. So enormous was this dome that it could contain the very Pantheon of Rome. Indeed, Brunelleschi had spent time in the Eternal City contemplating, measuring, and dissecting the ruins of Roman buildings in order to understand the manner of their construction and to plan the construction of his masterpiece. Most people assumed that the Roman ruins had been built by giants, or devils, or miracles; but Brunelleschi scoffed at such old wives' tales, and set to measuring the buildings themselves. When he returned to Florence he used what he had learned in order to surpass the buildings from which he had learned it.

So amazed was Alberti by the innovations of Filippo Brunelleschi and the other artificers of Florence that he wrote Latin treatises in their honour. *De Pictura* and *De Statua* gave literary expression to the crafts of painting and sculpture, and elevated them into the realm of intellectual speculation. In the

1440s Alberti began the long process of doing the same thing for architecture, modelling his *De Re Aedificatoria* on the only architectural treatise that had survived from antiquity: Vitruvius's *De Architectura*. Like Vitriuvius's work, *De Re Aedificatoria* is divided into ten books which deal with public and private buildings, engineering and the classical orders, liberally sprinkled with the writings of other authorities. But Alberti found Vitruvius himself a dubious source:

> What he handed down was in any case not refined; and his speech such that the Latins might think that he wanted to appear a Greek, while the Greeks might think that he gabbled Latin. However, his very text is evidence that he wrote neither Greek nor Latin, so that as far as we are concerned he might never have written at all, rather than write something that we cannot understand.

Alberti strove to restate what Vitruvius had written in a pure Latin, uncorrupted by Greek. His very title *De Re Aedificatoria* is a Latinization of *De Architectura*, which is, at its root, a Greek word. 'What we have written is (unless I am mistaken) in proper Latin, and in comprehensible form,' he noted. But it was not only a corrupted text with which Alberti had to deal, but also a corrupted architecture. He continued:

> Examples of ancient temples and theatres have survived that may teach us as much as any professor, but I see – not without sorrow – these very buildings being despoiled more each day. And anyone who happens to build nowadays draws his inspiration from inept modern nonsense rather than proven and much commended methods. Nobody would deny that as a result of all of this a whole section of our life and learning could disappear altogether.

Alberti's task was clear, and urgent: 'I felt it the duty of any gentleman or any person of learning to save from total extinction a discipline that our prudent ancestors had valued so highly.'

De Re Aedificatoria was an attempt to revive and preserve the architectural wisdom of the ancients, and the architectural world that Alberti described in the text was one from which 'inept modern nonsense' – meaning not only the work of his contemporaries, but indeed the entire architectural legacy of the Middle Ages – had been carefully excised. Alberti described cities filled with magnificent fora and porticoes and theatres – buildings which, in his time, were the mouldering haunts of thieves if they stood at all. He described churches as temples, the habitation of many gods rather than the one God of the Christians; and he wrote of the wisdom of Pliny or Herodotus as if they were speaking in his own time, and not from some remote and ruined past.

De Re Aedificatoria was the work of a theorist, rather than a practitioner; but as the composition of the book was drawing to a close, Alberti was given the opportunity to put his words into action. It is not recorded exactly how and where the humanist scholar met Sigismondo Malatesta, the tyrant of Rimini, but one of the first fruits of their meeting was a medal made by Matteo de' Pasti. It bears the date 1450, by which time the St Sigismund chapel was already under construction. The face of the medal shows, as ever, the profile of Sigismondo Malatesta, but the obverse depicts a building identified as 'the Famous Temple of Rimini'. The medal is small, but it is possible to distinguish the features of this Famous Temple well enough to observe that it was not one of the remains of antiquity that dotted the town but a new building, dominated by a huge dome.

The Famous Temple of Rimini was, of course, none other than the church of St Francis, whose interior was already in the process of being embellished by the medallist and his assistants. But while Matteo de' Pasti's interior was a crude exercise in classical collage, as corrupted as a medieval scribe's copy of Vitruvius, Alberti's design for the exterior of the church was as pure a statement of classical wisdom as the author of *De Re Aedificatoria* could make it. Alberti's façade wrapped the old brick church in a shroud of white Istrian stone. The original arched door was still there, but the scholar's design translated it into a triumphal arch dedicated to Sigismondo Malatesta. Alberti knew all about the ancient connection of arches to military glory:

> The greatest ornament to the forum or crossroad would be to have an arch at the mouth of each road. For the arch is a gate which is continually open … Spoils and victory standards captured from the enemy would be deposited by the gates, standing as they did in a busy place. Hence the practice developed of decorating the arches with inscriptions, statues and histories.

The triumphal arch that Alberti designed for Malatesta was framed by a pair of columns which, in size and in most details, were copied directly from the ruined city gate built by the Emperor Augustus over the entrance to the ancient Via Flaminia connecting Rimini to Rome. To either side of the arch there were niches in which, some say, Alberti intended to place the sarcophagi of Malatesta and Isotta. Above these, the clerestory window of the old building was framed by more pilasters and crowned with the sort of canopy that is held over the sacred relics of those who have been deified.

The sides of the church were similarly translated from a naive provincial Gothic into façades of the strictest classical probity. Each side was given seven rounded arches, each destined to contain the remains of one of the humanists of the court of Sigismondo Malatesta. For the east end of the church Alberti designed a great dome, not pointed in the manner of Brunelleschi's cupola at Florence, but rounded in the manner of the Pantheon in Rome; and the whole building was raised on a high plinth, like a Roman temple lifted up above the Forum.

Alberti's Famous Temple of Rimini was classical in its components, but it was also, unlike the interior, classical in its totality. Each and every part was carefully proportioned to each and every other part, so that they all sang in harmony, in accordance with the mathematical laws laid down by the Greeks. Alberti wrote: 'I affirm again with Pythagoras: it is absolutely certain that nature is wholly consistent. That is how things stand. The very same numbers that cause sounds to have that *concinnitas* [harmony], pleasing to the ear, can also fill the eyes with wonder and delight.'

Because each and every part of the Famous Temple of Rimini corresponded with each and every other part, it was beautiful; and because it was beautiful, it was perfect. 'Beauty is that reasoned harmony of all the parts within a body,' Alberti proclaimed, 'so that nothing may be added, taken away, or altered, but for the worse.' And if the Famous Temple of Rimini was perfect, was not also its creator divine, and numbered among the winged gods?

While Alberti was making his design in Rimini, Matteo de' Pasti made another medal, just for him. The face of this medal shows the proud profile of the humanist scholar, and the obverse depicts a typically gnomic emblem: the eye of knowledge, flashing with creative lightning and borne aloft by divine wings. It was surmounted by the inscription 'Quid tum?', which might be translated as: 'What next?'

* * *

Alberti was still secretary to the Papal Court. He was called back to Rome after a large wooden model of his design was completed, and the construction of the exterior of the Famous Temple of Rimini was entrusted to Matteo de' Pasti. A series of letters exchanged between the two men at the end of 1454 illustrates only too well what happens when theory is translated into practice. It is clear that de' Pasti and his provincial workmen did not understand the classical language of Alberti's design, and had rashly challenged his Pythagorean systems of proportion. Alberti brushed them aside:

> Greetings. Your letters were most welcome in many ways, and welcome in that my Lord has done what I wanted, that he has taken the best advice from everyone. But when you tell me that Manetto asserts that the dome should be two diameters high, then I prefer to believe those who built the Baths and the Pantheon and all those other great things rather than him; and reason more than any person. And if he relies on opinion, I will not be surprised if he is often in the wrong.

But besides the aesthetic problems there were also practical ones, physical obstacles placed in the way of the realization of his perfect design. Difficulties arose because Alberti was not building a new building but altering an old one, a building which, in his opinion, was clearly an example of 'inept modern nonsense'. Alberti wrote to de' Pasti:

> As for the business of the pier in my model, remember what I said to you: that the façade should be an independent structure because I find the widths and heights of those chapels [of the existing building] disturbing ... If you alter them [the new piers in Alberti's design], you will make a discord in all that music. And let us consider how to cover the church with something light. Do not trust the piers to carry any weight. And that is why it seemed to us that a wooden barrel vault would be more useful.

Alberti had decided to make his new façade entirely independent from the old building for two reasons. Firstly, he considered the old building so inelegant that he did not want his new one even to touch it. Secondly, he believed that the enlargement of the church – the new chapels of the muses and the planets, of St Sigismund and Isotta – had seriously weakened its structure, which was why he proposed that the ceiling of the nave should be made of timber rather than masonry. As a result, Alberti's new façade bears little relationship to the Gothic church behind it. Brick walls, medieval buttresses, and lancet windows appear in his new arches pell-mell, the old and the new marking out their own separate rhythms.

There were, furthermore, previously unobserved features of the church of St Francis that interfered with the realization of Alberti's design, as if the church itself was intent upon obstructing his grandiose project. There were buttresses protruding from the west front, for example, that interfered with the two niches intended for the bodies of Malatesta and Isotta. The original rectangular design for these niches would expose these ancient buttresses, and Alberti advised de' Pasti to make the niches round so that the buttresses would be concealed. But de' Pasti soon realized that this solution raised its own problems. The sarcophagi would not fit into round niches, and would protrude from the face of the building. In the end it was decided to abandon the niches on the west façade altogether, and to place the tombs of Malatesta and Isotta inside the church. The arrogant *condottiere* now lies in an obscure corner just to the right of the main door.

All along the project was plagued by Alberti's absence. Ever fearful of losing Malatesta's confidence, he wrote:

If someone will come here [to Rome] I will do my best to satisfy my Lord. As for you, I beg you to consider [all this] and listen to many and let me know. Someone might say something worthwhile.

Commend me, if you see him, or write to him, to my Lord to whom I would like to shew my gratitude. Commend me to the magnificent Roberto and monsignor the pronotary, and to all those you think love me.

All these difficulties are of the very stuff of architecture, today as in the fifteenth century; but the construction of the Famous Temple of Rimini also encountered problems beyond Alberti's design. Quite simply, Malatesta did not have enough money to complete the project. De' Pasti tried to save good facing stone to economize, but even so not enough material could be had. Rather than send to Istria or Carrara for limestone or marble to be hewn from the ground, Malatesta started to take stones from the Roman harbour of Rimini – not only a revered ruin, but also the city's prime economic asset. Indeed, one scandalized citizen wrote that 'wherever there was some noble stone that could be used for decorations or inscriptions', Malatesta took it, 'to the great detriment of the city's ancient monuments'. He induced the abbot of San Apollinare in Classe in Ravenna, built by the very Justinian who had made Hagia Sophia, to sell him chunks of his abbey; and the abbot sent him cartloads of porphyry and serpentine, which now adorn the arch around the west door of Malatesta's temple. The people of Ravenna were so outraged that they cancelled all the contracts they had with the *condottiere*, and called upon Venice to defend their honour.

The demigods of Alberti's dream had constructed rafts of learning from the flotsam they found in the River of Life, and now the Famous Temple of Rimini was being constructed by lashing together the relics of ancient buildings. The humanist had not envisaged that the construction of his classical masterpiece would be so destructive to the remains of antiquity he himself had sought to preserve.

* * *

Malatesta was an increasingly desperate man, and his enemies were multiplying by the day. In 1458, the new Pope Pius II engineered an alliance against him; they marched on the Rimini hinterland, capturing fifty-seven villages and executing all those who did not surrender. The next year Malatesta pawned all his jewels to raise troops and went into rebellion, laying siege to several Papal towns. One of his paid humanists, Valturius, defiantly compared him to the 'Divine Vespasian who built and completed the temple of Concord and Peace'; but by 1461 Malatesta was confined to Rimini, while in Rome the Pope convened the trial of his soul.

The verdict was a foregone conclusion. The Curia deposed Malatesta from his principality, excommunicated him from the church, and condemned him to Hell. He was burned in effigy at the cathedral doors of countless Italian towns. The Venetians, who thought he might come in useful to them, eventually negotiated a pardon for Malatesta, but he was required to fast for three days and then to kneel before the Papal legate in the forum at Rimini to beg forgiveness.

Malatesta's final campaign was far from his ephemeral principality. Three years after the condemnation and the pardon of his soul, the Venetians sent him to Greece to fight against the Turks. In the hills above ancient Sparta he found someone he had not thought he would encounter again: Gemistos Plethon, the Greek scholar whose paganism had so inspired him in his youth. Plethon was dead. Malatesta had his men collect the philosopher's bones and he shipped them back to Rimini, where they were placed in one of the side arches of the Famous Temple that Alberti had reserved for the remains of famous men.

The temple remained unfinished. All that was ever built of the dome were a few foundations. At the west end, the high tribune arch that was perhaps intended for Malatesta's own monument was never completed. The brick façade of the old church of St Francis still pokes through the hole where the tomb should have been. The sarcophagi that line the sides of the building remain half empty, Malatesta having been unable to gather around him the requisite number of famous men to fill them. The stone arches that house them peter out towards the east end, revealing the brick of the medieval structure they were built to conceal.

Malatesta died in 1468 of a malaria he had picked up in Greece. Seven years later, the bastard who succeeded him, Roberto, celebrated his wedding. The centrepiece of the table was a gigantic cake covered in sugar icing, made in the form of the Famous Temple of Rimini as his father and Alberti had imagined it. It didn't outlive the feast.

✳ ✳ ✳

Alberti, safe in the Papal circle, escaped the demise of his patron. He soon moved on to other projects in Florence, Mantua, and Rome; but none of Alberti's buildings were ever finished. They are as incomplete today as when the builders walked away from them, as ruined as the remains of antiquity Alberti sought to emulate.

Alberti had hoped that his buildings would be perfectly beautiful. When, in his dream, he stood atop the mountain and saw the gods flitting above the River of Life, he dreamed that he was one of them. He was punished for his blasphemy. The Famous Temple of Rimini, his statement of classical perfection, is nothing more than an incomplete sentence, a non sequitur, a stutter.

SANS SOUCI, POTSDAM

In Which Nothing Happens at All

CLASSICAL RUINS.
*View of the basin and the ruins at the top
of the hill opposite the palace of Sans Souci.*

Simulation

O*ne of the first tasks faced by the new Greek nation in 1833 was to invent its own history. The Greeks acquired themselves a king, and discussed turning the Parthenon into his residence. The design that Karl Friedrich Schinkel prepared for this palace was a collage of classical buildings clustered around their proto-type, the Parthenon. The latter was left in ruins as a memento mori, to remind the young nation that all civilizations will fall into ruin one day. Schinkel's design simulated a Greece that had never existed. His palace was, like* The Architect's Dream, *a history lesson, offered to a nation that possessed no history of its own.*

The Famous Temple of Rimini and the Alhambra were battlegrounds between the past and the present, the familiar and the other. There was no question in the minds of Alberti and Keiser Karel about which side to be on or, indeed, who was going to win. The course of history defeated them both, and the Temple and the Alhambra are no more perfect than all those other virgin shrines and temples to wisdom whose wrecks litter the history of architecture. Any architecture that aspires to completeness will eventually fall into what is, in the terms of its creators, lamentable decay and ruin.

Any architecture, that is, other than that of gardens. There, in the bosom of Natura naturans, *it has always been permitted to enjoy, rather than defy, the passage of time. At no period was this truer than in the Enlightenment, when Edward Gibbon was inspired to write* The Decline and Fall of the Roman Empire *by gazing at the ruins of the Roman Forum, and hearing the Franciscan friars sing the vespers on the site of the temple of Jupiter Optimus Maximus. His readers, men of taste and learning, would while away the boredom of their summer's ease by building follies, and these whimsical belvederes and ruins displayed precisely the altered states that architecture had traditionally sought to defy. They were, like* The Architect's Dream, *objects of speculation, miniature simulations of the processes of history, to be viewed from the summit of a colossal column, at a distance, without care.*

ONCE UPON A TIME, WHEN THE WORLD WAS WITHOUT CARE, THERE WAS a lake in a forest. The lake was still and dark, and was guarded by tall poplar trees; and by the side of this lake, the people of that country had made a shrine to the nymph who dwelt there. It is still there: a little niche in a wall, down by the water.

One day a wandering prince came upon this lake and this nymphaeum, and he made a garden; and in the garden he constructed two shrines: one to his father, the king, and the other to his mother, the queen. In time, the Greeks added a temple to this garden shrine; and in time the sanctuary was surrounded by a Doric colonnade.

In time the sanctuary must have grown wealthy, for the Romans built a complex of baths there, in which pilgrims to the sacred spot could refresh themselves. In the atrium there was a bath of Russian jasper, presided over by Apollo and Bacchus. In the next room, light and rainwater poured from the sky into an *impluvium* framed by four Doric columns; and in the third, all the things necessary for the bath were laid out on bronze consoles cast in the form of dragons. The golden gates of the *calidarium* would open in the aqueous gloom, and the pilgrim would descend between white marble caryatids into radiant steam.

It must also have been the Romans who added the arched gateway to the sanctuary, perhaps in the turbulent times of their decline and fall, for it is a crude structure, clearly built for defence. It was extended in the Dark Ages with a fortified Norman tower. In time the sanctuary fell into decay, and a farmhouse was constructed under the defensive aegis of the tower. This farmhouse is one of those ageless buildings that characterize the *campagna*: little more than a barn rendered in ochre, it is pierced with round-headed windows in the manner of the Tuscan *quattrocento*. Above the house proper there is a gallery under a pantiled roof, in which the cooling airs can be taken and the crops hung up to dry. To one side, a lean-to in the same style indicates where, in prosperous times, the farmer's family extended their dwelling.

These peasants were ignorant, no doubt, of the finer architectural points of the sanctuary whose remains they inhabited. With delightful insouciance they tethered their pigs and cattle against an ancient wall, and in order to provide themselves with a shady place to rest in the heat of the day they made a loggia on its other side. They took the Doric columns that had once surrounded the sanctuary, and placed them on top of the wall. Dispensing with the capitals and the frieze (now lost), they used their new colonnade to support a trellis for vines; and where this canopy required additional support, they propped it up with two wooden herms that they had found on the site.

And then the peasants who lived here gathered the remaining fragments of the sanctuary and used them to ornament their loggia. They took a Corinthian capital and turned it into a table; they took an ancient sarcophagus, broken as it was, and made it into a fountain, into which a bronze fish still dribbles cooling water; they set an old *basso relievo* into the wall, and placed a row of architectural fragments on the seat they had made around their table. And then, in the heat of the day, they rested.

It is a placid, timeless scene; but to those who would look for them, this complex of lake, temple, bath, tower, and farm is also an encyclopaedia of all the styles of architecture. And since the history of the art of building is nothing more nor less than the progression of style from one generation to the next, this humble home is nothing less than a history of architecture, written in crumbling brick and cracked mortar. Here, in one spot, had been a garden, the first of human habitations; simple shrines, which in time became the opulent temples of a great empire; and the refined monuments of antiquity, which fell to barbarism and were replaced by the crude dwellings of peasants. The chronicle of civilization is always such a story, of origin, establishment, construction, elaboration, and decay; and there can be no more powerful exposition of the cycles of history than a collection of buildings of many different dates, differently advanced in their artistry and in divers states of ruination.

In between the wandering prince, in his innocent state of nature, and the peasants, in theirs, had passed centuries; and it might be observed that both prince and peasants lived at times when the fortunes of civilization were at their lowest ebb. But the peasants possessed something that the prince did not: they had, however imperfectly, a memory, and, what is more, something to remember. Nothing is ever forgotten. Each cycle of history begins in advance of its predecessor: lessons, whether historical, technological, philosophical, or artistic, are learned which cannot be unlearned or lost. Thus we can speak of progress in civilization.

✳ ✳ ✳

Karl Friedrich Schinkel leant back on his sunny bench beneath the vine-clad trellis, and picked up his glass of wine from the top of the antique Corinthian capital. It was, as ever, a charming story, told by a charming storyteller. One of his friends later recalled: 'There was a nobility and harmony in his movements, a smile on his lips, a clarity in his brow, a depth and a fire in his eye ...

but still greater was the power of his word, when that which moved him came unbidden and unprepared to his lips. Then the doors of beauty opened.'

But Schinkel had not had to say a word. All he had done was to gesture, for the tale was all around him. Indeed, he was in it: sitting in the very same loggia, in front of the old *basso relievo* and other fragmentary antiquities of his story. It was a tale told in crumbling brick and stained ochre, assembled from shattered marbles, and hung with vines.

And the even more wonderful thing was Schinkel had invented it all. The lake was no more natural than the spouting fountains, and the ancient garden shrine no more primitive than the parterres of the palace gardens. The temple was no more Grecian and the baths no more Roman, the tower no more Norman and the farmhouse no more Tuscan than the barracks of Potsdam. The place was called Siam, and its ruined fragments and crumbling walls were fourteen years old at the most.

Karl Friedrich Schinkel was in the habit of conjuring fantasies. The sets he designed for *The Magic Flute*, in which the Queen of the Night rides a crescent moon through a galaxy of stars, are still used today. His *Panorama of Palermo* conjured a view of that city taken from a terrace at evening time, while his spectacles of the burning of Moscow and the Battle of the Nations inspired terror and awe in those who saw them. Their fame quickly reached the ears of the King and Queen of Prussia, who graciously engaged him to work for their family.

The bedroom he designed for Queen Luise, painted the most delicate shade of pink and hung with translucent muslin, evoked the delightful sensation of wakening at dawn in a gauzy tent. For her husband he made a replica of the Villa Chiaramonte, which the king wished to recall from a happy trip to Italy. Without even having seen the villa, Schinkel recreated it so convincingly that the king declared himself transported to the sunny Bay of Naples. For Karl and Wilhelm, the cadet princes of the family, Schinkel constructed another Italian villa, the Schloss Glienicke; and, facing it over the wide river Havel, the Gothic castle of Babelsberg, set high on a steep and wooded hill. But it was in Siam that Schinkel realized his most subtle flight of fancy – one so surely founded in history and philosophy as to be almost completely believable.

Alexander von Humboldt, who was sitting in the same dappled shade, was delighted with Schinkel's story, for it closely modelled his own thinking on the history of nature. As he would put it:

> The description of nature is intimately connected with its history; and the geologist, who is guided by the connection existing among the facts observed, cannot form a conception of the present without pursuing, through countless ages, the history of the past. In tracing the physical delineation of the globe, we behold the present and the past reciprocally incorporated, as it were, with one another; for the domain of nature is like that of languages, in which etymological research reveals a successive development, by showing us the primary condition of an idiom reflected in the forms of speech in use at the present day.

Schinkel's tapestry of light and shade, garden and interior, land and water expressed perfectly the natural philosopher's belief that nature and culture were not in opposition, but were rather symptomatic of – and sympathetic towards – one another.

Alexander von Humboldt was even more delighted that he had been invited to live in the farmhouse at Siam whenever he wished, and to use it as if it were his own. Humboldt never felt at home when he was at home. His scientific expeditions to Latin America and to Russia and his diplomatic and professorial visits to the capitals of Europe should have satisfied his wanderlust, but they only made him hungrier. To stay in Schinkel's confection would be to taste something of the joys of travel without any of its inconveniences: to recline under overgrown pergolas, in sight of Tuscan farmhouses, without actually having to go abroad. And here, free from the cares of city life, he could think, and write, and converse with wise and civilized men.

The Prince of Siam completed the small party that sat on the bench in that sunny afternoon of May 1840. He felt every bit as pleased with himself as did his learned and august friends, for that long post-prandial ramble through tall tales and elevated conversation was as much his creation as theirs.

Since his youth the Prince of Siam had dreamed of Italy. In 1828 he had gone to Rome for the first time, his progress to the Eternal City marked by stops in Venice, Florence, Naples, and all the other jewels in the crown of European civilization. He returned to the sandy plains of home determined that he could conjure from them the lush gardens and opulent villas of Tivoli. At his command, the gardener Peter Joseph Lenné laid out sinuous paths and elegant boskage, while expansive lawns and tall poplars called to mind the plains and cypress groves of the *campagna*.

And with Schinkel at his side, the Prince of Siam created himself a villa. Not for the first time, the architect was called upon to construct a building from happy reminiscence. This villa was designed to recall the prince's Grand Tour, as well as his readings of Pliny, who, in ancient times, had recalled his own villa with such pleasure. Its rooms were painted in the bold oxblood red and olive green of the houses of Pompeii, exquisitely decorated with grotteschi, and hung with painted scenes of the Bay of Naples. The furniture was designed to look as if it could be folded up and carried away to continue the prince's travels. One bedroom was even decorated as a large tent, lined in blue and white ticking, inhabited by camp beds with awnings over them supported on crossed spears. It was the perfect place for a summer holiday.

Siam was a place of cheerfulness and liberty. The people of Siam tripped lightly home through the sunlit fields, rather than trudging through the dark and stony streets of great cities. Dressed in loose robes, they were unrestricted by the corsetry of European manners and customs. Leading simple lives, they were unencumbered by the rows of medals, the military parades, and the court balls that suffocated the spirit. The people of Siam were free: free of drudgery, free of convention, free of politics and history. They were happy.

And the prince hoped that, in Siam, he could be the same. On that spring afternoon in 1840, his demesne had nearly been perfected. Schinkel's farmhouse completed the view from the terrace of the villa, its pleasing mélange of architectures provoking exactly the sort of idle speculation in which the prince liked to indulge when he was at leisure. And Humboldt had perfected the picture by agreeing to come and spend a few months in it: the natural philosopher in perfect harmony with his habitation and with nature itself. It was going to be a wonderful summer.

✳ ✳ ✳

The old man who had once been the Prince of Siam leaned back and sighed at the reminiscence. Wonderful summers are always cut short, he reflected. A month after that sunny May afternoon, the prince had inherited the throne of Prussia. Schinkel died that very autumn, and Siam faded into memory. It hadn't really been in far-off Siam anyway, but at the bottom of the royal garden in Potsdam. The prince had called his retreat Siam in a moment of whimsy, for he hoped that it would resemble what he supposed to be a land of freedom and pleasure.

The creation of Siam had been a rehearsal, nothing more, for it was but a small part of the magical demesne that would now be his home: a palace that had been made, the new king knew, so that he could be free of drudgery, free of convention, free of politics and history, free from care. That was why his new residence was called Sans Souci.

Sans Souci had been created a century before by the king's great-great-uncle, who liked to be known as Féderic. He had been a mercurial figure, and like his great-great-nephew he had longed to be anywhere else but at home. Unlike his descendant, however, he preferred France to Italy, dreaming of the elegant manners and witty conversation of the salons of Paris and the court of Versailles: so different, he imagined, from his dull life in the forests and sandy plains of Prussia. 'If God made the world for me,' he wrote, 'he put France there for my amusement'; and when he ascended the throne, Féderic decided to be amused. He couldn't absent himself from his royal duties, of course, but if he could not go to Versailles then he could at least make its Trianons come to him. He repaired to the salubrious airs of his gardens, where he could escape the cares of his kingly office, saying, 'Quand je serai là, je serai sans souci' (Once I am there, I shall be carefree).

In 1744, Féderic engaged an old friend from his military days, Georg Von Knobbelsdorf, to build him a palace where he could be *sans souci*. Like any happy couple, they argued constantly, and Féderic often took to the drawing board himself to correct his friend's design. Terraces were laid out on the hillside upon which the dwelling was to be built, and the king decided to cover them with greenhouses, to supply sweet figs and vines and peaches for the royal table. Sans Souci was finished in 1747, and Féderic took up residence immediately.

The palace was modest in scale, but its interiors were extraordinary confections, so delicate that they appeared to be spun from sugar, pink clouds, and sunsets rather than built in prosaic brick and plaster. In the music room there still stands the well-tempered clavier that was once played by Johann Sebastian Bach. In 1747, the irascible old man had been invited by Féderic to come and teach him the principles and the art of music. It is said that the composer was unimpressed by the effete young prince and was all too ready to criticize his musical efforts. Next to the clavier is the music stand at which

Féderic would play the flute to his guests after supper. The architecture of this room dissolves in kaleidoscopic pattern: mirrors are framed in writhing rocaille and hung with soft candles, and the sparkling crystal chandelier hangs from a ceiling ornamented with a gilded trellis, hung with vines among which roll laughing, drunken cherubs.

Féderic was an avid reader, and had always adored the wit of Voltaire. In 1750 he persuaded the luminary to come and live with him at Sans Souci. (Their affair didn't last long: the terrier-like writer could not resist biting the hand that fed him, and he fled after three years, returning to his niece – or, depending on whom you believe, his mistress – in Paris.) Voltaire's bedroom at Sans Souci was as witty and perverse as the writer himself. The ceiling was crazed with delicate tendrils of plaster roses, while the walls were inhabited by an exotic and arbitrary menagerie of monkeys, parrots, and ibises, garlanded with flowers and fruit. The philosopher might wake up on a summer's morning, the sun streaming in through the tall French windows, and imagine himself in far Cathay or Cipango, until he heard the bark of Féderic and his dogs on the terrace outside.

At the heart of Sans Souci was a dining room, for Féderic loved nothing so much as conversation around the dinner table. His dazzling repartee would flit from art to mathematics, engineering to liberty, as he neatly sliced the fruits that had been brought in from his garden. Lunches and suppers, prepared by his two French chefs, were legendarily long, and the king would down endless glasses of champagne and cups of coffee. His dining room was a veritable temple to the pleasures of the table, an oval colonnade of Corinthian columns of white and gold, its dome inhabited by the cherubs and muses who personified the subjects of their host's conversation.

The gardens of Sans Souci were filled with wonderful illusions of other times and other places. There was a Chinese pavilion for the taking of tea, whose roof, shaped like a gigantic tent, was supported by gilded palm trees, and whose verandahs were inhabited by mandarins and concubines frozen in gilded attitudes of pleasure. There was a temple of Friendship, to which Féderic would repair to remember his dearest sister Wilhemine. There was a fully functioning windmill, in which the royal children could play at peasants, and an endless forest of *allées* and *rondpoints* planted for the pleasures of the chase.

But the king reserved the best surprise for the departure of his guests. Leaving the sugary delights of the palace without care, they were presented with a mighty and sombre ruin. There was the broken wall of some great amphitheatre, reminiscent of nothing so much as the Colosseum in Rome; a dilapidated rotunda, formerly, perhaps, the residence of a philosopher; and a row of three Ionic columns that surely had formed part of the colonnade of some temple of Diana. It was as if the ancients had built a city upon this hill, once upon a time, and Féderic had made his residence in its shadow.

It was all a delightful *plaisanterie*, of course, a post-prandial memento mori, which the king hoped would provoke a wistful smile on the powdered faces of his philosophical guests. The ruin was conceived by Innocente Bellavite, a theatre set painter from Italy. Bellavite, like Schinkel after him, was a conjuror of the lonely plains and rocks of the Roman *campagna*, where shepherds corralled their flocks in the shadows of mighty aqueducts and peasants made their miserable habitations in broken shrines.

In his magical demesne, Féderic did nothing at all: he wrote, and played his flute, and held dazzling dinner parties, and ate the fruit that grew in his sparkling greenhouses, and contemplated the hazy mirage of ruins that closed the vista from his hallway. He lived without care: *sans souci*, as he hoped. It was as if, inside the gates of the park, time stood still, and history was a seductive mirage.

Sans Souci was a fantasy. It wasn't a real palace, a proper place to receive ambassadors and to undertake all the other tiresome duties of being a king.

Féderic had one of those sorts of places built at the bottom of the garden, so that he could do those sorts of things without interrupting his leisure. The Neues Palais was a baroque pile, topped by an arrogant dome and entered through a colossal hemicycle of Corinthian columns. It had countless bed-rooms, rich ballrooms, an opera house, a shell grotto, and an art museum; but Féderic couldn't be bothered to spend time there. 'It's just a *fanfaronnade*,' he said.

When his duties called him away from Sans Souci, Féderic dreamt of opening the French windows of his bedroom there and walking out into the morning sun with his favourite greyhound, named Madame de Pompadour for the mistress of the King of France. To quell his longing, he read and wrote: letters to Voltaire, poetry, histories of his own *res gestae*. It has been said that, were he not a king, he would be known as one of the finest French writers of the eighteenth century.

There was one book he always took with him: it was the only novel one could read again and again, he said. Voltaire had written *Candide* after he had fallen out with Féderic and had left Sans Souci, but the novel, in which a young naïf goes out into the world from his provincial chateau, struck a chord with a king whose inheritance had bound him to do the same. Perhaps Voltaire was thinking of Féderic when he wrote it, and the king is bound to have smiled and agreed when, at the end of the novel, Candide, having witnessed all the horrors of the 'best of all possible worlds', retires from it with the maxim: 'Il faut cultiver notre jardin.'

Féderic's descendant, once the Prince of Siam and now the King of Prussia, was only too ready to cultivate his ancestor's garden and to inhabit the palace which had lain dormant for half a century. Within months of his father's death, the shutters of Sans Souci were thrown open and the summer sun poured in through the French windows, surprising cherubs and monkeys that had slept for decades. Dust sheets were drawn back to reveal gilded reefs of rocaille, and soon the dining table in the great oval saloon groaned once more under fruits gathered from the garden. (Perhaps it groaned, too, at the earnest witticisms of the new king, who lacked something of Féderic's eighteenth-century lightness.)

The king engaged Ludwig Persius, who had assisted Schinkel in his later years, on a building programme that dwarfed anything Féderic had envisaged. On the crest of a ridge within the forest, Persius and the king conjured an apparition of the Villa Medici in Rome. Endless flights of steps and grottoes, rose gardens and nymphaea led to the villa itself, which was crowned with tall belvederes. To either side, huge greenhouses were filled with the heady scent of orange and lemon trees, so that not only the sights but the smells of Italy could be enjoyed; and in the summer the king could imagine that he was some Renaissance humanist, listening to the vespers bells as they rang out over the Eternal City. A pump house, built to power the fountains of the park, was disguised as an Egyptian mosque, reflected in the reservoir as if it were standing by some distant oasis. Nearby the king built a church in the form of a Romanesque monastery, complete with peaceful cloisters; and a little way away, on the top of a hill known as the Pfingstberg, he constructed a gigantic terrace from whose airy arcades and towers one could view the distant horizon.

In his youth, he had laboured to recreate Italy in the loggias of Siam; but the Sans Souci over which the king now ruled had become a panorama, a boundless hallucination, an insubstantial pageant of towers and gorgeous palaces, in which all times and all places were made present through the medium of architecture. At the heart of this magical demesne the King of Prussia was a Prospero calling forth visions of a universal history – in which, as Schinkel had once said, architecture 'ennobles all human relationships'. It was such stuff as dreams are made on.

* * *

In August 1945 three men sat on the terrace of the Cecilienhof, a half-timbered cottage overgrown with vines that the last of the royal house of Féderic had built for his daughter-in-law Cécile.

They had been there for a month, and a very nice month it had been. Their residences were close by, in the gardens of Schinkel's Gothic fortress of Babelsberg. One of their aides described them in his diary:

> They consisted of a series of villas, all facing onto the lake, and very
> pleasant. We have a house for the three Chiefs of Staff, and have Jumbo
> with us. Attlee is next door on one side and Bridges beyond him and
> PM beyond that. On the other side Pug. I spent the afternoon settling
> in and in the evening tried for a pike in the lake.

But the three men were there to do business rather than to go fishing or look at the scenery. The villas did not belong to them. As another of their secretaries recorded:

> All the Germans have of course been turned out. Where they've gone,
> no-one knows. Can you imagine what we would feel if Germans and
> Japanese were doing this in England, and if we had all been bundled
> out to make way for Hitler and Co.?

And their deliberations were not of the philosophical kind. The 'Big Three' – the leaders of Great Britain, the Soviet Union, and the United States of America – had come to Potsdam to resolve the German question once and for all, and to bring a particularly unsavoury historical episode to an end. They did not agree on much, but they did agree on one thing: the kings of Prussia had been careless. The follies they had built on their summer holidays were the stuff that nightmares are made of; and outside Sans Souci time had not stood still, history was anything but a mirage, and the world was full of care.

For outside his park Féderic had been far from a reluctant player on the historical stage: out of Sans Souci he was Frederick the Great, one of the most belligerent princes of the eighteenth century. Within a year of taking the throne he had sent his troops to annex neighbouring Silesia, and he spent most of the rest of his life trying to prevent his rival, the Empress Maria Theresa, from taking it back. His troops marched over the Oder to Breslau, down into Saxony, all the way to Prague, and nearly to the gates of Vienna itself. Frederick made and unmade counts and kings and even emperors; and at the end of his life, in a piece of extraordinary *Realpolitik*, he connived in the partition of Poland between himself and his erstwhile enemies the Empress Maria Theresa and the Tsar of Russia. The consequences were still playing themselves out in 1945. They still are.

Frederick spent much of his life outside the walls of Sans Souci not only living in a world of care and contemplating ruins, but also creating both. He was well aware of the senselessness of it. When his armies occupied Saxony in 1760, the king wrote: 'I spared that beautiful country as far as possible, but now it is utterly devastated. Miserable madmen that we are ... amusing ourselves with the destruction of masterpieces of industry and of time, we leave an odious memory of our ravages and the calamities that they cause.' Not that it stopped him. He wrote to his friend Catt: 'Admit that war is a cruel thing – what a life for the unhappy soldiers who receive more blows than bread, and who mostly retire with scars or missing limbs. The peasant is even worse off – he often dies of hunger – you must admit that the obstinacy of the Queen of Hungary and myself makes many people wretched.' Obstinate the king was; the Queen of Hungary, the Empress Maria Theresa, could only pray that 'in the end God will take pity on us and crush this monster'. So terrifying was the reputation of Frederick the Great that when Napoleon, having invaded Prussia, visited his tomb, he was moved to say to his officers: 'Hats off, gentlemen! If he were still alive, we would not be here.'

Frederick the Great's descendants followed him in his despotic militarism, as they did in his enlightened private life at Sans Souci. In 1848 King Friedrich Wilhelm IV, the very prince who had enjoyed the freedoms of Siam, was confronted by his subjects in Berlin, who demanded the same freedoms for themselves. They gathered in the streets, clamouring for the establishment of a constitution, a liberal government, and the unification of all the states of Germany into one nation state. History presented the king with the opportunity to turn his whole realm into a happy Siam.

On 18 March the enlightened and freedom-loving king sent his troops to disperse the demonstrators. Hundreds lost their lives that day in the streets of the city. But the people believed that history was on their side, and they did not return to their homes as the king had wished. Three days later, they forced him to leave Sans Souci and come back to the city. They draped him in the revolutionary tricolour and marched him to the graveyards, to honour the dead whose deaths he himself had ordered so recently. Perhaps at that moment the king also believed that history was on the side of the people, or perhaps he had no choice. Either way, he stood in front of them all, and agreed to their demands for liberty and progress. And then he returned to Sans Souci.

The new Prussia didn't last long. The king wandered in his park, and sat musing in the loggias of his Italian follies; and when autumn came he dissolved the democratically elected assembly of the people and the modern liberal constitution, and restored his own authority at the point of a gun. The next year, when the general assembly of all the Germans in Frankfurt offered him the imperial crown of all Germany, he dismissed it with disgust as a crown 'disgraced by the stink of revolution, baked of dirt and mud'. He retired to Sans Souci, and contemplated his latest folly. Entirely without irony, he named it the Friedenskirche: the church of Peace.

Frederick the Great dreamed of attending the French king at his toilette. Friedrich Wilhelm IV preferred dreams of Italy and Siam to the imperial crown. But in 1871, after a great victory over France, their successor, Wilhelm I, was crowned Kaiser of all Germany in the Galerie des Glaces at Versailles.

His grandson, Kaiser Wilhelm II, caught the imperial bug at that glittering occasion, and had little desire to be *sans souci*. When in Potsdam he stayed in the Neues Palais – that *fanfaronnade*, as his ancestor Féderic had called it. He arrived with electric lighting and all the most modern plumbing appliances. He even built a tunnel between the kitchens and the dining room of the palace, which were several hundred feet apart.

For Wilhelm II, *fanfaronnade* was a way of life. Living amid bombastic splendour, he began to believe his own propaganda. Like some Pharaonic inscription, he said of himself: 'Deep into the most distant jungles of other parts of the world, everyone should know the voice of the German Kaiser. Nothing should occur on this earth without having first heard him. His word must have its weight placed on every scale ... Also domestically the word of the Kaiser should be everything.' Just to make sure it was, he led his empire into war with his own cousins, the King of England and the Tsar of Russia, and, of course, with the old enemy, France; and the rest is mud, and shells, and poisoned gas, and ruins of the most unromantic kind. They are still digging up the bodies from the fields today, nearly a century later.

The *fanfaronnade* of Wilhelm II turned out to be just that, nothing more. Faced with utter defeat he refused to abdicate, and it took his chancellor, Prince Max of Baden, to do it for him. The Kaiser made sure he was safe in Holland before the announcement was made; but he sent a train to the royal station at the Neues Palais, and it returned with fifty-six carriages full of treasures. There was his vast collection of snuffboxes, hundreds of military uniforms, pieces of furniture designed for his ancestors by Schinkel and Persius, and of course portraits of Frederick the Great. Forced into peaceful country retreat at the modest Huis van Doorn, the former Kaiser of Germany was far from *sans souci*. He remained convinced that a call would come to return him to his rightful station, but it never did, and the old man spent his time venting his frustrations on the wooded garden around his house. In his exile he cut down some six hundred trees, leaving the landscape resembling nothing so much as the fields of Flanders.

Back in Berlin, on 9 November 1919, a Socialist Republic was declared from the balcony of his vacated palace, and the terrible history of modern Germany was set into motion. Stalin, Churchill, and Truman agreed: Hitler's *Gotterdämmerung* was the lineal descendant of the aristocratic vanity of Frederick the Great, the repressive conservatism of Friedrich Wilhelm IV, and the crass megalomania of Kaiser Wilhelm II. There was something in the Prussian spirit, wasn't there, that made them like this, something crude, and aggressive, and dangerous. The Germans needed to be cured of their obsession with making ruins and crazy follies, or else they'd do it all over again.

It was a convincing story, and it was a very convincing pretext. The Big Three had turned Germany into a landscape of ruins. Whole towns and cities had disappeared in the firestorms of an afternoon, and the palaces of the erstwhile rulers of Dresden, Stuttgart, Munich, and Berlin were wrecked shells. Even as the Big Three chatted away on the terrace of the Cecilienhof, their minions were carting away the paintings, the sculpture, the furniture, and all the other treasures they could find.

It was on the way to the Cecilienhof that Harry Truman, the President of the United States, made his decision to drop the atomic bomb on Japan, and it was on the terrace of that pretty cottage that he persuaded his allies to issue an ultimatum to the Japanese: surrender, or suffer the consequences. Suffer the consequences they did. The clocks stopped at the moment of detonation in Hiroshima, and the making of ruins was never the same again.

* * *

If the Big Three had had the leisure to wander outside the half-timbered farm-yard of the Cecilienhof, they would soon have come to Potsdam and the royal park of Sans Souci. The British Foreign Minister Anthony Eden jotted down: 'Devastation of Potsdam terrible and all this I am told in one raid of fifty minutes. What an hour of hell it must have been.' Frederick the Great's elaborate baroque Stadtschloss, Schinkel's noble Nikolaikirche, and the streets of the town now recalled the shattered remains of Rome. Here and there a column or a gesturing statue protruded from piles of smoking rubble, while women dressed in rags scrabbled for food among the remnants of their beautiful town. Even Winston Churchill, who had engineered their humiliation, was moved: 'My hate had died with their surrender and I was much moved by their demonstrations, and also by their haggard looks and threadbare clothes.'

Within Sans Souci, however, it seemed that the magical kingdom had only become more like itself. The gardens, which had not been tended in the last years of the war, were pleasingly overgrown, the setting for a melancholic *fête champêtre*. The palaces, whose paintings and furniture had been removed to distant bunkers for protection, had the desolate air of summer retreats shut up for the winter. The ruins that Frederick the Great had built to entertain his guests were only a little more ruined, the Norman tower having been damaged by a stray missile. A belvedere, similarly shelled, made a pleasing picture at the end of a long *allée* of trees. Only the western gate of the Neues Palais set a mournful, if picturesque note: the great triumphal arch was pitted with bullet holes, and the Corinthian columns of the great hemicycle around it had been shattered and lay in pieces in the long grass. They are still there.

And in Siam, the vines clambered over the pergola made of stolen antique columns, and water still dribbled into a broken sarcophagus from the mouth of a bronze fish. The windows of the farmhouse were shuttered, and the

Roman baths were dry and dusty. The Grecian temple was as elegant as it had always been; the garden shrine made by the Prince of Siam was a little over-grown, nothing more; and the tall poplars were quietly reflected in the dark waters of the lake. Nothing had happened at all.

NOTRE DAME DE PARIS

In Which the Temple of Reason is Restored

A NINETEENTH-CENTURY FICTION.
Frontispiece of Victor Hugo's Notre Dame de Paris.

Restoration

*T*he great buildings arrayed in The
Architect's Dream *date from many times and places, but in Thomas Cole's painted*
rapture each one of them has been made new and perfect, just as its makers intended. In
1834, Leo von Klenze stood before the Parthenon surrounded by men and women dressed
as ancient Athenians, and he likewise vowed to undo centuries of history – to restore the
temple to its original virginity. Over the next century interpolations were excised and exci-
sions reversed, and in the process many Byzantine and Ottoman remains were destroyed
for ever. Von Klenze's restoration was a selective affair, in which the temple of Athene
took precedence over every other incarnation of the Parthenon.

Restoration was, in the words of its greatest exponent, the French architect Viollet-
le-Duc, a modern idea and practice. While Renaissance architects studied ancient
buildings as exemplars, and Enlightenment historians meditated on them as lessons, the
architects of the nineteenth century were anxious to return them to their original states.

Their anxiety may perhaps be explained by the age in which they lived, which was
a time of unprecedented change. The French Revolution of 1789 brought the Ancien
Régime *to an end, and established an entirely new world from Year Zero. The Industrial*

Revolution gave that world new form, and altered the relationship between people and things for ever. At such a time, buildings raised by previous eras must have seemed like precious relics of a way of life that was rapidly disappearing from view.

The Parthenon was only ever restored to a ruined state, but Notre Dame de Paris, another shrine to a Virgin – and also, albeit briefly, a temple of Reason and Wisdom – is the example par excellence of nineteenth-century restoration carried to completion. While von Klenze stripped the Parthenon of barbarian excrescences, Viollet-le-Duc attempted to restore to Notre Dame the magnificence of which more recent barbarians had stripped her.

But Notre Dame was no Parthenon. Constructed over centuries, her design a moving target, the cathedral had never been a perfect virgin in the first place. The restored Notre Dame was an arbitrary fiction, a combination of romance and science that would have baffled the masons who had built it in the first place. Like The Architect's Dream, *it characterizes less the grand sweep of history than the moment of time in which it was made.*

IN 1962, THE WOULD-BE-REVOLUTIONARY WRITER GUY DEBORD RECALLED a small but telling historical footnote. Writing on the Commune of 1871 in a pamphlet entitled 'Into the Dustbin of History', he commented:

> The story of the arsonists who during the final days of the Commune went to destroy Notre Dame, only to find it defended by an armed battalion of Commune artists, is a richly provocative example of direct democracy ... Were those artists right to defend a cathedral in the name of eternal aesthetic values – and, in the final analysis, in the name of museum culture – while other people wanted to express themselves then and there by making this destruction symbolize their absolute defiance of a society that, in its moment of triumph, was about to consign their entire lives to silence and oblivion?

It was only a scrap of a story, and no-one really knows what happened. There are rumours that the Communards broke into the cathedral, piled up all the chairs in the nave, and set fire to them; but the building is still there, while the Commune is long gone. It's easy to see, though, why the Communards might have attacked Notre Dame: if ever they required a symbol for all the things that stood in the way of liberty, equality, fraternity – in the way of reason and progress and all the rest of it – they only had to look around them.

* * *

Notre Dame lowered over the Paris of the Commune as it had done for many centuries. The west front of the cathedral was a tottering city of building piled upon building, a vertical labyrinth infested with all the creatures of the medieval imagination. Each of the three doors of the west front was thronged with angels – choirs and choirs of them – and saints, martyrs, and personifications of the virtues and the seven deadly sins. Above the doors sat St Anne and her daughter Our Lady herself, with Christ presiding over the Last Judgement in the centre. Above these portals were arrayed all the kings of Israel, and above the Gallery of the Kings stood the Queen of Heaven flanked by two guardian angels. Behind her, like a halo, there was a rose window. Higher still, above the rose window, another gallery ran across the west front: a delicate forest of colonnettes and pointed arches, the eyrie of brooding gargoyles, misshapen, ugly, and hauntingly sad. Above this stone menagerie rose two towers, pierced by tall lancet windows so that the bells that hung within them could sound out over all of Paris; and as if in response to the music, tendrils, leaves, and strange beasts seemed to sprout from the architecture. On top of everything else, a spire dissolved into Parisian skies as grey as stone and lead.

The chief characteristic of the interior of Notre Dame was gloom. Against an architecture rendered almost inky black by contrast, tall stained-glass windows lined the nave of the church like colourful banners hung out for a procession. Beneath them opened two rows of aisles, and countless chapels:

richly painted, elaborately furnished stalls dedicated to the worship of multitudinous saints and cults. Halfway to the altar, the processional way of the nave was interrupted by a crossing. The south transept ended in a large rose window, a kaleidoscope of coloured glass and stone; the glowing colours of this miraculous wall told the stories of the New Testament, radiating in chapter and verse from the figure of Christ at the centre. The northern transept was also illuminated by a rose window, in the middle of which sat the Virgin in majesty with the Christ child on her knee. In concentric circles around this image of the new dispensation were arranged the representatives of the old: the prophets, kings, and high priests of Israel.

After the transepts, the nave terminated in a semicircular apse, and here was placed the high altar dedicated to Our Lady of Paris. Behind the altar rose high windows that glowed in the light of the morning sun. The apse was the head of the church, and the whole building took the form of Our Lord with his arms spread out on the Cross: the stone ribs of the vault made his skeleton, and the painted walls and coloured glass stretched between them were his living body.

This divine body contained within it images of all the things that could be known in Christendom. To the east, the rising sun shed its rays on the altar of the Resurrection. To the west, the setting sun cast its dying glow on visions of the Last Judgement. The prophets and patriarchs of the Old Testament were relegated to the gloomy north, while the apostles and saints of the New were bathed in southern light. The improving lessons of scripture were depicted close to the ground, where pilgrims might study them closely; while outside, perched atop the crags and bluffs of the building, were all the monsters of ancient lore, with their billy-goat horns and beards, their bats' wings, and their faces on their arses. No wonder the Communards wanted to destroy it.

* * *

The cathedral might have seemed medieval, but this incarnation of Notre Dame de Paris had in fact been completed only seven years before, in 1864. The architects, Eugène-Emmanuel Viollet-le-Duc and Jean-Baptiste Lassus, had been appointed to restore the existing cathedral by the Ministry of Justice and Religion in 1843, and they had taken great pains to ensure that their work would appear as authentically medieval as possible. In his report to the ministry regarding the project, Viollet-le-Duc explained: 'The artist must efface himself entirely, must forget his own tastes and instincts in order to study his subject, to recover and follow the thoughts that guided the construction of the work which he wishes to restore.' His approach was based not on imagination, but on the analysis of historical evidence. He continued:

> It was necessary to perform this minute analysis in order to explain, complete, and often correct opinions resulting solely from textual sources, for all too often a text can lend itself to diverse interpretations, or be in itself unintelligible. Archaeological evidence, on the other hand, written on the stones of the building itself, despite the difficulty of dating, remains incontrovertible, and provides us with detailed information.

Viollet's restoration involved, at root, two operations: the removal of the encrustations of ages, and the replacement of things that had been removed from the building over time. The former was an archaeological challenge in itself, but scientifically replacing those things that had been taken away was even more difficult. All the sculptures of the west front had been made by hands that had withered to dust centuries before, from stone hacked out of quarries long since exhausted or buried under new suburbs. All the stained-glass windows that had once lined the nave had contained images of which there now was no record. Not only had the contents of this encyclopaedic library of the medieval mind been lost, but also the very materials of which it had been made and the very skills that had made it.

Viollet deplored those who sought to replace what had been taken away with ornaments of their own devising, made in modern materials that did not match the original. 'It is impossible to conserve the form of something made in one material by making it in another,' he wrote; 'concrete cannot reproduce the appearance of stone any more than wood can pretend to be iron.' Accordingly, his restored Notre Dame was constructed using materials and techniques that matched as closely as possible those that he supposed to be authentic. As to the form of the sculptures and other pieces that had been removed, he wrote:

> We think therefore that the replacement of all the statues that adorned the great doors, the gallery of the kings, and the buttresses can only be carried out by carefully copying surviving sculptures on analogous monuments of the same era. Models exist at Chartres, Rheims, Amiens and in the many other churches that cover the Île de France. These same cathedrals also offer us models for the stained glass which needs to be replaced at Notre Dame: models which it is impossible to imitate, but wiser to copy.

The Notre Dame that was completed in 1864 was a work of painstaking research; and to the Communards who came to destroy it seven years later, it resembled absolutely the medieval cathedral whose phantom it was.

* * *

The restored Notre Dame was a masterly work of historical science, but the impulse for this operation was something else: a romance. Victor Hugo's *Notre Dame de Paris*, which he began writing in 1829, was set in 1482, and its hero had lived in the cathedral since he had been found on its steps as a baby. For Quasimodo, Notre Dame was the whole world, and he scarcely ever left it:

> The only espaliers he could conceive were the stained glass windows, which were always in flower, the only shade that of the stone foliage blossoming in clumps, laden with birds, on the Saxon capitals, the only mountains the colossal towers of the church, the only ocean the Paris that surged at their feet.

And, indeed, he resembled Notre Dame of Victor Hugo's day, for he 'looked like a giant, broken and badly reassembled'. The heroine of the novel was a dancing gypsy girl named Esmeralda; and she too resembled Notre Dame – or at least Notre Dame as Hugo imagined she had been in 1482, for she had a strange and exotic beauty that captivated all who saw her. But the real heroine of the story was Notre Dame de Paris herself, and Hugo knew how his novel would end: in the wreckage of the hopes of hunchback, gypsy girl, and cathedral.

Esmeralda was led astray by specious reasoning, and was violated by the unscrupulous men who had professed to adore her. Having been ruined, tried, and condemned to death as a whore, a witch, and a murderess, she stood in a loose white shift before the cathedral, awaiting her last shriving. Then, suddenly, without warning, Quasimodo swung down on a rope and swept her off her feet into the air. Up she flew, up past the portals, and the Gallery of the Kings, and the great western rose, up to the perches of the gargoyles, in whose hideous company Quasimodo was at home. Here Esmeralda found sanctuary, and Quasimodo took care of her.

But there would be no happy ending. The Parisian mob, convinced that

Quasimodo had kidnapped their beautiful gypsy girl, decided to rescue her from his clutches. They threw themselves upon the west front of Notre Dame; but the cathedral resisted their efforts, standing firm, like the gates of a great city closed against its besiegers. Indeed, Notre Dame did more than resist: she responded. Her gargoyles spewed forth a hellish bile of molten lead, and flames licked the sky between the two towers. The very stones of the cathedral joined in the defence, as slates and lintels began to rain down upon the besiegers. The mob was driven back.

But one young man made it up to the Gallery of the Kings. He laughed, flushed with success; but almost before he knew it, one of the stone kings rushed at him, grabbed him by his feet, swung him over the edge of the balcony and dashed his brains out on the wall below. Quasimodo appeared on the gallery, the limp body of his victim in his hand; for it had not been Our Lady of Paris who had defended herself, but her tutelary spirit, the hunchback. He turned away from the terrified crowd and ran back inside. He hurried through corridors, up turnpikes, along ledges, until he came to Esmeralda's sanctuary – only to find that his own gypsy lady of Paris was gone.

Soldiers dispersed the mob, and order was restored. The next morning, the bourgeoisie of Paris opened the doors and shutters of their houses. In the square in front of the cathedral,

> some goodwives, milk-jugs in hand, were pointing in astonishment to the strange devastation in the main portal of Notre Dame and to the two rivulets of congealed lead between the cracks in the sandstone. This was all that remained of the night's disturbance. The pyre lit by Quasimodo between the towers had died out.

Looking out from the gallery of the chimerae at the top of Notre Dame, Quasimodo surveyed the city and the sky before him. He 'raised his eye to the gypsy, whose body he could see in the distance, hanging from the gibbet, and shuddering beneath its white robe in the final throes of death ... and he said, with a sob that caused his chest to heave: "Oh, all that I have loved!"'

Hugo had composed an elegy for a Notre Dame that had long passed away; but his fictional cathedral was also a marvellous modern invention. The novel was finished in January 1831, and it was on the bookstands by March. It was a huge success, and thousands of people not only read the tragedy of the Ladies of Paris but went to visit the place where it had all happened. They could not help but construct in their minds what Hugo had described in words, ignoring the interventions of later ages and imagining splendours that had been destroyed. In 1837, the Duchesse d'Orléans told the author: 'I have visited *your* Notre Dame.'

Hugo had transformed the building into *Notre Dame de Paris*, and it was not long before his reading public demanded that the stones of the building be made to correspond to the words of the book. In 1845, Viollet-le-Duc and Jean-Baptiste Lassus began that very task.

* * *

There was much to do, for the Notre Dame de Paris of Hugo's novel was hidden under several centuries of what the writer called 'the blindness of time and the stupidity of man'. There is a spectacular canvas painted by Jacques-Louis David in 1804 that provides a record of what the church had looked like before Viollet-le-Duc began his work. In this picture, the medieval carvings and traceries that would become the imagined haunt of Quasimodo and Esmeralda are invisible under a layer of baroque marble, green and red and white, and the apse resembles nothing so much as a gilded salon at Versailles or a scene at the opera.

In the centre of David's painting, a diminutive man is gesturing before a golden throne. Napoleon Bonaparte, in deliberate imitation of Charlemagne, holds a laurel wreath aloft in his right arm; he is about to lower it onto the head of his wife, Josephine, to crown her as empress. The Pope himself is visible at the high altar, and the aisles of the church are filled with the great and the good of France.

David's painting suppressed their expressions of horror and fascination at Napoleon's shameless appropriation of the scenery and props of the *Ancién Regime*. It is said that one of them, a former general of the French Revolution, was heard to mutter: 'What a shame that the 300,000 Frenchmen who died to overthrow one throne are unable to enjoy the superb fruit of their sacrifice!' It is not recorded what happened to him after the ceremonies.

Ten years later, Louis XVIII – a real king – walked down the nave of Notre Dame, to give thanks for his own coronation and the restoration of the monarchy after a quarter-century of failed republic and ersatz empire. The cathedral was by then as exhausted and tawdry as a painted theatre set after the lights have come up and the show is over. In 1829, history almost repeated itself in miniature: Louis XVIII was deposed in 'three glorious days' of revolution, and for a moment it looked as if the republic might be restored. It was not. The king was replaced by his cousin Louis Philippe, of the house of Orléans.

That summer, the young Victor Hugo, alarmed by the apparent fragility of the restored monarchy, decided that if history would not take care of the preservation of Notre Dame de Paris then his fiction would. He locked himself into his apartment and started to write.

* * *

Hugo's fantasy of hunchbacks and gypsy girls was an exercise in romantic fiction. But, as his contemporary readers would have known all too well, it was closely based on history – and recent history at that.

On 23 October 1793, at the height of the revolution, the Commune of Paris sent the people to Notre Dame. The Archbishop of Paris appeared before them and rent his vestments and declared that there should be no religion but Liberty; and then, like the fools in Victor Hugo's novel, the mob climbed up to the gallery on the west front and cast down the twenty-eight statues of kings that stood there. The smashed monarchs, decapitated and mutilated, were thrown into the Seine, or planted in the paving of the Rue de Santé to be used as bollards.

The cathedral was already a wreck. Two years before, in February of 1790, the high altar of Notre Dame had been replaced with one dedicated to the Fatherland. The people assembled before it to take their oath to the Nation, and even Louis XVI, that Most Christian King, was forced to attend. In November of the same year, the clergy of the cathedral were handed an expulsion order. Soon after they had departed, the agents of the people came to Notre Dame and confiscated all the paraphernalia of Christian superstition. They tore down images of Christ and the Virgin, and the saints and the aristocrats and princes of the church who had worshipped them; and they sent these images off to the Museum of Antiquities they had created in an old monastery, for that was where they believed such nonsense belonged. The agents of the people ripped out candlesticks and thurifers and reliquaries and lamps, and took them down to the National Treasury, where the gold and the silver and the brass were melted down for the benefit of the republic. A year later the spire that crowned the crossing of the building was also taken down, and the lead melted for shot. But it wasn't until 10 November 1793 that the complete conversion of Notre Dame was finally achieved.

A diva of the Comédie Française crouched behind a pasteboard set, awaiting her entrance. It was dark and hot, the Phrygian cap on her head pinched her pretty curls, and her Grecian gown kept slipping down her shoulders; but Mlle Maillard was used to such privations. Anyway, it was all in the name of the revolution. Emerging on cue, Mlle Maillard found herself at the door of a hastily contrived belvedere inscribed with the words 'À la Philosophie', flanked by plaster busts of Rousseau and Voltaire. This temple stood atop a rocky mountain; and Mlle Maillard picked her way over to a throne, and took up the shield and spear of Athene. There she sat, still as a statue, while the chorus girls of the Comédie and the representatives of the people made offerings to her, crying her name: 'Reason! Reason!' The November sunshine that poured through the clerestories washed the goddess and her pale temple in a dispassionate, rational light.

After they had finished adoring her, the representatives of the people picked up the goddess of Reason and bore her westwards away from her altar, down the nave of her temple. Mlle Maillard bobbed from shoulder to shoulder, the light catching, from time to time, her pale Grecian robes. Then a pair of timber portals swung open and the goddess of Reason found herself in the chilly autumn air, borne high above the stinking mud of the street outside and the malodorous mob who were still chanting her name.

Behind the goddess rose the façade of her temple, like a great city of building piled upon ruined building, to which clung the mutilated remains of the vanquished foes of Reason. The gates were flanked by sculpted figures whose wings had been removed, whose heads had been chopped off, whose anachronistic sceptres had been ripped from their hands. Above the central portal, a relief of Christ dispensing the arbitrary religious justice of the Last Judgement had been defaced. The gallery above was bare of all figures, and the pedestal at the heart of the rose window was empty. The towers were freckled with stumps of stone: here and there, a claw or a bat's wing protruded from the buttresses, reminders to the people gathered below that the sleep of Reason engenders monsters.

A year later, Jacques-Louis David, the arbiter of taste for the revolution – who would go on to become the arbiter of taste for Napoleon's empire – proposed a monument to the conversion of the cathedral into a republican temple. Hercules, the symbol of revolutionary might, would stand at the prow of the Île de la Cité, perched on top of a mountain; and that mountain would be made of all the smashed angels and saints that had been thrown down from Notre Dame. The victory of reason over the reactionary forces of religion would be complete.

* * *

It was a victory that had been nearly a hundred years in coming. The Cardinal de Noailles, archbishop of Paris at the beginning of the eighteenth century, had charm, an easy wit, and vast amounts of money. He was an adherent of the Jansenist doctrine, which decried the theatrics of traditional religion and argued for a Christianity that would enlighten its adherents with reason rather than stupefy them with mystery and ritual. By the time that Noailles took the episcopal throne, Notre Dame was filled with the instruments of mystery and ritual. Successive kings, aristocrats, clergymen, and guilds had filled the nave with votive gifts: paintings, statues, tombstones, and metalwork. Louis XIV had even encased the entire sanctuary of the cathedral in the baroque marble arcades that would later provide the backdrop to the operatic moments of glory of Napoleon and Mlle Maillard. The cathedral was dark and cluttered, and, in the opinion of Noailles, in severe need of enlightenment.

In the 1720s, Noailles ordered the floor of Notre Dame, uneven with countless burials and worn with centuries of shuffling feet, to be repaved in marble, smooth and white, so that the light which fell into the nave would be reflected from it. He had his men whitewash the walls of the cathedral, which had been blackened with centuries of candle wax, smoke, and incense, so that sunbeams might fall upon radiant surfaces and illuminate the congregation in their devotions. The successors of Noailles followed his lead. In 1741 the cathedral authorities arranged to have the stained glass of the clerestory windows removed and replaced with clear glass. Most of the glass itself – which, after all, depicted childish stories for the illiterate – was taken away and smashed, and never seen again. They also removed the crumbling gargoyles that disfigured the exterior of the cathedral, for by the 1770s it was not unknown for some hideous beast to crash down on to the pavement, terrifying the ladies. Now, when the spring drizzle and the summer storms fell on Paris, the rainwater no longer spouted from the mouths of monsters, but was discreetly conducted away in lead downpipes of the most modern design.

By the time of the revolution of 1789, most of the barbaric features of the cathedral of Notre Dame had already been covered up and cleared away. All the revolutionaries had needed to do was to add the finishing touches to their temple of Reason.

✳ ✳ ✳

Viollet-le-Duc's task was to restore Notre Dame to the state that had existed before time and man had wrought their destruction upon it. Once upon a time, he supposed, Notre Dame had been the building her original makers had desired her to be; that was the state to which Viollet-le-Duc and Lassus now hoped to restore her. The problem lay in ascertaining who those original makers had been, and what they had desired. For this temple of the Holy Virgin, quite unlike the one on the Acropolis, had never been built to a single design.

Notre Dame had been started in 1163, when Maurice de Sully, the bishop of Paris, traced his crozier in the ground of the Île de la Cité. Sully's cathedral, however, differed in important respects from the Notre Dame that Hugo and Viollet knew and loved. Where they looked up and saw tall clerestories, and imagined them sparkling with coloured glass, Sully had placed an expanse of solid wall pierced with much smaller windows. Where Hugo and Viollet marvelled at the cathedral's complex external armature of flying buttresses, Sully's workmen had made a simple pile of heavy masonry to stabilize the thrust of the vaults within. The original Notre Dame had not been the vessel of light, the skeleton of thin stone ribs and glittering glass, that the nineteenth century admired; nor had its originator, Maurice de Sully, ever imagined it so.

Sully died in 1196, thirty-three years after he had traced his crozier in the ground, and work stopped briefly, with only the sanctuary and three bays of the nave of Notre Dame having been finished. Construction began again in 1200, and a new generation of masons set themselves to the completion of the nave. As the great hole in the west end of the cathedral was closed, the interior became darker and darker. Soon it became apparent that the clerestory windows in the side walls were too small to admit enough light into the nave; and so the masons decided to enlarge them.

This change in the design of the building raised its own problems. When the high windows of the nave had been small, the structure of the cathedral had been strong, since there was a large expanse of wall under the high vaults. As the masons set about enlarging the clerestory windows, they soon realized that they were turning this expanse of wall into an expanse of glass, ill suited to holding up great loads. Unless the masons desired the vaults to fall, they would have to invent another way of supporting them.

They devised half bridges – *arcs boutants*, they called them – that carried the weight of the vaults away from the walls and out to external buttresses. These buttresses, towers of solid masonry, then transferred the load vertically down to the ground. In combination, the buttresses, the *arc boutants*, and the ribs of the vaults formed a stone cage so strong that it required no walls to stabilize it. Now the masons were able to turn what had once been heavy heaps of stone into luminous banners of glass that glowed high above the nave.

And so the design of Notre Dame de Paris departed from the intentions of Maurice de Sully: by the application of reason and experience the masons had been able to improve on the original. The final bays of the nave of the cathedral were filled with light on the inside, while on the outside they formed a fantastical skeleton of stone arches and buttresses pointing upwards to the sky. And the masons of Notre Dame were so impressed at what they had done that even before they had finished the building they started to rebuild it – or, at least, to alter what they had already built to match their new design. They worked their way back up the nave to the original altar of Maurice de Sully, and they enlarged all the high clerestory windows so that light began to pour into what had previously been dark. They worked their way down the side walls of the cathedral, adding their *arcs boutants* and their buttresses, and where previously there had been only heavy masonry the very building itself gradually seemed to dissolve into the lightness of air.

Decade after decade passed, and still the masons kept on with their labor of altering the unfinished cathedral. As Victor Hugo wrote of their work:

> Great buildings, like great mountains, are the work of centuries. Often architecture is transformed while they are still under construction: *pendent opera interrupta*, they proceed quickly in keeping with the transformation. The new architecture takes the monument as it finds it, is incrusted on it, assimilates it to itself, develops it as it wants ... The man, the individual and the artist are erased from these great piles, which bear no author's name; they are the summary and summation of human intelligence. Time is the architect, the nation the builder.

Time never stopped being the architect of Notre Dame: through the hundreds of years since Maurice de Sully's death, the cathedral was reimagined and remade over and over again. If Viollet-le-Duc wanted to find an original state to which the cathedral could be restored, he was going to have to invent it.

✷ ✷ ✷

Viollet prepared a drawing of the sanctuary of the cathedral as he imagined it had been when Quasimodo and Esmeralda had haunted it. Napoleon's throne was cast out, and the temple to Philosophy vanished. The yellowed distemper with which the Cardinal de Noailles had covered the stone was stripped away. At the heart of the sanctuary he sketched a Gothic altar, covered in beaten copper and studded with gems. It was as if four centuries had never happened.

And then the drawing was set into practice. The scenery of Louis XIV's baroque sanctuary was prised away, and behind it was revealed a ring of pointed gothic arches that matched those of the nave. Viollet ordered his workmen to scrape away all the eighteenth-century whitewash, and soon walls which had appeared to be made of nothing more substantial than painted pasteboard took on the weight and the integrity of stone.

Viollet prepared another drawing, presenting the west front of Notre Dame as he imagined it had been before the revolutionaries had destroyed its statuary. Then he set his masons to work to restore to their original habitations all the disappeared inhabitants of that great City of God, from the angels and the saints to the vilest of the gargoyles. The west front became once more an image of the medieval universe itself, 'that divine creation,' as Hugo wrote, 'whose twin characteristics of variety and eternity it seems to have purloined'.

Viollet's most difficult problem, however, was what to do with the flying buttresses and the tall clerestory windows of the nave. These had not been part of the original conception of Bishop de Sully, so they presented Viollet with a choice. He could remove all traces of any later, lighter design, restoring the cathedral to the state intended by Sully. Alternatively, he could leave the buttresses intact, and repair the building in its altered form.

Viollet chose neither option. Instead, he adopted an ingenious strategy: he invented a design that combined, for practical and archaeological advantages, the various different states of the cathedral from its long course of construction. He retained the thirteenth-century improvements – the *arcs boutants* and tall clerestories – around the entire nave and apse except for the areas around the crossing. In the bays that adjoined the crossing he reinstated Sully's original scheme, with large expanses of solid wall pierced by small windows. The bays rebuilt according to Sully's design were symmetrically disposed around the centre of the cathedral, lending it both literal and visual strength, drawing the building together towards its heart. Above the crossing, Viollet replaced the spire that had been torn down in the Revolution, further reinforcing the symmetry of the composition and further suggesting that the building was complete and whole, a virgin.

* * *

Notre Dame had never been whole before. There never had been an original, completed state to which it could be restored. The Notre Dame which Viollet-le-Duc finished in 1864 was an attempt to fix a moving target in time, and archaeologists and historians still lament the restoration as they attempt to untangle the story of the cathedral. Despite his best efforts, Viollet's work was less an operation of historical science than a romantic fiction, an allegory, a manifesto that destroyed as much as it preserved.

Of this, Viollet himself was quite aware. 'The term *restoration* and the thing itself are both modern,' he wrote. 'To restore a building is not to preserve it, to repair, or rebuild it; it is to reinstate in a condition of completeness that could never have existed at any given time.'

John Ruskin, the celebrated English art critic, was appalled, describing restoration as 'a destruction accompanied by the false description of the thing destroyed'. If Notre Dame was the work of centuries, then there was no particular scientific reason to strip away the contribution of the eighteenth century, say, than any other. Removing those layers that former ages had deemed necessary to add to a building was a violation of their trust in posterity. And restoring the things that had been taken away was also a crime, for it falsely pretended to resurrect the obsolete societies that had originally made them. As Ruskin's disciple William Morris commented, 'Surely it is a curious thing that we are ready to laugh at the idea of the possibility of the Greek workman turning out a Gothic building, or a Gothic workman turning out a Greek one, but we see nothing preposterous in the Victorian workman producing a Gothic one.'

Ruskin proposed a much more radical strategy. Do nothing, he said, or rather do as little as possible. 'Watch an old building with an anxious care; guard it as best you may, and at any cost, from every influence of dilapidation ... bind it together with iron where it loosens; stay it with timber where it declines; do not care about the unsightliness of the aid.' Morris was even more radical: 'If it has become inconvenient for its present use ... raise another building rather than alter or enlarge the old one.'

'We understand the rigour of these principles,' Viollet retorted, 'and we accept them completely: but only when we are dealing with a curious ruin, without a future or an actual use.' Notre Dame de Paris was no curious ruin, but the chief temple of the most advanced nation on earth. She had been desecrated amid the disasters of the revolution, those years of tumult that divided the ancient from the modern regime; and just as it had proved necessary to restore the monarchy, so was it necessary to restore the seat of its religious authority.

But just as the restored monarchy (and then the Second Empire) was nothing like the *Ancien Régime*, so the restored Notre Dame was no copy of the original. It was a very nineteenth-century romance, a manifesto of the modern rather than the medieval era. 'Gothic construction ... is supple, free, and as enquiring as the modern spirit,' Viollet had written, and he pressed the architects of his own day to be as inventive as the masons of Notre Dame.

To Viollet, Gothic architecture *was* modern architecture: he prophesied buildings whose luminosity and thinness would rival the stained-glass filigree of the clerestories of Notre Dame, whose rigorous structural logic would be inspired by the vaults and the flying buttresses of medieval masons. His Notre Dame de Paris was every bit as typical of the Paris of the nineteenth century as the Galeries Lafayette and the engineered glass roofs of the Gare d'Orsay.

It is ironic that some of the Communards chose to vent their fury on the cathedral in 1871. If they required a monument to reason and progress and all the rest of it, they only had to look around them at the vaults and buttresses of Notre Dame.

THE HULME CRESCENTS, MANCHESTER

In Which the Prophecies of the Future are Fulfilled

REMEMBER TOMORROW.
Faked cover of a 1971 issue of The Architects' Journal, *made*
for an exhibition about the Hulme Crescents in 2004.

Prophecy

Lord Byron *wished that the dilettanti and the scholars of his time would leave the Parthenon to die alone. Now his wish is coming true. The building is melting into air, and all the restoration and conservation in the world can only postpone its disappearance.*

Restoration was, as Viollet-le-Duc pointed out, an entirely modern approach to old buildings. It was founded in a consciousness that the past, having been detached from the present by historic upheaval, was the legitimate object of disinterested study. The group of architects who succeeded Viollet (and saw him as a prophet of modernity) turned his methods back to front: they wrote histories of what was still to come, documenting the future with the same rigour that their nineteenth-century forebears had devoted to the investigations of bygone days. It was as if Thomas Cole's architect, reclining on his column, had turned away from the monuments of Egypt, Greece, and Rome to dream instead about splendours yet to be built.

In the timeless dream of the architect, all ages appear simultaneous before him. But in the waking world, each generation supplants the ones before it, only to be supplanted by others in turn. The realization of the avant-garde utopias of Modernism involved the destruction of everything that had preceded them; yet soon these new worlds became old themselves, ready to be devoured by other visions.

The Hulme Crescents in Manchester were just such a utopia once, the fulfilment of Modernist prophecy; and alone among all the buildings in this book, they have now passed away. Today they are just memories, preserved behind screens of liquid crystal. Logging on to scattered websites, the Crescents' former residents swap stories about what the future was like, once upon a time.

'HELLO, GOOD EVENING, AND WELCOME TO HULME, MANCHESTER, Great Britain! It is my immense honour to say to all you slum dwellers: your prayers have been answered. Welcome to Paradiiiiise!'

It's March 1993, and it certainly doesn't look like paradise. Peering into darkness, the video camera finds no purchase in the light that flickers over burning grass. A hooded procession emerges from the flames and the lens zooms in on a vacant face crudely daubed in black and white, animated, if by anything at all, only by a mixture of pity and contempt. A strangled cry pierces the night as a solitary muffled drum beats out a doleful march.

Then the solemn scene explodes into flashing strobes and thrashing music, and the slum dwellers of the Hulme Crescents burst into dance. Searchlights bring a vast building into focus: sliding flashes of stained concrete, glittering shards of glass, and dully gleaming security fences. A white sheet has been hung across the front of this building, stretching from the roof to the ground, and at the top of this shroud a small group of people is struggling with some unwieldy object.

One by one the searchlights move into position; the beat intensifies, and so does the roar of the crowd. The spectral figures gather at the parapet and briefly hold still. Then they all move in concert, pushing their burden – a small white car – to the edge of the roof. It teeters there for a moment, and then the concrete parapet shatters. The car falls past the screen, so slowly that it might be sinking in water. The crowd roars and rushes forward, the mob submerging the wreck under their bodies. They scarcely notice the explosions in the air above them.

✳ ✳ ✳

It wasn't meant to happen that way. No one could have predicted it back in 1971, when the Crescents were first opened and everybody gathered at the Zion Centre for tea. Then it was as though some wonderful revelation had been delivered, on time, on budget, and looking fantastic. The *Manchester Evening News* ran an article entitled A MINI TOWN WITH ALL MOD CONS. It hailed the 'complex of overways, underways, and linkways … houses with central heating and double glazed windows' as a self-contained 'quiet refuge', complete with their own 'walks, shops and a library'.

There were four crescents, each half a mile long, set amid a vast open park. Each crescent was seven stories tall, with hundreds of flats, all of them designed to the latest ergonomic space standards and all of them accessed by open decks that overlooked acres of grass. The designers of the Crescents, Hugh Wilson and Lewis Womersley, had named each of the four buildings for a great British architect – William Kent, John Wood, John Nash, and Charles Barry – and Wilson and Womersley clearly hoped to join their august company. 'It is our endeavour at Hulme,' they announced, 'to achieve a solution to the problems of twentieth-century living which would be the equivalent in quality of that reached for the requirements of eighteenth-century living in Bloomsbury and Bath.' It was a bold claim: the smart Georgian terraces of

Bloomsbury and Bath were a long way from Hulme. But in 1971 anything seemed possible.

* * *

The Crescents had been a long time in coming; but the future always is, isn't it? It had been more than a hundred years since a young German businessman named Friedrich Engels first arrived in Manchester. His father had sent him to that white-hot crucible of the Industrial Revolution hoping that a good dose of work at the family mill would make the young man abandon his naive idealism; but Engels junior loathed his new job, and it did nothing to moderate his radical views. He took up with a certain Mary Burns, who brought him to all the parts of Manchester that weren't on his father's itinerary. Engels was so horrified that he published a book describing what he saw. *The Condition of the Working Class in England in 1844* painted a vivid picture:

> In a rather deep hole, in a curve of the Medlock and surrounded on all sides by tall factories and high embankments covered with buildings, stand two groups of about two hundred cottages, built chiefly back to back, in which live about four thousand human beings ... Masses of refuse, offal and sickening filth lie among standing pools in all directions; the atmosphere is poisoned by the effluvia from these, and laden and darkened by the smoke of a dozen factory chimneys ... In this atmosphere, penned in as if with a purpose, this race must really have reached the lowest stage of humanity.

Engels left the city and his father's job soon afterwards and ran away with Mary Burns to Paris, where he met Karl Marx. In 1848, as revolutions swept across Europe, they published *The Communist Manifesto*, in which they demanded, among other things:

- Abolition of property in land and application of all rents of land to public purposes.
- A heavy progressive or graduated income tax.
- Abolition of all rights of inheritance.
- Centralization of the means of communication and transport in the hands of the State.
- Extension of factories and instruments of production owned by the State; the bringing into cultivation of waste-lands, and the improvement of the soil generally in accordance with a common plan.
- Equal liability of all to work. Establishment of industrial armies, especially for agriculture.
- Combination of agriculture with manufacturing industries; gradual abolition of all the distinction between town and country by a more equable distribution of the populace over the country.
- Free education for all children in public schools. Abolition of children's factory labour in its present form. Combination of education with industrial production, &c, &c.

By 1971, many of these demands had been met. If you required a monument to Marx and Engels, all you had to do was go to Hulme. All property belonged to the City Corporation of Manchester, and everyone drew their state benefits from the state-owned post office. No-one inherited anything: they had nothing to pass on, and if they had it would have gone to taxes. People travelled into town on the state-run public transport system, the unions and corporations formed industrial armies, and comprehensive education was available to all children. The Hulme Crescents, gigantic concrete buildings in a sea of greenery, even completed the 'gradual abolition of all the distinction between town and country'.

* * *

The new order that Marx and Engels predicted was a utopia of sorts, but they didn't expect that the fulfilment of their vision would come about peacefully. 'Communists know only too well,' they wrote, 'that the development of the proletariat in nearly all civilized countries has been violently suppressed … If the oppressed proletariat is finally driven to revolution, then we communists will defend the interests of the proletarians with deeds as we now defend them with words.'

And the communists weren't the only ones who believed that the world needed a strong push in the right direction. Indeed, calls for a violent upheaval became the standard *Leitmotif* of modernist manifestos all across Europe – and not just in the field of politics. One crazy night in 1909, a group of young men who called themselves the Futurists sat up in their flat, writing down anything that came into their heads. They were in backward Italy, and they were bored. What had horrified Engels at first hand intoxicated them at a distance. They might as well have been dreaming of Manchester:

We will sing of great crowds excited by work, by pleasure, and by riot; we will sing of the multicolored, polyphonic tides of revolution in the modern capitals; we will sing of the vibrant nightly fervor of arsenals and shipyards blazing with violent electric moons; greedy railway stations that devour smoke-plumed serpents; factories hung on clouds by the crooked lines of their smoke; bridges that stride the rivers like giant gymnasts, flashing in the sun with a glitter of knives; adventurous steamers that sniff the horizon; deep-chested locomotives whose wheels paw the tracks like the hooves of enormous steel horses bridled by tubing; and the sleek flight of planes whose propellers chatter in the wind like banners and seem to cheer like an enthusiastic crowd.

And after they'd had enough of whatever they were having, they went out and totalled a sports car in a ditch. Standing amid the wreckage, covered in oil, they issued their manifesto. It involved the total vandalism and destruction of the past:

> We stand on the last promontory of the centuries! ... Why should we look back, when what we want is to break down the mysterious doors of the Impossible? ... Come on! Set fire to the library shelves! Turn aside the canals to flood the museums! ... Oh, the joy of seeing the glorious old canvases bobbing adrift on those waters, discolored and shredded! ... Take up your pickaxes, your axes and hammers and wreck, wreck the venerable cities, pitilessly!

A quarter of a century later, pickaxes and hammers were exactly what the city fathers of Manchester decided would be best for Hulme. They weren't motivated by their love of 'the polyphonic tides of revolution'; in fact, the city fathers decided to obliterate Hulme precisely because they were afraid of an uprising. 'In spite of disease and death and tottering houses,' the *Manchester Guardian* had reported, 'the population has been compelled since the [1918] armistice to huddle into the area in even greater numbers than ever.' Such a huddled mass of humanity was all too liable to turn into one of the great crowds the Futurists had described, excited, if not by work or pleasure, then by riot.

So the city fathers bought the whole of Hulme, lock, stock, and barrel. They relocated all the slum dwellers out to brick cottages in the suburbs, softening the blow by calling the houses 'homes for heroes'. Then they flattened the entire district, leaving an empty wasteland behind. The old high street became nothing more than a dusty path through the yellowed summer grass. No-one had any idea what to do with it.

* * *

The answer was already on its way. In 1933, the year before Manchester's city council began to clear away the slums of Hulme, a group of young architects, fired with the passion that only youth can provide, had hired a steamer and set sail from Marseilles into the future. By the time the boat docked in Athens, the Congrès Internationale d'Architecture Moderne had worked out what that future was going to be. Standing in the shadow of the Acropolis before fifteen hundred representatives of the government of Greece, the CIAM announced 'a reply to the present chaos of the cities', a proposal that 'unlocks all the doors to the urbanism of modern times ... In the hands of the authorities, itemized, annotated, clarified with an adequate explanation, the Athens Charter is the implement by which the destiny of cities will be set right.'

The charter began with a warning and a vision, framed in portentous fragments: 'An immense, total mutation takes hold of the world: the machinist civilization is moving in amid disorder, improvisation, ruins ... It has been going on for a century! ... But a century also in which a new sap is rising ... A century in which visionaries have brought forth ideas, thoughts, and made proposals ... A day will come, perhaps ....' It continued with a doctrine of twenty-five points, which set out with scientific precision what the city of the future would and should be. And the city of the future wasn't going to be theoretical. The Congress added a political injunction to their scientific analysis: 'the Charter must be placed on the table of authority, in both the municipalities and the councils of state'.

Scientific as it sounded, the charter had been inspired by a spate of prophecies every bit as crazed as the ravings of the Futurists. In the heady first days of the Russian revolution, Soviet architects had sketched out gigantic collective dwellings that would literally float above the steppe, suspended by the awesome power of nuclear fusion. In Germany, the poet Paul Scheerbart foresaw cities made of transparent glass, and the architect Bruno Taut imagined a crystal citadel sparkling in the clear alpine air. No wonder the architects of CIAM set sail to Athens in confident expectation that the destiny of cities was within their grasp.

The principles of the Athens Charter were given definitive form in a book published soon after the CIAM gathering by its leading light. Le Corbusier's *The Radiant City* was the blueprint for a New Jerusalem, adorned as a bride for her husband. At her feet lay her smoky factories, connected to the rest of the world by an elaborate system of railway sidings. Her head was crowned with crystal towers, from which the intellectual elite of the city would govern like the philosopher-kings of Plato's *Republic*. Her body was made of the dwellings of the people, and her lungs were great green parks.

This Radiant City was the purest demonstration of the charter's description of urbanism as 'a three-dimensional, not a two-dimensional, science'. Elevated roads were suspended above the liberated verdure, feeding their traffic into great apartment buildings that sailed above the treetops. On the roofs and balconies of these towers, their inhabitants disported themselves in the sun like first-class passengers on great white ocean liners. They looked out over a seemingly empty greensward, an immaculate forest without a trace of human history. The palaces and temples of former times had been swept away, and the streets and squares of Le Corbusier's own day had likewise disappeared, leaving only the future: an expanse, as Le Corbusier put it, of 'sunlight, space, and greenery'. It was a paradise that could not appear until the End of Days.

But the architects of the Congrès Internationale d'Architecture Moderne weren't going to have to wait for the end of days for their paradise to appear. Their utopia was not consigned to an inaccessible island – the 'no place' of Thomas More. It was just round the corner. Within a decade, the Second World War had swept the old cities away, more completely, perhaps, than the communists and the Futurists could ever have imagined; and the world was ready to be made anew.

* * *

And made anew it was – or most of it, at least. In the years following the war the devastated cities of Europe rebuilt themselves with remarkable speed in the image of the Radiant City, but for three decades nothing happened in the empty space that had once been Hulme. In 1964, Robert Mellish, who had been appointed by the Housing Minister as 'progress chaser', visited the inner-city wasteland and cried out, 'Why are you showing me this desolation? Why don't you put some houses on it?'

The city councillors of Manchester, stung by the progress chaser's outburst, went over the Pennines to see what had been going on in nearby Sheffield. They were awestruck and envious: on top of a hill in the city centre, their rivals had built the prophesied city of the Modernists. Great stretches of apartments afforded sunlight, space, greenery, and indoor toilet facilities to a proletariat that until lately had barely had access to running water. What's more, Sheffield had built a very British version of the Radiant City. British architects of the postwar period were certainly enamoured of dazzling liners sailing through oceans of greenery, but they were also concerned to pre-serve something of the sociability of the old slums that they were so busy replacing. They were, despite themselves, nostalgic for the cobbled lanes and back-to-back cottages that had once been Engels's nightmare, for they were learning that Modernist architecture could engender the most modern of afflictions: loneliness and alienation.

The Park Hill estate in Sheffield provided the definitive solution. Huge concrete buildings bestrode the ruins of what had once been dense inner city, leaving vast areas of open green space between them. But these buildings were linked by broad concrete decks that formed a network of 'streets in the sky', with the flats opening onto them as cottages had opened onto the lanes of old. Soon, the architects confidently predicted, the decks would be filled with playing children, their mothers gossiping around the rubbish chute as if it were the village well.

The city fathers of Manchester saw what they had to do. They poached J.S. Millar, who had been instrumental in the implementation of Park Hill, to take charge of their planning department; and Millar approached Lewis Womersley, who had also worked on the Sheffield project, to transform the wastelands of Hulme. Womersley and his partner Hugh Wilson were efficient operators. They had already provided, or were in the process of providing, plans for the Modernist expansion and transformation of Skelmersdale, Redditch, Northampton, and Nottingham. In 1966, the pair presented their designs for Hulme to Manchester city council. The bald minutes of the meeting convey little of the excitement that the design aroused in the panjandrums of the committee:

> The planning brief for Hulme stage 5 asked that densities should increase near to the neighbourhood centre and stated that the aim should be to create an urban environment on a city scale. The solution to this problem proposed by the consultants to achieve larger scale and high density is to build continuous blocks of maisonettes at six stories high in a few bold and simple forms so as to develop large open spaces.

These continuous blocks were laid out in the form of four crescents – reminiscent, the architects claimed, of the Royal Crescent in Bath and the Nash terraces around Regent's Park in London. The councillors, who had been to neither, were suitably impressed.

It wasn't all about nostalgia for Georgian elegance, though. Hulme was going to be a modern sort of place built in a modern sort of way, using the latest industrial processes. The architects' report explained how 'a high quality of finish, both internally and externally, can be obtained because structural components, fittings and services will be manufactured and supervised under factory conditions and not subjected to climatic and other hazards of an open site'. In plain terms, this meant that the entire building complex was constructed out of precast concrete. Five years after Wilson and Womersley's presentation, the Hulme Crescents – prophesied, in their various ways, by everyone from Engels to Le Corbusier – were ready for their first inhabitants.

* * *

Some people can still remember what the Crescents were supposed to have been like. A visitor to a website funereally named 'exHulme' posts a message signed 'Caroline'. She writes:

> I was four when we moved there. My family moved to Hulme because Broughton in Salford was being cleared. We were promised from what I have been told by my mam 'a bright new future in the new deck access flats'. At first and I have to say for the first few years we lived there they were lovely flats to live in ... I remember watching what I thought was really posh the man over the way cleaning 'is Avenger, and thinking *cur that's posh*. He did that every Sunday. We made friends easy and it did seem like a real community ... we had shops, and a wash house. Cos in those days it was dead posh to have a washing machine. I watched the Crescents of Robert Adam and John Nash go up ... and like I say for the first few years things were lovely we had every facility we could ask for ... they were wonderful places. Full of really new ideas and loads of hope for the people living in them. People talked to each other. And I can remember laughter with a family that lived in them. They asked me and my grandad in for a cup of tea.

Showed us round the strange way the flats were designed. But the flat was so clean and nice and they were so proud of it.

But when people started to live in them, the Crescents started to lose a little of their shine. 'Caroline' continues:

> Then suddenly about 1972 I think it was things started to go wrong. And like I say people started to move out. I remember walking over to the shops with my mam, and running across the green in front of the crescent cos there were strange people hanging about in the stairwells of the crescent. But it was all there, parks in front of the flats shops and the lot. But it all went so wrong, don't know how but it did. As the crescents started to get bad, the badness started to come.

The badness: it began with damp patches on the wall. In the winter of 1971, some tenants had started complaining about condensation in their flats, dark blotches disfiguring their bright modern wallpapers. The architects and the housing officers came to see the damage, and roundly berated the tenants for not opening their windows while they cooked or dried their clothes. The tenants opened the windows, and put up with the icy draughts; but the dampness didn't go away.

In 1973, the oil crisis precipitated a massive rise in the costs of power. The Crescents were heated by electricity, so the people who lived in them were particularly badly affected: in some cases heating bills rocketed to £500 a quarter. Many tenants simply disconnected themselves from the electrical supply. They saw out the dark winter in their modern flats by old-fashioned candlelight, warming themselves around paraffin heaters. At least the gloom concealed the stains.

But these were just technical difficulties. There were management problems as well. The Crescents had been designed to rehouse a particularly deprived portion of the citizens of Manchester: 70% of the residents had come there as a result of slum clearance elsewhere, and 30% of them were on welfare benefits provided by the city council. The rent they owed was thus paid to the city by the city itself, and as their proportion increased – within two years, 44% of the residents of the Crescents were on benefits – the city's income diminished accordingly. And on this ever-shrinking budget, the city fathers had somehow to manage the maintenance of two miles of building: replacing the lights, cleaning the walkways, clearing away the rubbish that fluttered along the concrete decks and littered the greenery. They were unprepared to handle even the basic upkeep, let alone the plagues of rats and cockroaches that seemed to spread along the Crescents like wildfire.

And these were just the management problems. There were serious design flaws to deal with, too. As in Sheffield's Park Hill, all the flats in the Crescents were accessed by great decks, which stretched, in total, for several miles; and these 'streets in the sky' proved to be just as sociable as the architects had hoped. Kids loved to run along their length, pushing on doorbells and running away when someone answered. They loved to climb up on the balustrades, peering over the edge to sniff the air that lay beyond. The way the balustrades were detailed just seemed to invite it, with plenty of footholds and big fat ledges to lean on. It was only a matter of time before someone fell off them. He was a little boy of four: one year older than the Crescents themselves.

That was the last straw. In 1975 the families of the Hulme Crescents presented a petition to the Housing Committee of the city of Manchester. They were scared for their children, and their demands were clear:

- A list to be drawn up of all the families who want to be rehoused.
- These must be listed in order of priority.
- Dates must be given for rehousing.

- No new families to be put into any properties. Any flats left empty by tenants to be given to single tenants, couples without children, or students.

- All tenants should have the right to get on the transfer list regardless of rent arrears.

'Why should we have to pay to live here in these dangerous prisons?' the petition asked, and it proclaimed emphatically: 'Rehousing must start *now*.'

The Housing Committee agreed with them. The families moved out, and the Crescents were left empty, ready for single tenants, couples without children, and students to move in. One of these new inhabitants recalls: 'The day I moved in was 11th Dec. 1981, and there was deep snow everywhere – unusual for Manchester at any time. As we tiptoed around the crescents the vibe was awesome – monolithic magnificence – a complete void. I don't think even seeing the pyramids for the first time could compare.'

A complete void the Crescents had indeed become. So few people actually wanted to live in Hulme that the city started giving the flats away. Well, not exactly giving, as 'Karen' recalls on the exHulme site:

Moved to Hulme in 1982 and lived on each of the crescents ... moving regularly with *the* shopping trolley that everyone used, a mains fuse and a wire to get round the meter and my Yale lock. Seemed very normal back then – choose a flat and move. It went wrong one time though when it seemed I had picked the same flat as two guys who proceeded to try and kill me with a hammer.

All you had to do was break into an empty apartment and lock yourself in for a while. You wouldn't need to bother with rent or landlords: by the time the authorities found out about you, you would have moved on. That was the difference between the new tenants and the families that had moved out, you see: there was nothing to tie them down.

After the first inhabitants of the Crescents had left, the Manchester city council had installed steel gates at regular intervals along the access decks to the flats. These gates could only be opened by security codes – codes that the tenants knew, the housing officers soon forgot, and the police never found out. The council being the council, it took them some time to realize they had locked themselves out. There was no way they could keep up with the new residents, who started, in the absence of any visible authority, to invent a society all of their own. They were young, shiftless, feckless, and free, they didn't have families and jobs and possessions. The laws of property were suspended in Hulme: nothing belonged to anybody, and everything belonged to everybody. Everything was stolen, scammed, joyridden, totalled, and given away. They told one another that it was exactly what Engels had prophesied.

The Hulmans of Hulme did whatever what they wanted. The accepted modes of behaviour didn't just break down in the Crescents: they were rejected wholesale, gobbed on, and told to fuck off. Karen recalls a *déjeuner sur l'herbe*:

Remember Queenie? We were sat on the grass outside the Zion one hot sunny day, about 15–20 of us all drinking and smoking when Queenie came along swearing and shouting and offering to sit on anyone's face! Poor Shaun (not with us now I'm afraid) was pinned to the grass whilst she did it … Yes, I remember Rizzla too at the precinct but also remember vividly the day he jumped off the top walkway between Robert Adam and William Kent opposite the Spinners. We all ran out of the pub expecting him to be splatted on the road when he suddenly got up, started swearing and went off to do it again! Crazy guy.

By the mid-eighties, the Hulmans were a scurvy bunch that is still recalled with wistful nostalgia. Someone has even set up a MySpace page for the Crescents, a mock personal profile in which the buildings describe whom they would 'like to meet':

Punks, goths, ratios, scum, dickheads, junkies, bums, bummers, animals, wasters, prats, knobheads, alkies, speedfreaks, perry boys, crusties, salts, pissheads, muggers, mugs, moonies, rastas, weirdos, wannabees, the grants, mohawks, psycho billies, spikey's mum, cock-roaches, methadone queuers, arsebandits, violent bastards, depressed hippies, pidgeons, barbed up scallies, wankers, acid heads, pigs, robbers, crusties, the psv, indie kids, e-heads, dopeheads, trustafar-ians, the scream team, stringies ...

That wasn't in the prophecies, was it?

✱ ✱ ✱

In 1976, a young music journalist called Tony Wilson attended a concert at the Free Trade Hall in the centre of Manchester. It was a thinly attended event, with just forty people in the audience. They had come to see an unknown new band called the Sex Pistols.

An hour or so later, Wilson left the hall burning with a messianic fervour for punk rock. He hadn't experienced anything so exciting since reading Engels and hearing about Tristan Tzara at the Cabaret Voltaire. He found an old working men's club on the edge of the Crescents and opened it as the Russell Club, a place for the new music that was beginning to pour out of the housing estates. It might not have looked like much, but Wilson's factory of art – made very much in the mould of Andy Warhol's cooperative, or the Bauhaus – proved to be a glasshouse that germinated a new avant-garde, self-consciously reminiscent of the great age of Modernist prophecy. The Fall, Joy Division, and all the rest of them played in the club in their early days; and Wilson went on to found Factory Records, a record label that put Manchester on the international map. He employed the graphic designer Peter Saville to do the club posters and the album covers, and Saville did exactly what Laszlo Moholy Nagy and Marcel Duchamp and Georges Braque had done in the twenties: he ripped things off, collaged them together, and passed them on, a stream of achingly hip images of a shattered past and an incomplete future.

Time and time again, the residents of the Crescents remember the music. 'James' writes:

> My fondest memory might be the solitary one of placing the needle on *Power Corruption and Lies* for the first time after buying the album the day it came out. To me, barely in my 20s, that record summed up the existential dread of Hulme, along with the freedom and creative possibilities it incited in anyone who could cope with the quotidian smell of piss in the stairwells and lifts and the dog shit everywhere, like a magic carpet of despair.

'James' shared his flat with a drummer, and together they blacked out the front room and lined it with egg cartons to form a makeshift recording studio. They weren't the only ones: 'Lloyd' ran two pirate radio stations out of the third floor in the Charles Barry crescent, moving his gear to empty and inaccessible flats every time he got wind of a visit from the police. Joy Division came to pose for grainy, grey photographs on the concrete decks; bIG*FLAME, 'Britain's premier jazz fuck trio', were born in the Crescents in 1982. A Certain Ratio, A Guy Called Gerald, Finlaye Quaye, the Inspiral Carpets, and many other bands jammed in the Crescents, recording and performing in the makeshift studios and clubs that riddled the buildings with endless thrashing, thumping, pulsating noise.

Around the middle of the eighties, the music of Hulme started to change. The new bands weren't beautiful and their lyrics weren't deep. An album from the Happy Mondays was entitled *Pills 'n' Thrills and Bellyaches*, and that's more or less what it was about: it was a drugs thing. Punk rock had been a beer thing – at least you threw your pint across the room when you were listening (if that is the word) to it. Tony Wilson's brand of post-punk was a weed thing: you reverently placed the needle on the record and lay back on your bed, waiting for that sense of existential dread to surge through you. But the new rave music of the late eighties was all about the pills: speed, acid, and, above all, ecstasy – chemicals that kept you dancing and gurning all night, all the next day, and all the way through the night after that. It didn't matter how stupid the music was.

And that's when the Crescents started to eat themselves. It began at a party in 1989. It was just an after-party at first, a few folk getting together in a kitchen after the clubs had closed to dance off the last of their drugs; but before long things got out of hand. Everyone had brought their mates, and soon the kitchen was so crowded that no-one could breathe, let alone dance. 'Bruce' can just about remember what happened: 'I recall Jamie taking a jackhammer to the wall of his flat to start a club? ... but that resulted in him getting all his studio gear nicked?' They had knocked a hole through the wall to the flat next door, you see. And when more people showed up they did it again. And when still more people turned up they did it a third time. By the time Jamie put his jackhammer away, they had knocked through several walls and floors, so that the former kitchen was now an infernal cavern rammed with sweaty bodies and thumping bass:

There was a massive sound system in the front room – the downstairs kitchen had been turned into a bar selling Red Stripe, and the whole block seemed to ooze spliff. Not that it matters because every one is E'd up – gonzoid-eyed and scrunched-up faces leering into the dark haze. Careful as you wander around that staircase that sort of goes to the second floor.

Soon enough the parties started taking over the whole place, making it more or less uninhabitable for anyone who wasn't dancing. 'Gonnie' recalls

the memorable Hulme Demolition Sound System, not so much because of their music selection, but more because they set up in the little shopping precinct to play techno from Wednesday into Thursday morning, after the clubs had closed until the shops had opened, with just one police patrol car popping by to check the proceedings. Desert Storm Danny on the decks and his mate Joe running around to motivate people. While elderly people shuffled past to get their breakfast milk on a grey Thursday morning, there would still be a few people dancing on the precinct roofs and others sitting around on sofas and easy chairs that had been abandoned in flats ready for demo-lition.

The city fathers who had destroyed the slums of Hulme in 1934 in fear of crowds excited by pleasure and riot could not, in their worst nightmares, have imagined the brave new world that had taken their place.

* * *

As early as 1986 the Manchester city council had hosted a conference in which they tried to work out what to do with the Crescents. They clearly didn't hold out much hope for a happy ending: the meeting was entitled 'Deck Access Disaster'. They'd tried everything. They had established a Housing Action

Trust to deal with the renovation of the complex, but the residents ransacked the offices of the team that had been detailed to help them. They paid for a study to examine the social, economic, environmental, and housing situation of the area, but they soon gave up on the effort. Hulme didn't look like a problem that could be solved, they said.

It couldn't be solved by Manchester on its own, anyway, and eventually the city turned to the central government for help. In 1991, Manchester was given a grant to address its biggest problem – not quite enough money, mind, to sort everything out, but at least enough to get the city council out of the landlord business. The official goal of the project, stated in bland bureaucratese, was the creation of a 'safe, clean, and attractive' physical environment where people could have 'accommodation which meets both their housing needs and their aspirations'. Ultimately, the planners hoped, 'the local population ... will have a long-term commitment to the area'.

It was not too much to ask, one might think, compared to the demands of the Communist Manifesto or the Athens Charter. But for a place like the Hulme Crescents it was a marvellous vision, a future that for years had seemed possible only in the realms of fantasy.

There was a price to pay, of course: this was a future in which the Crescents themselves could play no part. The city council approached the Dogs of Heaven, a local theatre group, and asked them to concoct a crowning send-off, a fitting finale for the hell that the Crescents had become. On a clear night in March 1993, they pushed a car off the roof of the John Nash crescent and lit the funeral pyre of a utopia that hadn't turned out as anyone had planned. It was televised on the BBC's *Late Show*.

There is another film, a home movie, that records the events of the day after. It is blustery, but the music is still pulsing away. A ragged crowd is pulling bastard wagons cobbled together from doors and windows, car parts and kitchen units. They pile these fragments at the foot of a gigantic phoenix made from fragments of the concrete building behind them, and they dance as the firebird consumes the offered remnants of their homes.

The Hulmans said goodbye to their Crescents in time-honoured fashion. Graffiti on a concrete wall parodied the pronouncements of a council notice:

Madchester City Council, cutting jobs, destroying services, selling your home ...

We have democratically decided that your homes are not important. Big business and yuppies have offered us large sums of money to have offices, posh shops, car parks, wine bars etc. in Hulme. One or two of you paid the poll tax. We have a few flats to offer you in Wythenshawe. You will not be able to come to the city and spoil our chances of attracting big business and the Olympics. For you scum who pay no poll tax, squat, or are too young or too old to be bothered with, we have a wide selection of park benches and cardboard boxes to offer you as accommodation. We apologize for any inconvenience.

Go to Hulme today and you won't find a trace of the Crescents. Instead you'll see a neat suburb of brick terraces and tidy gardens which look remarkably like the back-to-back cottages that Engels described, give or take a filthy urchin or two. The future of Hulme resembles nothing else so much as its past.

* * *

That doesn't sound much like the prophecies, does it? But one should always be careful with prophecies. Engels knew that the fulfilment of his dreams could only come after a destructive revolution, and so did Le Corbusier, whose Radiant City would have obliterated the cities of his own time. The New Jerusalem, they knew, could only appear at the Apocalypse.

But what they forgot was that every future is followed by another – that their blueprints for everlasting utopia would, like all plans, be cast aside in the pursuit of others they could not possibly foresee. It's something the residents of Hulme found out again and again over the course of a century, as vision after vision was visited on them: crucible of revolution, Modernist showcase, anarchist free-for-all, chemical paradise. Each of these futures is remembered with simultaneous nostalgia and horror by the people who were there.

'No future, no future,' the Sex Pistols sang in one of their biggest hits. But it was the Futurists who put it best:

The oldest of us is thirty: so we have at least a decade for finishing our work. When we are forty, other younger and stronger men will probably throw us in the wastebasket like useless manuscripts – we want it to happen!

They will come against us, our successors, will come from far away, from every quarter, dancing to the winged cadence of their first songs, flexing the hooked claws of predators, sniffing doglike at the academy doors the strong odor of our decaying minds, which will have already been promised to the literary catacombs.

But we won't be there ... At last they'll find us – one winter's night – in open country, beneath a sad roof drummed by a monotonous rain. They'll see us crouched beside our trembling aeroplanes in the act of warming our hands at the poor little blaze that our books of today will give out when they take fire from the flight of our images.

They'll storm around us, panting with scorn and anguish, and all of them, exasperated by our proud daring, will hurtle to kill us, driven by a hatred the more implacable the more their hearts will be drunk with love and admiration for us.

Injustice, strong and sane, will break out radiantly in their eyes.

Art, in fact, can be nothing but violence, cruelty, and injustice.

The Futurists. It sounds like a band from Manchester, doesn't it?

THE BERLIN WALL

In Which History Comes to an End

HISTORY FOR SALE.
A young boy sells pieces of the Berlin Wall, Potsdam Square, Berlin, 10 March 1990.

The End of History

The Parthenon is dissolving into the atmosphere,
but preparations have been made for the conclusion of its story. Bernard Tschumi's new
museum at the foot of the Acropolis contains an empty space the same size as the temple,
ready to receive its remains should it ever become necessary to transfer them indoors. This
museum already houses all of the sculptures of the Parthenon that remain in Greece, and
other plinths in it await the return of the marbles held in London and elsewhere. Once the
temple has disappeared from its original location, its history will terminate in this mausoleum.

The prophets of Modernism tried to push the future towards a definitive end, seeking
a utopian solution to all human strivings. Marx and Engels, for their part, posited
history as a dialectic: a battle of ideas in the process of progressive resolution, century
by century, iteration by iteration. The Architect's Dream *is the very image of such a*
process, in which building follows building in a sequence of improvements, from the
pharaoh's authoritarian tomb to the cathedral made by the willing hands of inspired
craftsmen. Once the final revolution had been enacted and the human condition perfected,
history itself would come to an end. Then the architect could rest on his column and gaze
upon a world made complete, in which nothing need ever change again.

History did come to an end of sorts, but not quite as the Marxists or the Modernists had planned. The fall of the Berlin Wall on 10 November 1989 concluded what the historian Eric Hobsbawm calls 'the little twentieth century', which began with the assassination of Archduke Franz Ferdinand in 1914, ran through the horrors of the trenches, Auschwitz, and Hiroshima, through Nuremberg and the Prague Spring, and finished in Berlin. The events of that night represent 'the end of history', a term invented by the political economist Francis Fukuyama. Democratic capitalism defeated autocratic communism, bringing the last great ideological conflict to a close once and for all.

But unlike the Hulme Crescents, the Berlin Wall, whose spectacular destruction marked Fukuyama's 'end of history', was not obliterated. Indeed, as hated as it had been, the Wall soon took on something of the preciousness of the marble of the Parthenon, which dissolves and crumbles even as it is gathered. The strange afterlife of the Berlin Wall is the history of the end of history.

ONCE UPON A TIME, AN OBSCURE WOMAN STOOD ON AN OBSCURE STREET in an obscure corner of Berlin. In front of her, section after section of concrete slab stretched away in a space devoid of buildings and people.

The woman, who had hennaed hair, a broad face, a long black coat, and a cigarette in her mouth, stood on the cobbles looking to the West. She was scanning the concrete wall in front of her. Suddenly her eyes lit up, and she smiled. She waved at whatever, or whoever, she saw; and then she glanced to the left and to the right, and her face fell. She turned on her heel with her head down and walked away, back to the East.

Ute had never seen the Antifascist Protection Rampart before. Although she lived only a few hundred yards away, her journey to it had been dangerous, and had involved months of preparation. She was not meant to be there. She had no idea what was behind the Antifascist Protection Rampart – other than fascists, she supposed, if that was what it was meant to be protecting them from. Ute had a map of Berlin in which, beyond the rampart, there was only a *terra incognita*. The rampart was the western horizon of the world, and on winter evenings whatever was behind it cast a baleful light into the sky, as if even the sunsets had been organized on the cheap by the border guards. No-one walked up to, touched, or crossed over the Antifascist Protection Rampart. At least, no-one did any of those things and ever came back to tell the tale.

✳ ✳ ✳

One bright Sunday morning in 1961, a young officer of the German Democratic Republic put on a pair of walking boots. He packed his map, a bucket of white paint, and a paintbrush, and headed towards the centre of Berlin. Hagen Koch's path began at the junction of Friedrichstrasse and Zimmerstrasse, and a crowd soon gathered there to watch him begin. He took out his can of white paint and the paintbrush, dipped the brush into the can of paint, and began a line on the cobbles.

Hagen Koch was drawing a new meridian, a new equator, a new edge of the world, at which one ideological, political, economic, social, historical system came to an end and another began. The line he had painted was the line of the Berlin Wall.

The government of the German Democratic Republic issued a pamphlet that attempted to answer questions about the Wall for those who might happen to be curious.

Did the wall fall out of the sky?
No. It was the result of developments of many years' standing in West Germany and West Berlin.

Did the wall have to come?
Yes and no ... The wall had to come because they (the West) were bringing about the danger of a conflict. Those who do not want to hear, must feel.

What did the wall prevent?

We no longer wanted to stand by passively and see how doctors, engineers and skilled workers were induced by refined methods unworthy of the dignity of man to give up their secure existence in the GDR and work in West Germany or West Berlin ... But we prevented something much more important with the wall: West Berlin's becoming the starting point for a military conflict. The measures we introduced on 13 August in conjunction with the Warsaw Treaty states have cooled off a number of hotheads in Bonn and West Berlin. For the first time in German history the match which was to set fire to another war was extinguished before it had fulfilled its purpose.

Was peace really threatened?

It (the protective wall of the GDR) served the cause of world peace since it halted the advance of the German neo-Hitlerites towards the East.

Who is walled in?

According to the exceedingly intelligent explanations of the West Berlin Senate we have walled ourselves in and are living in a concentration camp ... Does something not occur to you? West Berlin Mayor Brandt wails that half of the GDR, including the workers in the enterprise militia groups, is armed. What do you think of a concentration camp whose inmates have weapons in their hands?

Who breaks off human contacts?

Of course, it is bitter for many Berliners not to be able to visit each other at present. But it would be more bitter if a new war were to separate them for ever.

Does the wall threaten anyone?

Bonn propaganda describes the wall as a 'monstrous evidence of the aggressiveness of world communism'. Have you ever considered it to be a sign of aggressiveness when someone builds a fence around his property?

Who is aggravating the situation?

The wall? It stands there quite calmly.

Is the wall a gymnastic apparatus?

The wall is the state frontier of the German Democratic Republic. The state frontier of a sovereign state must be respected. That is so the world over. He who does not treat it with respect cannot complain if he comes to harm.

So that was why the line had been drawn. It protected the Socialist Workers' Paradise of the German Democratic Republic from the rest of the world.

∗ ∗ ∗

According to Ute, the Socialist Workers' Paradise wasn't that bad. There were libraries and swimming pools, holiday resorts and good public transportation. There were protected rents, and safe jobs, and secure pensions. Life was predictable. In fact, Ute's family had moved to the GDR in the late fifties of their own volition. Her grandfather had been one of those communists who'd held out against Hitler throughout the Nazi years, and he had persuaded them all to come and join him in the democratic republic they were building out in the East.

'There's everything you need,' he'd said, and so there was, in the village where Ute and her sister grew up. It was the things you wanted that took more time. If you wanted a car or a TV you put yourself on a waiting list for about ten years, and you saved. If you wanted bananas, then once a year you went to the town square and queued up for them all night. Ute and her sister were taught to make do, to expect little, and to be satisfied with what they had. They weren't satisfied, though, and they decided they were going to do something about it.

* * *

Hagen Koch's path ran through Berlin like a herald with a bell. It ran over the pile of rubble that had been the Gestapo headquarters in Niederkirchner-strasse. It ran past the wasteland under which lay the remains of Hitler's Chancellery and the department stores of Potsdamer Platz. It ran under the bombed-out ruins of the Reichstag and the Brandenburg Gate, and through the quiet war veterans' cemetery at Invalidenstrasse. It ran down Bernauer-strasse, turned the corner by the old railway station at Schwedterstrasse, and then came out to the bridge over the tracks at Bornholmerstrasse.

As it passed by them, the residents of Bernauerstrasse woke up to find that the wall between their flats and the street outside – the one they'd just repapered, the one with the window with net curtains and flower boxes, the one with the front door that jammed a little every day – yes, that wall – had become the Wall.

They were taken by surprise. 'There are no plans to build a wall,' their president had said just a few weeks before. The tenants of Bernauerstrasse saw their lives stretch out before them, and they knew what they had to do. They hurried to their windows on the first floor, and the second, and the third. They opened the casements and they jumped, and their bodies rained down onto the capitalist paving stones of the West below them. They had to be quick to beat the guards running up the stairs. Some people were too scared to jump, and spent the rest of their lives as citizens of the German Democratic Republic.

Others were too bold and jumped too soon, smashing their bodies on the cobbles. Others were not quite quick enough.

There is a photograph in which a woman hangs from a window. She is in her fifties, her hair dyed black and set neatly in a perm. She is wearing a long dark coat. East German police or soldiers are leaning out of the window, holding her arms so that she cannot fall; but this isn't a rescue operation. Bystanders – her relatives who have already escaped, perhaps? – are on the ground outside. They are gripping her feet, trying to pull her down into the West.

Perhaps she lived happily ever after. The Wall stood there quite calmly, aggravating no-one, guaranteeing world peace, and preventing skilled workers from being lured into a life of capitalist wage slavery. But the woman and her neighbours jumped out of their windows rather than stay at home in paradise.

No wonder the government felt the need to get everyone out. The inhabitants of Bernauerstrasse were evacuated, and the doors and windows of their flats were hurriedly bricked up. The streets that ran between the buildings were barricaded with whatever came to hand: a jumble of concrete blocks, kerbstones, and bricks, garnished with unruly coils of barbed wire.

∗ ∗ ∗

Ute and her sister moved to Berlin as soon as they were old enough. According to Ute, the capital of the Socialist Workers' Paradise wasn't that bad. You could go anywhere you needed – to the shops in Alexanderplatz, to the Pergamon Museum, to the rallies in Marx-Engels-Platz. You could visit the fine hospitals and the opera houses and the libraries. You could take a lift to the top of the impressive TV tower, and from the round café at the summit you could see all the way to the western horizon.

It was going where you wanted that was more difficult. There were some streets that didn't seem to lead anywhere – all that could be seen at the end of them was some empty ground and a concrete wall. If you tried to get a closer look, guards would appear and turn you away. 'It's dangerous for you here,' they'd say. 'Go back home.' And that would make you want to walk down there all the more.

There was a clock in Alexanderplatz called the *Weltuhr*, the world clock, which showed the time in all the capital cities of the world. Ute always looked upon it with irony. 'What's the bloody point of knowing the time in all these places you'll never visit?' she'd say. Her geography is still terrible.

* * *

A few months after Hagen Koch's walk with his paintbrush, a young man found his way into number 44 Bernauerstrasse. He crossed courtyards that moaned in the autumn wind and climbed up empty staircases that creaked and squeaked under his weight. He wandered around the vacated homes, his shoes echoing on the bare floorboards. He made his way into one of the attics, and then he climbed out onto the roof.

It didn't take long for the border guards to spot him and give chase. They climbed up the vertiginous little iron ladders on the sides of chimneys, ran past urns and statues and balustrades, and tripped through gutters that squelched underfoot. Dislodged tiles fell to the street below, and Bernd Lunser's plans and dreams fell away with them. He reached an ornate cornice, and then there was nowhere else for him to go. He jumped.

The Wall stood there quite calmly, guaranteeing world peace and protecting socialist workers from a life of wage slavery. But Bernd Lunser jumped to his certain death rather than enjoy its protection.

No wonder the authorities knocked down the old flats along Bernauerstrasse. There is a photograph of the street taken a little later, showing what at first glance looks like a boulevard or a park. On the East side, gigantic windowless walls rise from the grass. The peeling wallpaper, the empty holes left by the floor joists, the marks where pictures had once been, and the mantelpieces suspended high above the ground all indicate that until recently these walls had been inside the rooms of people's homes.

On the other side of the expanse there are two smaller walls, standing very close to one another. One, brand new, is made of H-shaped concrete posts set firmly into the ground at uniform centres. Prefabricated sections of concrete slab have been set vertically between the posts, topped with a rounded concrete pipe and a coil of barbed wire. Next to it, standing closest to the inhabitants of West Berlin, is a crumbling, rambling structure about six feet tall. Plants sprout from its shattered masonry, and all the ornamental good manners of pilaster and caryatid are flaking off the brickwork. Look carefully, and you can still just see the front doors and the parlour windows, hastily sealed with crude blockwork.

In between all these walls the ground is empty, except for thousands of grey rabbits. It is known as No Man's Land.

* * *

According to Ute, things weren't that bad until her sister disappeared. Then the police came for her and told her all about it. Her sister had gone over to the fascists, they said. It was Ute's fault, they said; and then she found out what happened to people who went behind that concrete wall at the end of the road. The police locked her up, and they tortured her for six months. She was made to sit in pools of freezing water for hours, for days, until she couldn't even shiver any more. She was forced to crouch naked on a mirror and urinate, while the guards stood over her and pointed and laughed. She listened to the horrible cries that echoed down the corridors from God knows where. She didn't sleep: the lights were always on, and she didn't know whether it was day or night. After a while her hair and her teeth started to go, her periods stopped, and her body began to wither away. The police tried to make Ute say that she had helped her sister, but she said nothing. She still won't say what she knew.

✳ ✳ ✳

The year after Hagen Koch had painted his line, a teenage boy managed to climb into the empty expanse. Peter Fechter made a dash for it, but as he reached up to grab the top of the wall on the other side the border guards shot him in the back.

He lay there for three hours, screaming for help, but nobody knew what to do. People poked their heads over the wall from the West and looked at him. Some of them threw bandages down to him, but he was too weak to pick them up. The border guards just stood and watched. He had brought it all on himself, they said. Eventually they released a smoke bomb; and when the air had cleared, the guards and the body of Peter Fechter were gone.

The Wall was aggravating no-one, guaranteeing world peace and protecting the socialist workers against the neo-Hitlerites in the West. But still Peter Fechter made a dash for it across No Man's Land, and died in the sand rather than stay at home.

No wonder the authorities felt the need to improve the Wall. Year by year it evolved, and by 1975 it was perfected. There is a diagram of Grenzmauer '75, as the structure was officially known. It looks like some magical fortress designed by a child, with its strange perspective, its absurd, fantastical multiplication of defensive devices, and its sketchy little Alsatian ready to attack.

Each prefabricated concrete slab of Grenzmauer '75 was L-shaped, precisely 3.683 metres tall. The vertical outer face of the slab faced West, and the inner angle of the 'L' faced East. The inner angle was carefully curved, so that it was impossible to gain a foothold on it. The top of the slab was covered with a rounded concrete pipe, so that it was impossible to gain a handhold on it. The concrete itself was smooth and slippery.

These concrete slabs formed the western face of Grenzmauer '75. Behind them there was a row of tank traps. Behind the tank traps was a ditch. Behind the ditch there was a patrol track for vehicles, and then a marching track for infantry. Behind the marching track there was a row of street lamps, and behind the street lamps was a row of watchtowers. Behind the watchtowers was a barbed-wire corridor inhabited by attack dogs, and then a low-tension electric fence. Behind the electric fence was a 'fakir's bed' of nails that protruded from the ground, and another concrete wall. Behind this rear wall was a border area cleared of buildings, which the citizens of the German Democratic Republic were not allowed to visit. And behind the border area was an entire society that had been told nothing of the true nature of the Wall.

* * *

Things weren't that bad after Ute was finally allowed to go home. Her sister was gone for ever, and Ute thought of her as if she were dead. She mourned her, she grieved, but she went back to work and saw her friends. It would have been madness to do otherwise. Life went on.

Then one day she received a message: 'Come to Bernauerstrasse, and I will see you there.' So Ute went and peered over the rampart. She saw a figure standing on a little steel tower, waving at her. And because it was dangerous even to approach Bernauerstrasse, Ute had to drop her hand, turn on her heel, and walk away – as if she had seen nothing, not even an apparition waving from the other side. 'It was the bitterest day of my life,' she says. She wishes she'd never gone.

* * *

Günther Schabowski lives happily ever after with a modest career behind him as the editor of a local newspaper in Hesse. But once upon a time he was the

Minister for State Propaganda in the German Democratic Republic; and one day he'd made a mistake at work.

It was 9 November 1989. Schabowski had been called to a news conference. There was a crisis: what had once been a trickle of escapees over the Wall had become a flood, and no-one knew how to deal with it. He had just returned from his holidays, and he was exhausted, but no-one else would speak to the press that day – they'd left it up to him. No-one had told him what he had to say, so he improvised:

> We know about this tendency in the population, this need of the population, to travel or to leave the GDR. And (um) we have ideas about what we have to bring about ... namely a complex renewal of the society (um) and thereby achieve that many of these elements ... (um) that people do not feel compelled to solve their personal problems in this way.
>
> We have decided today (um) to implement a regulation that allows every citizen of the German Democratic Republic (um) to (um) leave the GDR through any of the border crossings.

The room erupted. Would people need visas or passports to leave? When would this regulation come into force? 'It comes into effect,' ad-libbed Schabowski, 'according to my information, immediately.' 'That has to be decided by the Council of Ministers,' an aide murmured, but he was not heard above the hubbub. The subsequent questions were inaudible, but Schabowski repeated four times: 'I haven't heard anything to the contrary.'

The press conference was broadcast live on GDR stations, but no-one watched them in those days – not if they actually wanted to know what was going on. Four hours later, a West German news programme reported the press conference under a sensational headline:

> This ninth of November is a historic day: the GDR has announced that its borders are open to everyone, with immediate effect, and the gates of the wall stand wide open.

It wasn't quite what Günther Schabowski had said, but that didn't stop anyone. The people of the GDR got up from their sofas, put on their coats, and walked out to the gates of the Wall, expecting to find them wide open. The queues at the Bornholmerstrasse checkpoint were soon overwhelming, and the guards didn't know what do to do. They telephoned their bosses, and their bosses reminded them that the Council of Ministers had in fact recommended nothing more than a review of travel restrictions. Headlines on the West German news did not constitute official East German government policy, they said.

Except that this time they did. No matter what the guards said, the people refused to go home. At about half past eleven, as if prompted by some hidden signal – or perhaps just because they didn't know what else to do – the guards began to wave people over the old railway bridge into the West. They marked their papers with an 'exit with no right of return' stamp, as if they were sentencing them to death. But from that moment, the Wall ceased to be the Wall and became a wall. It ceased to be the boundary between states and ideologies and hemispheres and became a length of concrete, twelve feet tall and only a few inches thick.

* * *

Ute, too, had been listening to the West German news that night. She rose slowly from her chair, went into the bedroom, and opened her suitcase. She packed some underwear, a few shirts and trousers, and a jumper, because it was cold. She switched off the light, tiptoed down the stair, crossed the courtyard, picked her way to the front door, and dropped the key as her shaking hands felt for the lock. She made her way to her workplace and left a note on the little roll of paper hanging by the door that people used in the absence of telephones. She apologized: she wouldn't be back for a while.

One day later, Ute was sitting on the doorstep of her long-lost sister's house in West Germany, waiting for her to come home from work. They didn't talk about the Wall. They had dealt with quite enough history for now.

✶ ✶ ✶

Volker Pawlowski lives happily ever after in Bernau, the town outside Berlin for which Bernauerstrasse is named. He is the proud owner of a building yard, a huge silver Chrysler cruiser, and US patent number 6076675, issued to him for

> a presentation and holding device for small-format objects that has at least two transparent joinable halves that form a hollow body when fitted together into a corresponding opening in a presentation surface, such as a picture postcard. The hollow body is effectively used to contain an object which has some connection with the motif presented on the picture postcard.

Once upon a time Pawlowski was a construction worker in East Berlin, but he slipped a disc around the time when the gates of the Wall were opened. Stuck at home, he came up with the modest device that has made his fortune. Pawlowski's invention is only half the secret of his wealth, for it is the specific motif presented on the picture postcards he sells, and the 'small-format objects' that have a connection with it, that lend patent 6076675 its awesome power.

Every so often, Volker Pawlowski drives his truck into Berlin and picks up sections of the Wall. Then he brings them back to his building yard, where they are unloaded and showered in bright spray-paint to make it appear as if they have been covered in graffiti. When the paint has dried, workers chip away at the slabs until there is a pile of little concrete shards on the ground. These are sorted into different sizes; and then, in accordance with patent number 6076675, they are attached to postcards of famous sections of the Berlin Wall in its heyday.

In pieces pinned to postcards, the Wall is taken back into town. Alongside old Russian army uniforms and GDR badges, it is piled up on souvenir stalls around Checkpoint Charlie, the Brandenburg Gate, and Potsdamer Platz. At the height of his business, Pawlowski was shifting between 30,000 and 40,000 postcards a year. That's a lot of wall. 'It's worthless,' he says, 'but people seem to want it, and who am I to complain?'

Pawlowski isn't the only one to profit from the destruction of the Wall. The very morning after Günther Schabowski's mistake, bulldozers turned up in Bernauerstrasse. Although the gates of the Wall had already been thrown wide open, they forced a new opening in it; and then the giant machines rumbled away, and left the people to continue their work.

Some of them started with graffiti. For a long time people had been coming from around the world to deface the Berlin Wall. The border guards might have kept a close watch on the eastern side, but they could effect no jurisdiction over its western face, which by 1989 had become a riot of abusive colour. When the bulldozers broke down the Wall, artists streamed through to attack its inner, eastern face, which had hitherto remained pristine. They created *trompe l'oeil* murals that poked gaps in the structure upon which they had been drawn. A painted desert glimpsed through a painted hole evoked the sandy void of No Man's Land. A tinny little East German car – the Trabant – crashed through the concrete. The President of the Soviet Union locked himself in a passionate tongue kiss with the President of the German Democratic Republic. The stories painted on the surface of the Wall challenged its very right to exist.

But for others, paint seemed like weak punishment. The people took their hammers and chisels, their sledgehammers and crowbars, and they went to the Wall. Berlin in winter is a city of extraordinary echoes, particularly at night, and people didn't sleep much in those days. The pecking of metal against concrete echoed down the dark, treeless streets of the city centre, and those who chipped away at the Wall that had contained them became known as the *Mauerspechte*: the 'wall woodpeckers'.

The *Mauerspechte* were destroying the Wall in anger, but they did not discard their peckings. Many of them carefully collected, catalogued, and bagged their fragments. Sometimes they set up little stalls and sold their harvest to wandering tourists, complete with hastily contrived certificates of authenticity. Others hired their home tools out to visitors, who could then proudly display their bag of chips and honestly say that they had helped bring down the Berlin Wall. Some, like Volker Pawlowski, were more ambitious.

All over the world there are tiny pieces of the Berlin Wall, hoarded and revered as if they were fragments of something awesome and numinous. The Japanese ceramicist Tokusen Nishimura once ground a chunk of the Wall into dust, mixed it with clay, and fashioned it into a vessel for the solemn tea ceremonies of Kyoto. The writer Araminta Matthews recounts the tale of a piece of the Wall that was passed from Berlin to lover to lover to her – until she offered it to her intended, and he, not understanding its significance, handed it back. Reader, she dumped him.

Six months after the opening of the Wall, the East German government itself joined the ranks of the Wall profiteers. At a gala event at the Metropole Palace Hotel in Monaco, the Antifascist Protection Rampart was auctioned off to help pay the debts accumulated by the Socialist Workers' Paradise it had been built to protect. Three hundred and sixty chunks of the Wall were photographed and listed in a glossy catalogue, with the provenance of each fragment carefully noted. Pieces covered with beautiful graffiti fetched particularly high bids.

The Wall can now be found in a bewildering array of locations: the CIA headquarters in Washington, DC, the campus of Honolulu Community College in Hawaii, the urinals in the Main Street Station Hotel in Las Vegas. A slab of Grenzmauer '75 adorns the piazza of the small Italian hill town of Albinea, and another decorates a children's playground at Trelleborg in Sweden. A segment of the Wall in Moscow carries the graffiti 'BER'. The 'LIN' is on a separate slab in Riga, Latvia.

As the bidding was going on in Monaco, bulldozers returned to the ruins in Berlin and resumed their work. It took them about four months to clear away what was left. (Most of it was ground down into the rubble that now lies under the roads which reconnected Berlin to itself.) Then, three months after the auction of its border rampart, the German Democratic Republic reached the end of its own history. In October 1990 it abolished itself, and ceased to exist.

* * *

Ute didn't stay with her sister for too long; their reunion wasn't what she had expected it to be. Her sister looked drawn and nervous. She still had nightmares, she said, about what the border guards had done when they'd caught her. She told the same torture stories as Ute: there had been the pool of freezing water, the humiliating exercise with the mirror, the cries echoing down the corridor. She suffered from terrible migraines, too. But the government of the German Democratic Republic had treated Ute's sister to one additional debasement. They had sold her: she had been dumped in West Germany in exchange for hard currency, along with a load of dissidents and criminals. The police had packed her on her way with a warning. 'Our agents are everywhere,' they said: 'Keep your trap shut, or what happened to you will happen to everyone in your family.'

Ute didn't stay with her sister, but she didn't go back to Berlin either. Like the fragments of the Wall, she went off to discover the world and make her fortune.

✷ ✷ ✷

In the present-day happily ever after, Jacqueline Röber is a community councillor and lawyer who lives and works at one end of Bernauerstrasse. Röber is an expert on property law – something of a burning issue in a neighbourhood like hers, where rents were capped at GDR prices until the pressures of gentrification blew the Berlin housing market wide open. A child of the East zone, Röber didn't expect much from the newly unified Germany, and although she's done well for herself she hasn't forgotten her roots. These days, she is an advocate for the erstwhile citizens of her vanished nation.

Her campaigning has led her into direct confrontation with another inheritor of the same legacy. When Germany was reunified and the state railway corporations of the East and the West were merged, a company called Vivico was established to run the railways' extensive property portfolio. It has since become a major player in the German real estate market.

Once upon a time, decades before the Wall, there had been a railway station at the end of Bernauerstrasse. The railway tracks divided the inner districts of the city in two: to the west was Wedding, to the east Prenzlauerberg. The station was flattened in the war, and Hagen Koch's line ran between the two districts along the centre of the deserted railway tracks. As the Wall grew, the tracks to the East disappeared beneath concrete and sand and barbed wire, while a makeshift labyrinth of vegetable plots was planted over them to the West. Everyone forgot that there had ever been a railway station in No Man's Land, or that the area had belonged to anybody in the first place.

After the *Mauerspechte* and the bulldozers had done their work, there was nothing left of the Wall – nothing apart from nothing, that is. And with the border guards no longer tending No Man's Land, the ground began to bloom with the pigeons of the plant kingdom: purple mallow, lilac, yellow goldenrod, and all those other scruffy, colourful species that thrive on abandoned urban soil. Where the attack dogs had raced up and down, old ladies now ventured for a walk. Where two world systems had faced one another across the sand, rival Turkish gangs showed up to play their evening football. Where search-lights had raked the void, lovers came to conceal themselves in the foliage.

In 1994, as part of a bid for the Olympic Games, the city had the No Man's Land landscaped to a design by the Hamburg architect Gustav Lange. Berlin didn't get the Olympics, but it did get a new park. The Mauerpark became a hangout for punks and teenagers, who drank and smoked and did deals on the hill. Occasionally they rioted. Mostly they did nothing. There is a wall in the Mauerpark that might or might not have been the Wall. This wall blazes with colourful graffiti, but it is not the art of protest and satire. It is a gallery of abstract hieroglyphs meaningful only to the impenetrable coteries of local delinquents who stake their ever-changing, arbitrary claims to a territory that belongs to no-one.

No-one except Vivico, that is, since it owns all the land that had once belonged to the railways on both sides of the Wall. The company donated some of its parcels to the Berlin city council for the Mauerpark, with the land-scaping funded by the city on the basis of environmental conservation. Now Vivico wants to build houses on the remainder of the land it owns, but the city won't give it a construction permit: they say that it will harm the ecosystem of the park. The people, represented by Jacqueline Röber, are campaigning for the city to buy the land to protect and expand the park, but Vivico is asking for a market rate that the city can't possibly afford. The city can't buy. Vivico can't build. The people make do with half a park; and the land is suspended, as it has always been, in limbo.

* * *

Ute went to London, to make her fortune and see the world. She found work as a pastry chef in a smart restaurant, she worked hard, and she made good money. She could buy whatever she wanted, but she wasn't happy. Ute had never been abroad before, and she didn't speak English easily. She found people false and cold. 'They always ask you over for a cup of tea, and say how nice it is to see you,' she'd complain, 'but they don't mean it.'

About five years ago, Ute went home. She moved back into the flat in East Berlin she'd left a decade before. The plumber came round and removed the old coal boiler in the living room and put in central heating instead. She bought a new kitchen, painted the bathroom, had a telephone installed, and got a television. The street outside was unrecognizable: all the buildings had been replastered and painted in bright colours. There was a shopping mall over the road, incomprehensible computerized ticket machines at the U-bahn station, and endless, endless coffee shops.

At least her old friends were the same, she thought. But, actually, they weren't: they were as emptily friendly as the people she'd met in England. Once upon a time they had all lived in one another's pockets, hand to mouth, closely connected to one another by their mutual fear of the state. Now they'd say, 'Let's go for a drink sometime,' and then she'd never hear from them. Berlin felt like nowhere in particular, inhabited by millions of people who were no-one in particular. While she was away, it had turned into a No Man's Land.

* * *

Hagen Koch now lives happily ever after as a tour guide in Berlin. He works in the old Secret Police headquarters, which is now a museum, and takes children and tourists on walks around the city looking for traces of the Wall. He has amassed the largest collection of Wall memorabilia in existence, including histories, photographs, and, of course, maps, marked again and again with the line he painted on the pavement that summer morning in 1961. It was the same Hagen Koch who, twenty-nine years later, coordinated the removal of the fragments of his Wall to Monaco, where they were sold off to the highest bidder and dispersed across the globe. Now he is the guide and the guardian of what's left of his creation. There's not much.

There is still one section of the Wall on Bernauerstrasse. Back in 1989 it was decided to cordon off a piece from the bulldozers and the chisels just in case someone, somewhere, at some point in the future might want to know what it was like. Nothing happened for years, until in 1995 a competition was held to solicit proposals for this fragment that had somehow managed to survive the end of history.

There were no winners, which pleased the locals. They didn't want anything to happen. They had been imprisoned behind the Wall and had torn it down; they couldn't see the point in trying to preserve it now. Eventually, though, the contract was awarded to one of the runners-up in the competition, a Berlin firm by the name of Kolhoff and Kolhoff, and exactly nine years after the Wall had come down its memorial was completed.

The memorial is precise in every detail. There is the post-and-slab construction of the hinterland wall. There is the void of No Man's Land, with its raked sand, its crooked concrete path, and its lights on their tall curved stalks. There is the proud outer face of Grenzmauer '75, standing there calmly, aggravating no-one, resisting fascism. But this is just a wall, an exhibit in a minor suburban museum. At either end it is book-ended by gigantic sheets of steel, their polished surfaces reflecting the concrete back and forth to an infinity that no longer exists.

There are monuments to the Wall all over Berlin now, as people struggle to remember what it had all been like not so very long ago. The oldest of these attractions was established just two days after the Wall was built, in a flat on the western side of Bernauerstrasse. (It moved a couple of months later to

Checkpoint Charlie.) Its owner, the enterprising Rainer Hildebrandt, used to help people escape over the Wall, and then used their stories as exhibits in his museum.

In 2004 his even more enterprising widow, Alexandra, tried to rebuild the Wall. In a vacant lot across the road from their museum, about thirty feet away from where the actual Wall had stood, she cobbled together some 450 feet of wall from broken chunks she'd picked up here and there. But her No Man's Land belonged to someone else; and soon this second wall, too, was brought down.

Checkpoint Charlie is now one of the chief sights of Berlin. Students dress up as border guards, American or Russian, and pose for photographs with tourists. The little shed the Americans had used as a guardhouse has been reconstructed, and so has the famous sign that warns 'You are now leaving the American sector' in English, French, Russian, and German. The original placard was stolen in 1989, and now hangs over a sofa somewhere in the United States.

Behind the Ostbahnhof station, a section of the Wall that graffiti artists flocked to in 1989 is now known as the East Side Gallery. Conservators are hard at work on the murals. They have begun the painstaking task of restoring the flaking paint and the crumbling concrete, as if it bore a priceless cycle of Renaissance frescoes.

There are remembrances of the Wall further afield as well. In Sweden there is a collection of hand-crafted models of the Wall made by a woman who calls herself Eija Riitta Berliner-Mauer. She married the Wall, she says, back in 1979, in a small ceremony at Gross Ziethenerstrasse. Now she laments his demise by writing him love poetry. She reconstructs him again and again in balsa wood on her living-room floor, as her cat jumps from East to West on the carpet.

Once upon a time it was dangerous even to look at the Wall, but now it has been made safe by all the prophylaxis of the curated exhibit. The glass case, the tasteful lighting, the souvenir shop, and the audio guide sanitize the squalor and the cruelty and the sheer strangeness of what actually happened. And because it is safe now, the Wall is not readily forgotten. There is even a word for the longing that the former inhabitants of Ostdeutschland, the erstwhile socialist workers of the East, experience for their vanished paradise. They call it *Ostalgie*.

✳ ✳ ✳

Ute doesn't suffer from *Ostalgie* very much. When she was a child, she says, she was forced to go on endless history trips to museums and memorials – to gaze at the piles of hair and teeth in concentration camps, to see the war graves of Russian soldiers and the empty ground above Hitler's bunker, to look at the bridge from which the communist revolutionary Rosa Luxemburg had been thrown. She couldn't bear it then, and she can't bear it now. It all seems so intrusive. People's teeth and hair, their dead bodies, the places where they died should be private to them, she thinks; and so should their lives. The Wall has joined all the other abominations in the whole 'lest we forget' parade, the circus of German horrors with which Ute's generation was punished for the sins of their fathers.

Ute takes her granddaughter out walking in the evening. 'I'll show you where I saw my sister over the Wall,' she says. 'It's not far.' They wander in the old No Man's Land for hours, but for the life of her Ute can't find the place. She looks around, takes a drag on her cigarette, and utters a throaty laugh: 'Scheisse!' She can't remember.

THE VENETIAN, LAS VEGAS

In Which History is So, Like, Over

Venice to Macao.
Image created by Ludovico de Luigi, Venetian painter of impossible views.

Heritage

*T*urn *away from the Parthenon and you'll*
encounter countless souvenir stands selling marble statuettes of gods and satyrs and, of
course, the Parthenon itself. The temple swims in snow domes, adorns tea towels, and
crowns countless paperweights and ashtrays.

Nearly all the other buildings whose secret lives have been recounted in this book have
suffered the same fate. The Berlin Wall was once the edge of the world, but since the 'end
of history' it has become a quarry of souvenir chips and scraps. Ayasofya is now a
museum, Gloucester Cathedral serves as Hogwarts in the film versions of Harry Potter,
and the Alhambra is such a popular attraction that visits to it must be booked online
three months in advance. Venice, meanwhile, has become a museum of itself, maintained
more for the delectation of tourists than for the use of the people who live there.

Buildings that our barbarian ancestors ruined, stole, and appropriated, that our
medieval forebears transformed through repetitive rituals, that our Renaissance progeni-
tors translated into classical languages, that our more modern predecessors imitated and
restored are now displayed as heritage, to be viewed with the impassivity of Thomas Cole's
architect reclining on his isolated column. The Architect's Dream *itself, which was*

painted to hang in an architect's studio, is now safely housed in the climatically controlled conditions of a museum.

It has been argued that the prototype of the contemporary city is the expo and the theme park. Nowhere is this clearer than in Las Vegas, a city of spectacles, whose chief reason for existence is the provision of amusements for the jaded visitor. Ironically, Vegas is filled with attractions modelled on European cities that have themselves become tourist traps. Cruise the Vegas Strip today and you will find a Bellagio, a Monaco, a Paris, and a Venice as packed with trippers as the originals. It is The Architect's Dream *made real – or as real as can be fabricated out of fibreglass in the middle of a desert.*

Vegas is an extreme case, a mirage, a desert oasis. But now, in a further irony, it is itself being imitated for the pleasure of tourists. The Vegas brand of Venice has just arrived in China, where centuries ago Marco Polo stood before Kublai Khan and described the unlikely city from which he had come. Translated through centuries and transported across continents, this Venice is nothing like the robber republic that Marco Polo described. It's a place for a minibreak, nothing else. After the end of history, we take a break, sip a coffee, and take our snaps of monuments that used to change with history – and used to change it, too. They don't seem to, any more.

IT IS TWELVE YEARS AFTER THE END OF HISTORY IN BERLIN. A WESTERN merchant stands before an Eastern potentate in the Hall of Purple Lights in the Zhongnanhai Palace. The brightly lacquered columns and glazed tiles of the old pleasure pavilion still evoke hours of imperial leisure. Dragons and lions disport themselves among the architecture, and outside, the Grand Liquid Sea wrinkles and slides in the listless summer air.

Sheldon G. Adelson, self-made billionaire, the third-richest man in the United States, turns to his CEO and chuckles: 'A very regal-looking environment.' The lights go down, the projector fires up, and Adelson gets ready to make the presentation of his life. He's trying to get permission to build a Vegas casino made in the image of Venice on the Cotai Strip in Macao. Just like everyone else he wants to get into China, real bad. 'It'll be like getting the brass ring,' he says.

Qian Qichen, a Vice-Premier of the People's Republic of China, is not, perhaps, the most attentive of audiences. He can't understand much of what Adelson is saying, and the air-conditioning is making him drowsy. Besides, he has already decided what's going to happen. The pixels of Adelson's presentation swim before his eyes, and he gives himself up to dreaming of a time when another merchant of the West stood before an oriental potentate in Beijing. It could be a scene from Italo Calvino:

> Kublai Khan does not necessarily believe everything Marco Polo says when he describes the cities visited on his expeditions, but the Emperor of the Tartars does continue listening to the young Venetian with greater attention and curiosity than he shows any other messenger or explorer of his. In the lives of emperors there is a moment which follows pride in the boundless extension of the territories we have conquered … It is the desperate moment when we discover that this empire, which had seemed to us the sum of all wonders, is an endless, formless ruin, that corruption's gangrene has spread too far to be healed by our sceptre, that the triumph over enemy sovereigns has made us the heirs of their long undoing. Only in Marco Polo's accounts was Kublai Khan able to discern, through the walls on towers destined to crumble, the tracery of a pattern so subtle it could escape the termite's gnawing.

Qian Qichen allows himself to suppose for a moment that he is Kublai Khan and that Sheldon G. Adelson is constructing *Invisible Cities* for him in Power-Point. As photographs and artists' impressions follow one another, a fruity voiceover tells the stories of Venice and of Vegas.

*   *   *

'Beginnings,' the voice intones, and the first image appears on the screen: an empty expanse of water. Rivo Alto is just what it's called, says the voice: a high bank in a desert of brine. The people who live there dig crabs and shellfish from the mud, and they dwell in brick cottages on stilts suspended above the brackish murk. Blocks of marble are set at random into the bricks of their houses, and the citizens of Rivo Alto tell stories about them. 'We carried them over the water when we ran away from the barbarians,' they say. 'They are the remnants of our former city. They remind us that we were Romans, once upon a time.' They dream that, one day, they will be again.

On the screen, the watery void dissolves into an image of empty desert, and the voice continues. Ragtown is just that: a ragged encampment set by a well in a sea of sand. Old Helen Stewart has run the place ever since Schuyler Henry shot her man dead in 1884. Her ranch house is built from the remains of the Mormon fort that used to stand there. The Mormons didn't stay long: the heat and the Indians drove them away. Now old Helen rents out her dusty patch to prospectors. She knows that they'll need water from her well, and she earns more from them than she'd ever make from trying to grow anything. Sitting around their campfires they tell one another stories about where they've come from. They dream of going home.

* * *

Qian looks at Sheldon G. Adelson, self-made billionaire. He was, Qian already knows, once a prospector of sorts himself. Adelson's parents had come from the Ukraine and Lithuania, and he'd started out real humble – selling news-papers on street corners, toiletry kits by mail order, de-icers for windshields. He has no intention of going back to the place he came from.

Qian is dreaming of a spit of sand in the distant south of the People's Republic. The Cotai Peninsula is empty of anyone but a few fishermen. They live in simple cottages, digging for crabs and shellfish. He knows they won't be for long.

* * *

'Consummation,' the voice intones, and another image appears in the darkness. A beautiful city emerges from the dunes of water where Rivo Alto had once floated in the void.

The improbable towers and domes of La Serenissima hover like a reverie above the watery heat haze, but it is not a dream: it is Rivo Alto, five hundred years after its first people arrived there in flight from the barbarians. The air is filled with the cries of stevedores and the clanging of church bells. Marble palaces of every describable colour crowd the foaming brine, embroidered with balustrades, cornices, and castellations, fringed by the red and white candy-striped poles to which the boatmen moor their craft.

La Serenissima is beautiful, but it's also a place to get down to business. The docks in front of the Doge's Palace, a gigantic block of pink marzipan dripping with icing, are piled high with the treasures of the Levant. The heads of executed criminals are displayed on richly carved columns beside the palace, for it is both the treasure house of the republic and her seat of justice. The colourful palaces that ride the waves are the dwellings of merchants, whose galleys are fitted and armed in the Arsenale at the city's eastern edge.

Every year the Doge casts a golden ring into the water, to renew the marriage of La Serenissima with the element that has served her so well. It isn't an empty gesture, for all her wealth has come over the sea. Nothing in La Serenissima is an empty gesture: every part of the city performs a function and expresses that purpose with splendour. The customs house, the entrepôt of all the world's treasures, is surmounted by four Atlases who support a globe on their shoulders. On top of the globe is a bronze image of La Serenissima herself, in the guise of Fortune, twisting and turning in the sea breeze.

Up on the screen, the dunes of water around La Serenissima turn into waves of sand that lap the pleasure domes of another city – the place that used to be Ragtown.

The improbable towers and pleasure domes of Glitter Gulch wink away in the vast sea of the desert twilight. Around the corner of Tropicana and the Strip is a speeding jam of open-top cars with massive sound systems, full of cheering girls in T-shirts. It's sixty years since the prospectors pitched their tents on Helen Stewart's ranch. A cacophony of signs shimmers away up the Strip, neon words promising exotic escape and instant magic: Tropicana, Barbary Coast, Dunes, Desert Inn, Sahara, Hacienda, El Rancho, Stardust, Silver Slipper, Bonanza, Slots-a-Fun.

A limo pulls off the Strip under one such sign, emblazoned in a vaguely Arabic script with the single word 'Sands'. The car purrs to a halt in the parking lot. The tarmac is flooded with the glow of the casino within: a form-less electric twilight, dotted here and there with pools of brightness that suffuse the faces above the green baize with an anticipatory glow.

They call the casino floor the 'grind joint', because that's just what it is: hour after hour the slot machines and the gaming tables grind cash out of the guests. The Sands provides free meals to anyone who'll stay at the tables long enough, and cheap all-you-can-eats to everyone else. In 1955, one man plays blackjack for twenty-seven hours and wins $77,000. He loses it again instantly, autographing hundred-dollar bills and handing them out to admiring by-standers. The hotel that towers above the casino is only there to give the poor hucksters somewhere to sleep between games. To keep everyone gambling all the time, there are roulette wheels and one-armed bandits by the swimming pool.

There's entertainment, too. The Copa lounge is inhabited by 'The Most Beautiful Girls in the World', recruited directly from Hollywood. Tallulah Bankhead has played there, and so have Dean Martin, Jerry Lewis, Nat King Cole, and Frank Sinatra. *Ocean's Eleven* was filmed at the Sands in 1960. It's all there to keep the ladies happy while their men are at the card tables.

Glitter Gulch is a factory of desire. It is the destination to which the road leads across the desert, the thing that all the flashing signs signify. The citizens of Glitter Gulch remember that once upon a time they were prospecting for gold, and they intend to enjoy every cent of it now.

∗ ∗ ∗

Qian's advisors have already informed him that Sheldon G. Adelson made his fortune in Glitter Gulch. He built his empire running COMDEX, an annual Las Vegas expo for computer goods. Talk about being in the right place at the right time: COMDEX was so successful in the 1980s that delegates booked up all the rooms within a forty-five-mile radius of the event. Sheldon G. Adelson bought himself a casino – the Sands – in 1988, and married a new wife the following year. They went to La Serenissima on their honeymoon.

Qian Qichen is daydreaming about office towers and shopping malls. He was born outside Shanghai; when he was young his parents would take him to the bund by the river, where they would look across the Yangtze River at empty marshland. Now Pudong bristles with skyscrapers. Qian Qichen imagines the blank sands of the Cotai Strip and wonders if one day they will look the same.

And then he remembers that he is a Vice-Premier of China and that he has a job to do. He jerks awake and puts his hands on the desk. He eyes Adelson levelly: 'Tell me about Steve Wynn.' Adelson's round face reddens slightly, as it is apt to do when he is pricked. He coughs, and the presentation rolls on.

∗ ∗ ∗

'Decadence,' says the disembodied voice, and an eighteenth-century painting by Canaletto appears in the gloom. A gilded barge floats in the water in front of a pink palace. The water around it is filled with smaller craft, and the steps of the palace are thronged with revellers in silken costumes, their faces hidden behind elaborate masks.

Carnival roisterers ride the dark waters from palace to palace in search of new pleasures. In a fresco on a ballroom wall Cleopatra dissolves a pearl in vinegar and drinks it, while on a painted ceiling the clowns of the *Commedia dell' Arte* disport themselves on swings. Lovers who pretend not to recognize one another hop through the gavotte and arrange assignations *sotto voce*. Later they embrace in boats plying the dark tangle of canals that lace the city, as the songs of gondoliers echo off the shuttered arcades of silent palaces.

The revellers rise late to hear Mass in the church of the Scalzi, and peer up at the gilded screen suspended on the wings of laughing cherubs. They wonder whether the beauty of the nuns hidden behind it matches the beauty of their voices. Casanova plots his elopement with one of them. After Mass, friends go to the casino to gossip.

Once a year the Doge still emerges from his pink palace and casts a ring into the waves, to remind his city that once upon a time the riches of the sea paid for the pleasures of the Carnival. They don't any more. Canaletto makes a fortune from painting the event for the English *milordi*. He realizes long before anyone else does that the Carnival's future rests not on water or trade, but on the attractive images that can be conjured out of it.

The shipyards of the Arsenale have fallen quiet, and the treasures of the Levant no longer spill onto the docks by the Doge's Palace. On the last day of the city's existence, a council is called to determine the future of the place that once was Rivo Alto and became La Serenissima. Few of the aristocratic families bother to turn up. The Doge returns to his apartments and hands his glittering insignia to a servant with a wry smile. The party is over.

* * *

'Very salutary,' says Qian Qichen, 'but I asked about Steve Wynn.' Sheldon G. Adelson doesn't miss a beat, and the slides keep coming. Canaletto's rich canvas dissolves into an image of Atlantis, where tropical fish swim amid the towers and domes of a submerged civilization.

The Mirage is a city housed in three golden towers that rise from a lush jungle. Every fifteen minutes a volcano erupts amid the palms, and the air is filled with the tropical scent of piña colada. The people who have gathered to watch the eruption applaud and whoop, and then they wander off to explore. In a giant fish tank at the reception area, sharks and angel fish swarm through the ruins of a sunken city. Dolphins disport themselves in a private sea, and in a secret garden Siegfried and Roy perform magic tricks with the white tigers of Timbavati. Of course, to get there, one has to pass the slots and the gaming tables. The Mirage is just what it says it is: an illusion. It's a grind joint in disguise.

Those who try to leave the Mirage only encounter more mirages. The bridge to Treasure Island crosses a Caribbean lagoon, around which a ragged village of white houses tumbles down to the water. Two galleons carved with buxom bowsprits are moored by the dock, their rigging and sails torn by tempests. At the same time every evening, a band of dreadlocked pirates defend themselves against a bevy of scantily clad sirens; the sirens always win. After the show the crowds whoop and applaud, and continue over the bridge to the roulette wheels and the fruit machines.

Those who try to leave Treasure Island only encounter another one. The path to the Wynn winds through tropical foliage to a hidden lake where a thundering waterfall cools the air. Endless corridors are lined with impressionist paintings, exquisite porcelains, and fragments of antiquities. These corridors lead to a golf course whose lush grasses and whispering pines dissolve into the hot desert air. Along the way is shop after designer shop, all 'tailored to one lifestyle – *yours*'. Later, those who've played enough golf or bought enough in the boutiques make their way to the theatre and watch the Cirque du Soleil perform La Rêve. 'Dream with your eyes open,' the billboards say, and that's just what happens. The dream they are all dreaming is the dream of Steve Wynn.

* * *

Qichen doesn't really need to ask about Steve Wynn: he already knows everything he needs to know. He just did it to make Adelson feel like he was paying attention. Handsome, funny, and clever, Wynn started small, just like everyone else: he ran a bingo parlour in Maryland. After a while he made his way to Glitter Gulch to seek his fortune, working his way up from grind joints to hotels. He seemed to be able to attract the sort who hadn't been interested in Las Vegas before: respectable family folks from out east with plenty of money.

And Wynn soon realized that they weren't coming for the gambling. The Mirage and Treasure Island were considered great risks in the early nineties: they weren't really casinos but resorts, aimed squarely at Wynn's well-heeled market. Wynn later said of the Mirage: 'Our goal was to build a hotel so over-riding in its nature that it would be a reason in and of itself for visitors to come ... in the same way that Disney attracts visitors to Orlando, Florida.' Like Disney World, the Mirage and Treasure Island were constructed as endless, magnificent, spectacular carnivals. It wasn't an easy task, but it was well worth the work. 'It's much more difficult to give a party than a roll of quarters,' Wynn explained: 'any damn fool can hand over a roll of quarters, and we have a lot of damn fools handing over rolls of quarters.'

Qian casts his eye over the Hall of the Purple Lights and listens to the murmur of the waves of the Grand Liquid Sea outside. It is ironic, he reflects, that an imperial pleasure palace has become the seat of a regime that once tried to abolish pleasure. Qian remembers the Red Guards stoning the idle songbirds and ripping up the useless grass in the name of the Cultural Revolution. His mind wanders south to the Cotai Strip. It is part of the old Portuguese colony of Macao, which had long been a hedonistic refuge from the People's Republic before being transferred back to China in 1999. There's nothing there now, but the Cotai Strip is ripe for pleasure.

Sheldon G. Adelson is of the same opinion. He is determined that he'll make it to Cotai before Wynn does. He's sick of following him around, and Qian knows that he has been for some time. Three years after Adelson bought it, the Sands was looking more and more like a losing proposition. It had made its name on the backs of its great entertainers, but by 1991 it couldn't afford to attract new talent. The president of the hotel said: 'What was famous then is not famous today. You can see by the headliners. We are almost a waxwork museum now. There's nothing new anymore.'

By comparison with Wynn's Mirage, Adelson's Sands felt like a dusty truckstop. He wasn't happy: 'Their reception desk looks better than our entire hotel!' He had to do something. On 30 June 1996, the last gamblers were ushered, blinking, out of the artificial gloom of the Sands. For five months the place stood empty; the only visitors were the film crew for *Con Air*, who resurrected the casino for a week or so and then crashed a plane into it. Then, at 9 p.m. on 26 November 1996, the old neon sign was switched off for the last time, and the Sands crumpled in a cloud of dust.

The photo of the implosion slides into view on the PowerPoint presentation. It disappears, and the Hall of the Purple Lights goes dark for a moment. There is a silence. From the shadows, the rich voice of the narrator speaks: 'What stood in its place three years later was someplace else altogether.' A videotape starts to roll before the glazed eyes of Qian Qichen.

* * *

A self-made American billionaire hands a beautiful woman down into a gondola. She turns and smiles at him graciously, and he chuckles a little, because it is Sophia Loren who reclines on the cushion by his ageing side. Their gondolier, dressed in a straw hat and a candy-striped shirt, sings to them as he steers his craft through the canals of the Venetian.

The happy couple ascend the marble steps into the Piazza San Marco, where they drink champagne and watch the masked figures of the Carnival amuse the crowd. They wander through gardens thick with cypresses and scented jasmine where the moonlight sparkles on countless pools of water. They pause to listen to soft music echoing from a hidden source around the vaults of a stone cloister; they crane their necks to admire the frescoes that adorn the ceiling of a great cupola. Then they stroll down the crooked streets, peering through shop windows at glittering carnival masks and fauns spun from glass.

They pass through doors whose bronze handles have been wrought in the form of the *ferro* that adorns the prow of a gondola, and find themselves in the upper loggia of the Doge's Palace. All around them, Venetian monuments glow in the gloom. On the hour, the deep bell of San Marco resounds in the night air, and as it subsides it is joined by the peal of hundreds of church bells. Amid the clamour, the ageing American billionaire and the ageless Italian film star watch fireworks scatter their coloured gems on the rippling lagoon.

They scarcely notice the volcano across the road, spewing out its piña colada-scented lava. They don't care about sirens battling pirates or about the dreams of Steve Wynn. They go back inside, where Cher belts out 'If I Could Turn Back Time' to a packed auditorium.

The camera pans around the scene and takes in the assembled stars. The Doge's Palace is centre stage, framed on one side by the Ca' d'Oro and on the other by the Rialto Bridge, which in turn leads straight to the bell tower of San Marco. It is as if the chief monuments of La Serenissima have huddled together for a group snap. Together, they resemble the seductive canvases that Canaletto painted to help his English *milordi* remember their grand tours.

It's all a set, of course, and the fanciest camerawork can't hide it. The Grand Canal, the narrow lanes, and the Piazza San Marco have been turned into interiors: vast sound stages where the soft evening is carefully lit, air-conditioned, and set to the muted strains of Vivaldi. It is always dusk here, the time when it is no longer necessary to do anything other than stroll, sit down with a drink, and imagine the pleasures of the night to come. This interior city has been freed from the four seasons and then set to their soundtrack.

The Venetian is Venice as it should be: a delightful sequence of spectacles, a city that will never flood, never grow old or cold, a place where nothing untoward ever happens. Nobody says it's real — the receptionist carefully points that fact out to arriving guests — but it's a helluva show, thought through right down to the very last detail. Even the candy-striped mooring posts for the gondolas are made to lean slightly, as if they had spent decades sinking into the Venetian mud. The canals have been repainted several times to get the blue just right, and there were fierce debates about the sky in the Piazza San Marco: should the clouds be projected, painted, or made of fluff hung on fishing wire?

The Venetian is not just a great set. The extras are perfect as well: the valets in the porte cochère are dressed as gondoliers, the security guards as *carabinieri*, and the cocktail waitresses as scantily clad harlequins. Characters from the *Commedia dell' Arte* stroll down the narrow lanes and perform in the piazza. They are listed in the hotel brochure as 'Streetmosphere'. At the Enoteca San Marco, brusque waiters are clad in stonewashed jeans and crisp white shirts; they sport Gucci sunglasses on top of their heads, and will serve only Peroni lager. The tourists, of course, are picture-perfect too, as they peer from the windows of the Bridge of Sighs, and lean, sighing, on the Ponte della Paglia.

* * *

A motto appears on the screen: 'Authenticity is the basis for fantasy.' The Venetian is both at the same time, reflects Qian Qichen. It's a film of a city, a place of edited highlights spliced together with all the boring bits left on the cutting-room floor. It's Venice turned inside out, illuminated and set to music for dramatic effect. It's a story with a happy ending, told just as a Hollywood director might tell it.

And Venice is only one among many locations that have been through the elaborate Las Vegas post-production process. As the Venetian dissolves on the screen, another video begins.

Catherine Deneuve drives up the Champs Elysées, rides to the top of the Eiffel Tower and presses a button that launches a floral explosion of fireworks into the Vegas sky. Leaning out into the hot night she sees Lake Como, surrounded by a rocky shore dotted with Roman pines and romantic villas. She just has time to hear the piped chirruping of cicadas before the scene bursts into song. As the voices of Céline Dion and Andrea Bocelli rise into the night, so does the lake itself, in hundreds of fountains dancing in time to the music. The elegant French actress espies the Brooklyn Bridge decked out in fairy lights; the Statue of Liberty; the façade of Grand Central Station; and, rising above them all, the New York skyline, glittering as romantically as ever it might over the East River. She can hear the cries of the taxicab passengers as, strapped into their seats, they career on crazy rollercoaster tracks that twist around the great towers. Further out, beyond the Statue of Liberty, she can make out visions of other places and times: the towers and battlements of the Excalibur, the gnomic black pyramid of the Luxor, the gilded towers of Mandalay Bay.

And somewhere beyond them all, down there in the desert, is an old sign that now stands more or less on its own by Route 91. In cheery, obsolete Perspex letters it says: 'Welcome to Las Vegas.'

When they first put the sign out there, Vegas had looked like Vegas: a strip of flashing neon in the desert. It was Glitter Gulch. Now Vegas looks like everywhere else. It's just like Venice, a city confected from the stolen images of others.

* * *

Qian Qichen looks at the palace his People's Republic has stolen from its imperial past. He thinks of the portrait of Chairman Mao hung over the central entrance to the Forbidden City. Now the people stream in and out under Mao's image through a portal that only the emperor was allowed to use, before history disposed of him.

Once upon a time no-one left the Middle Kingdom of the emperor, and his millions of subjects were unaware of the existence of other worlds. They did not believe Marco Polo when he told them stories about Venice. Perhaps they still wouldn't. Unless, that is, someone rebuilt it in front of their very eyes.

Sheldon G. Adelson sees a smile flicker over the impassive face of Qian Qichen, and the potentate watches Adelson's eyes widen as he sees it happen. It feels good being able to manipulate the third-richest man in the US with a twitch. The construction of the Venetian in Las Vegas cost Adelson hundreds of millions of dollars; but he's sure earned them back, as he might say. As he stands in front of the Vice-Premier of China, his Sands Corporation boasts 28,000 employees. It has a stock value of around $100 a share, and there are some 355 million shares; Adelson controls at least two-thirds of them. Sheldon G. Adelson is the ruler of an extensive empire, whose heart is in the Doge's Palace in the Venetian. His reach extends to Singapore, Israel, and Pennsylvania; and now he's got his eye on the Cotai Peninsula.

* * *

'The business case,' says the voice. Facts and figures flash over the screen; but good communist that he is, Qian Qichen gets the feeling that he might not have quite the same spin on them as the one Adelson would like him to.

The Venetian contains some 14,000 inhabitants, who live in three towers some thirty-five storeys tall. Every morning they awake and fumble for the remote, switching on the TV in the bathroom when they meant to open the curtains. They stumble down the corridors and wait for one of eighty lifts to arrive. The lifts are always crowded.

Downstairs they sip a coffee and watch the people go by on the Grand Canal, or they gorge themselves in the Grand Lux Café, or they eat a McBreakfast in the Food Court. If they have to work they make their way to the convention centre, where five vast floors of meeting space are designed to anticipate every one of their needs. If they don't, they lie by one of ten swimming pools and watch Kevin Federline being thrown out of the Tao Beach Club, or they retire to an air-conditioned cabana where they watch it on TV.

If they are bored of the pool they visit the casino, all 120,000 square feet of it. High rollers can retreat to private suites where cocktail waitresses have their favourite drink ready before they have even thought of asking for it. If they are bored of gambling they shop at Barneys and Bottega Veneta, dawdling over handbags, shoes, and executive toys. If they are bored of shopping they eat at one of eleven fine dining restaurants, or at one of the nine more casual establishments and two food courts nearby. All tastes are catered for by the extensive army of talented chefs overseen by Wolfgang Puck.

If the resort guests get bored of shopping and eating, there is always the theatre – *The Phantom of the Opera*, or the *Blue Man Group*, or the Cirque du Soleil, or just some cabaret. Afterwards, if they don't head back to gambling, they go clubbing at Tao, to check out whether the sisters at the bar are Olsen or Hilton.

There used to be an art gallery at the Venetian, a branch of the Guggenheim. Designed by the prominent European architect Rem Koolhaas, it was a casket of treasures clad in corten steel. The first exhibition showcased masterpieces of Impressionism. The second, curated by the *enfant terrible* Frank Gehry, addressed itself to *The Art of the Motorcycle*. The gallery is closed now. No-one needs to look at art when they're in Las Vegas.

The 14,000 citizens of the Venetian are looked after by about the same number of servants. Silent Mexicans push cleaning trollies up and down the carpeted corridors; punchy actors read the incomprehensible menus in the restaurants; inscrutable Eurasian girls deal cards and spin the wheels of fortune. They are the permanent inhabitants of the city; but their sole reason for existence is to service the temporary guests.

And while the citizens of the Venetian wallow in luxury, their every move is tracked by security cameras discreetly mounted into chandeliers and the belt buckles of frescoed goddesses. No sooner have they opened the minibar, or lifted a box of cookies from the tray, than infrared sensors have charged their credit cards. If they've maxed out their cards at the tables, they can't even get back into the lift to return to their rooms and pack.

Not that there's any point in leaving. If they do, they find only more Venetians. Across the moats of freeway that surround the resort is just another casino floor where beautiful Eurasian waitresses pollinate the gaming tables with brightly coloured cocktails. Wolfgang Puck is running the high-end restaurants here too, and the Cirque du Soleil is once again performing in the theatre. Every business need is met in the convention centre, and there are air-conditioned cabanas by the pool.

None of the 14,000 citizens of the Venetian stay there for more than a few days. After their holiday, they fly home to Boston or Pittsburgh or Minneapolis, relieved to see the rainy sky. But even weeks later, as they leisure-shop in the heritage mall, or listen to Vivaldi while on hold with a customer-service representative, they're still in Vegas.

∗ ∗ ∗

They're still in Vegas even if they go to Venice, moored like a cruise liner in an Adriatic lagoon. Some 74,000 people arrive there every morning. If they have to work, they catch the early train or bus to avoid those who wander in later. If they don't, they sit in a café and sip a coffee and nibble a croissant, watching the people go by.

When they have had enough of watching other tourists, the guests stroll the streets and shop. They dawdle over shoes and handbags, glittery masks and fauns of spun glass. They rummage through junk stalls, hoping to find some forgotten treasure of La Serenissima or the Carnival. When they are tired of shopping they queue up to pay the entry fees for the galleries and the *scuole* and the churches: the Guggenheim, the Accademia, the Frari, San Giovanni e Paolo, San Zaccaria. If the attraction is crowded, they are allowed ten minutes to look around, wandering through interiors piled with the relicts of a Serenissima that no longer exists.

When they are sated with art they eat carpaccio and drink bellinis in the innumerable restaurants that line the squares and the canals; and when they are finished with eating they go to the Fenice to see an opera. They don't go to the cinema: outside the annual Film Festival, there isn't one. They don't go clubbing: there aren't any clubs.

And then they fumble their way to bed. There are countless accommodations to choose from, ranging from the smart efficiency of the Danieli Business and the isolated luxury of the Cipriani to the rather more spartan arrangements of the youth hostel on the Giudecca. That's in addition to the thousands of bed and breakfasts and furnished flats available for short-term letting.

The permanent residents of Venice are a tiny number compared to the 11 million that visit them every year. There were 150,000 of them in 1950, but by 2008 there were only 58,000. Twice as many people die as are born here. At this rate, the city will be completely empty of permanent inhabitants by the year 2034

People can't afford to stay: many of the flats have been turned into holiday lets, and the prices of the ones that are left have skyrocketed. There's a dwindling number of schools and precious little space for children. The residents depart in droves for the suburbs on the mainland, where houses are cheaper and there are actually things to do.

One might imagine that a place confronted by certain and imminent extinction might devise radical strategies for its survival. But the inhabitants of Venice envisage no such progressive future. Instead they address themselves to the restoration of churches whose congregations have long since withered away, and the refurbishment of palazzi whose families are long defunct. When they discuss affordable housing, the construction of new buildings is not even considered.

And why would it be? The city is booming, sustained by tourists who come in their millions to see the paintings of Canaletto in three dimensions. Every two years there is a Biennale, a showcase for all that is modern and innovative in architecture, design, and the arts. Yet this festival inhabits a place that hasn't changed in centuries.

Early each morning, the former residents of Venice commute back to what was once their home. While their guests are sleeping, they walk to the districts and the houses where they were raised. They turn down the beds in their old bedrooms, set out the breakfasts in their old dining rooms, and polish the glasses in the bars in which they used to drink.

In April 2008, the last few permanent inhabitants staged a demonstration in the Piazza San Marco. They unfurled a banner upon which was written 'Venice is not a hotel'; but it is, for all their protestations. After a few days their guests fly home to Paris, Edinburgh, or Munich. Perhaps they are relieved to see the rainy skies. It is only a few months later, as they wander round the old factory sensitively reconditioned as an arts space, or drink in the elegant bar that used to be a bank, or drive out to their weekend cottage in a village full of other weekend cottages, that they realize that they are still in Venice.

* * *

Qian Qichen is well schooled in Marxist philosophy, and he calls to mind a few snatches of Guy Debord. The citizens of the Venetian, he thinks, live lives 'presented as an immense accumulation of spectacles', where 'everything that was directly lived has receded into a representation'. Their world has become 'a separate pseudo-world that can only be looked at. The specialization of images of the world evolves into a world of autonomized images where even the deceivers are deceived. The spectacle is a concrete inversion of life, an autonomous movement of the nonliving.'

It's not so bad, thinks Qian, that separate pseudo-world, that autonomous movement of the nonliving. He is considering the millions of his subjects who have never travelled anywhere except to migrate to the great cities in search of work. They have never been on holiday. They have never had the luxury of wandering about, bored, wondering what to look at next. They have never been able to be the quiescent consumers of spectacles. Perhaps it would be good for them.

Sheldon G. Adelson senses that the brass ring is nearly within his grasp. He went to a soirée once with a load of intellectual scientists, but he didn't think much of their endless discussions about the meaning of life. He later told an interviewer: 'If I make other people feel good, I feel good! I literally, mentally, went like – it's over with! I don't have to think about that issue ever again in my life.'

The Eastern potentate and the Western purveyor of invisible cities both think of something Steve Wynn once said of his creations: 'We start with one question. "Who are these people and what do they want?" The answer controls everything we do. We respond to the emotional and psychological desires of our visitors. If this place has any other redeeming feature, I don't know what it is.'

If you already know everything that people want, and if the sole purpose of everything you do is to deliver it, then you have a created a world in which every desire is anticipated, satisfied, and ultimately dictated. God gave mankind free will in the Garden of Eden. The creators of Vegas didn't. Wynn once said, 'Las Vegas is sort of like how God would do it if he had money.' He wasn't joking.

Sheldon G. Adelson conjures up one last invisible city. He hands Qian Qichen the mockup of a glossy brochure that bears the image of the Venetian and the subtitle 'Macao':

> Even as this city moves forward, it has preserved its rich, European legacy for future generations to relive the past as they walk along cobble-stoned paths and gaze up at centuries-old temples and churches ...
>
> The fully integrated resort-hotel features 3000 all-suite guest rooms, one million square feet of Grand Canal Shoppes, a 15,000-seat Cotaistrip® CotaiArena™, 1.2 million square feet of convention and meeting facilities and a purpose-built theater for ZAIA™, the new resident show from the world-renowned Cirque du Soleil® ...
>
> The Venetian Macao is a fully integrated resort where you can wine, dine, shop, stay, play and still do some serious business.

Qian Qichen's face brightens. 'Now you're speaking my language!' he says.

* * *

Once Adelson is safely installed in the car back to the airport, Qian Qichen stares at the empty Hall of the Purple Lights with its tawdry porcelain and its cracked tiles. The lights have gone up, and they expose centuries of the termites' gnawing. The oriental potentate reflects upon a conversation between Marco Polo and Kublai Khan.

> 'Sire, now I have told you about all the cities I know.'
>
> 'There is still one of which you never speak.'
>
> Marco Polo bowed his head.

'Venice,' the Khan said.

Marco smiled. 'What else do you believe I have been talking to you about?'

The emperor did not turn a hair. 'And yet I have never heard you mention that name.'

And Polo said: 'Every time I describe a city I am saying something about Venice ... To distinguish the other cities' qualities, I must speak of a first city that remains implicit. For me it is Venice.'

'You should then begin each tale of your travels from the departure, describing Venice as it is, all of it, not omitting anything you remember of it.'

The lake's surface was barely wrinkled; the copper reflection of the ancient palace of the Sung was shattered into sparkling glints like floating leaves.

'Memory's images, once they are fixed in words, are erased,' Polo said. 'Perhaps I am afraid of losing Venice all at once, if I speak of it. Or perhaps, speaking of other cities, I have already lost it, little by little.'

✳ ✳ ✳

It's August 2007, and the CEO of the Sands Corporation is talking to the press. 'The Venetian represents that first massive step in changing Macao ... to a full-fledged international, multi-day, multifaceted destination resort,' he says. 'It's like truncating the 76 years of development of Las Vegas into one place under one roof.'

Or a millennium and a half of Venetian history, perhaps. A week later, Adelson hands a beautiful woman down into a gondola. She smiles at him and he chuckles a little, because it is Diana Ross who reclines on the cushion by his ageing side. Their gondolier sings to them as he steers through the canals, and on the hour the deep bell of San Marco resounds in the night air. They scarcely notice the waves of the South China Sea lapping on the sands of the Cotai Strip outside.

THE WESTERN WALL, JERUSALEM

In Which Nothing, and Everything, Has Changed

THE ARCHITECTURE OF FAILED DIPLOMACY.
Scheme for Palestinian access to the Haram e-Sharif,
prepared by Eyal Weizman and Rafi Segal. Image cropped by the author.

Inheritance

*T*he last place whose secret life is recounted in
this book is older by far than the Parthenon, and in some quarters much better known;
but it makes an odd sort of tourist attraction. It is surrounded by a security cordon
tighter than most airports. Closed-circuit cameras focus on its crumbling stones, and every
visitor must pass through a metal detector manned by soldiers. The T-shirts sold by local
hawkers are not just the usual cheery souvenirs. 'Guns 'n' Moses', some of them say; 'Uzi
Does It, Israel'. Many guided tours around the excavations at this site culminate in
communal prayers and group photographs under the Israeli flag. Nearby, exhibits are
inscribed with the names of soldiers who died to make it possible for Jews to visit this
place at all.

The Parthenon is a ruin in two senses. Its stones are crumbling, and the original
reason for its existence has receded far into the past: it has become heritage. This place is,
on the other hand, for better or for worse, a living inheritance. It is so controversial that
no-one even knows what to call it, for every name is loaded with sectarian significance.
To the Jews the site is Har Babyait, the Temple Mount; to the Muslims it is the Haram
e-Sharif, the Noble Sanctuary. The British administrators of the Palestine Mandate

referred to its western boundary as the Wailing Wall. The term used by BBC newscasters today is the Western Wall. On Al Jazeera they call it the Al-Buraq Wall, after Muhammad's winged steed. To Jews, it's simply the Kotel — the wall.

Jews are forbidden by rabbinical edict to visit the interior of their Temple Mount; and anyone who does so, dissident Jew or curious Gentile, is subjected to the most stringent security checks. The bridge that leads into the enclosure is scattered with confiscated Bibles and Torahs, for it is forbidden to take them onto the Muslim Haram. Riot shields are stacked by the door, ready for the next bout of sectarian violence. Once you're in, there is no museum, no guidebook, no souvenir shop. The Noble Sanctuary is a rare thing in the contemporary world: a historic site that has resisted the siren call of tourism.

At the Western Wall just outside the sanctuary, meanwhile, are people who have travelled thousands of miles to touch its stones. If they can't come themselves, they email messages which are posted between the cracks on their behalf. Skiploads of them are burned every day. In Colorado Springs, an evangelical Christian organization is building a 50-tonne scale model of the wall at its headquarters. It expresses its solidarity with Israel, it says.

The cities of Western Europe have turned into a realization of the architect's dream: the buildings of their past have become static exhibits in a monumental museum. Elsewhere, however, ancient buildings are still stolen, appropriated, copied, translated, simulated, restored, and prophesied. They still change as they have always done, and they do so because they still excite passions beyond the merely aesthetic. In a reversal of the story of the Parthenon, Hindu extremists tear down a mosque in Ayodhya and build a temple in its ruins. In Japan, Shinto devotees rebuild the holy house of the Ise shrine every twenty years to exactly the same design — they have been doing so for nearly two millennia. In Indonesia, whole villages are dismantled, transported, and rebuilt as dining pavilions in luxury resorts, where the waiters are dressed like peasants in some eighteenth-century capriccio. Outside the confines of the West, historic buildings are not imprisoned in the timeless rapture of the architect's dream, but overflow its fixed frame and impose themselves on the present. History has not come to an end.

ON THE AFTERNOON OF 14 FEBRUARY 2004, THE SKY TURNED DARK OVER Jerusalem and it started to snow. In the middle of the city there was an open plaza with an ancient wall on one side of it; and high up in this wall, at the summit of a cobbled ramp leading up to it from the plaza, there was a door. As the snow turned to rain, the walls supporting the ramp started to bulge and seep. Two days later they crumbled, exposing a huge scar of raw earth and scattering a heap of rubble on the shiny paving stones of the plaza.

The authorities closed the door and cordoned off the area at the base of the ramp. It was too dangerous for tourists to use it, they said. The problem was, the ramp had been the only way that tourists could get to the door that led to the other side of the wall. The authorities couldn't just leave the ramp the way it was; but they couldn't make up their minds as to what to do about it, either. Nothing happened until December, when they announced that they'd be building a timber walkway between the plaza and the door in the next few months.

This wooden structure was only a temporary solution, and about a year after the storm a local architect submitted plans for a more permanent replacement. The remains of the collapsed ramp would be removed, enlarging the open space at the foot of the wall, and the walkway would be replaced by a concrete bridge over the plaza that would take visitors right up to the door.

The only difficulty was that the ramp, like everything else in Jerusalem, was an antiquity. It was known as the Mugrabi path, and a thorough archaeological survey of the site would be required before work could begin. This was another source of delay; but the interim wooden walkway was still in place, and the wall had been standing there for two thousand years. There was plenty of time, it seemed. Then another blizzard in early 2007 raised the spectre of further collapse, and the archaeologists were forced to begin on 6 February.

Suddenly things started to move very fast. On 7 February thousands of Palestinians gathered around the ramp to protest against the excavations. Their imams threatened an uprising, and the Palestinian Authority claimed that Israeli bulldozers were trying to undermine the great Al-Aqsa Mosque on the other side of the wall, inside the Noble Sanctuary. Abas Zkoor, an Arab member of the Israeli legislature, supported them: he visited the excavation site and pointed out the remains of a modest medieval mosque buried amid the ruins of the ramp earmarked for removal. There was a riot at Friday prayers and the police fired rubber bullets into the crowd. On 9 February a crowd in Nazareth waved banners accusing Israel of starting the Third World War.

The Prime Minister of Israel was forced to make a statement:

The restoration of the Mugrabi path after the place collapsed and was declared a dangerous structure was done in complete coordination with all parties, including foreign countries, relevant Muslim officials, and international bodies. As has been explained, this work is being

carried on outside the Temple Mount, and the repairs do not constitute any damage to the Mount or Islamic holy places.

But that didn't seem to satisfy anyone. Ayatollah Khamenei, the religious
leader of Iran, thundered: 'Islam should show a serious reaction to the Zionist
regime's insult.' The Israeli ambassador in Cairo was given a dressing-down,
while Egypt's parliament discussed whether to rescind their 1979 treaty with
Israel. One member of the ruling Egyptian party proclaimed that 'nothing will
work with Israel except for a nuclear bomb that wipes it out of existence'. King
Abdullah of Jordan called on the US to prevent Israel from continuing the
excavations. The President of Turkey sent a group of Islamic archaeologists to
inspect the site; they found no wrongdoing, but were dismissed by the rest of
the Arab world as Zionist patsies. UNESCO, the cultural arm of the United
Nations, demanded that the excavations cease until they had been able to
prepare a report.

A week after the archaeologists had begun, work stopped, and the scheme
for the replacement bridge was withdrawn. An Israeli Minister suggested that
the project be suspended to avoid compromising Israeli interests at an upcom-
ing Middle East Peace Conference. But once that conference was over, it was
back to business as usual. Another plan for the bridge was submitted; it too
was denounced at Friday prayers, rubber bullets were fired once more, and the
head of UNESCO had to be called in to mediate. At the time of this writing,
the excavation, conservation, alteration – call it what you will – of the
Mugrabi path remains incomplete. It's an insoluble problem for now, but a
stalemate cannot be sustained for long. The temporary wooden walkway itself
is deteriorating, and all it will take is another storm for the whole structure to
collapse.

Still, neither side in the dispute will budge. The wall, and the holy sites
on the other side of it, have an awesome fascination for both of them. For the

Jews, the wall is the boundary around the habitation of what they call the *Shekhinah*. The Muslims speak of the *Sakina*. It is something for which there is no word in modern English; we used to call it the Glory of the Lord.

✳ ✳ ✳

It's not the first time that archaeology has sparked a dispute between Israel and Islam. The Waqf, the Muslim authority that controls the day-to-day affairs of the Noble Sanctuary, has consistently opposed Israeli attempts to excavate the wall that surrounds it.

There is a warren of tunnels running alongside the foundations of the Western Wall, hollowed out by an Israeli archaeological team under the leadership of Benjamin Mazar. They had started by digging at the southern end of the Western Wall, cutting away Ottoman, Mameluke, Crusader, Ummayad, Byzantine, and Roman remains to reveal a paved street running along the base of the Kotel. Both street and wall, they claimed, had been built by King Herod the Great in biblical times.

Further north, these Herodian remains are buried under the heart of the old city of Jerusalem – the Muslim quarter. If Mazar's archaeologists had tried digging from the surface there, they would have provoked the same sort of apocalyptic reaction that later attended the archaeological dig around the Mugrabi path. Instead, they proceeded horizontally along the base of the wall by clearing out one ancient cellar after another, removing tons of rubbish from Roman vaults entombed beneath the Muslim quarter buildings. The underground passage thus excavated stretches for half a mile or so, until the wall turns at the northwest corner of the Noble Sanctuary.

The Western Wall tunnels, as they are known, are open to the public. To tour them is to map the city from beneath: here and there a hole cut into the vaults overhead indicates the location of a well in a square above, or perhaps a trapdoor into somebody's house. The gigantic stones of the Kotel appear huger still when discovered in the rat runs that lead from cellar to cellar. Eventually the tour comes to an end. 'There is a door out here,' says the guide, 'but it's closed' – she pauses – 'for security reasons. You'll have to go back the way you came.'

The Israeli authorities tried to open the northern exit from the tunnels in 1996, but the inhabitants of the Muslim quarter erupted in protest at what they saw as an Israeli incursion into their part of the city. Fifteen Israeli soldiers and seventy of their own people were killed in the ensuing riots. Eventually the Israelis reached a deal with the Waqf. They would be allowed to open their door during daylight hours, and in return the Waqf would be granted permission to create a new mosque in the Haram.

The Waqf sent in the bulldozers, and by 2000 some six thousand tonnes of earth had been removed from the southwest corner of the Noble Sanctuary. Now Israel reacted with outrage. An archaeologist at Bar Ilan University demanded to know: 'Would anyone in the civilized world agree if some bulldozers were working on the Acropolis in Athens or the Pantheon in Rome, particularly without any type of archeological supervision?' The director of the Waqf replied that all work 'has been done under the close supervision of a team of professional Palestinian archaeologists ... They have examined samples of the excavated dirt and found no structures, artifacts or archaeological remains from any era.' But the Israeli authorities placed an embargo on the Waqf, ordering them to stop all work.

To this day the Haram is piled high with rubble and soil, which the Israeli authorities have decreed will remain there until Israeli archaeologists have been given access to sift through the evidence. The Waqf won't let them anywhere near it. Again and again the Muslim authorities have obstructed Israeli archaeology around the Western Wall. It raises the question, doesn't it, of what it is that Israel is trying to dig up – of what is buried under the Noble Sanctuary of the Dome of the Rock.

✳ ✳ ✳

Everyone knows the answer. About halfway down the tunnel that runs along the side of the Kotel, there is a small cave furnished with religious books. 'This is the holiest spot on the wall,' the guide whispers in the darkness. 'You can say a prayer if you like. There was a rose garden here, whose petals were used to make the incense the priests of the Temple of the Jews used in their ceremonies. It was just behind this section of the Kotel that the Holy of Holies once stood. The room behind this wall was the dwelling place of the *Shekhinah*.'

The Palestinians are convinced that the Israelis intend to restore the Temple of the Jews, and they point to a bewildering array of organizations established to that very end. The Yeshiva of the Crown of the Priests exists to conduct research into the rituals of the Temple. The society of the Temple Mount Faithful raises funds for the reconstruction of the temple from fundamentalist Christians in the United States. The Temple Institute runs a museum in which all the ritual vestments of the Temple are on display, waiting for the day that they can be put into use; they have been adorned with gems and jewellery collected from the devout by the Temple Women. Another group runs a rota system to ensure that there will always be a rabbi standing by the entrance to the Temple Mount dressed in the white robes of an ancient Levite; and yet another meets to discuss the breeding of a perfectly red heifer, the sacrifice of which was considered by all the ancient texts of Judaism to be the highest form of offering. Every few years, these groups gather under the auspices of the Temple Lovers to discuss their research and to organize visits to the Temple site. They dream of rebuilding the Temple and of making it ready for the *Shekhinah*, so that God may once more dwell among men.

This is not an innocent affair of restoration: unlike the Acropolis in Athens, the Temple Mount is not covered in obsolete ruins. The Temple of the Jews cannot be rebuilt unless the Dome of the Rock and the Al-Aqsa Mosque are demolished. That's all part of the plan of the Temple Lovers. There have already been countless attempts to destroy the shrines of the Haram e-Sharif with mortar attacks, machine gun fire, and arson. It's not just mindless aggression: some of the attacks have been deliberately encouraged by rabbis who mutter that, in their observation of historical niceties, 'the archeologists sold out to the enemy'. Leaflets handed out by activists are clear in their demands: 'The time has come to do what should have been done a long time ago. Government of Israel, remove the Gentiles and the Arabs from the Temple Mount.'

The government of Israel officially condemns this sort of extremism and tells the Waqf that it has nothing to fear. The Waqf doesn't believe it, for of all the assaults on the Haram e-Sharif, the most extreme was that committed by the government of Israel itself.

* * *

At dawn on 7 June 1967, the third day of the Six Day War, the Israeli army invaded the Arab part of Jerusalem. By eleven o'clock the chief army rabbi, Shlomo Goren, was blowing the *shofar* at the Kotel. His young soldiers, exhausted and bloodstained, fell on the stones and wept. Then they went up to the door high in the ancient wall and they forced it open. They found themselves in the Haram e-Sharif, standing before the Dome of the Rock; but to them it was the Temple Mount, the site of the Holy of Holies, the dwelling place of the *Shekhinah*. One young man later recalled: 'I stood there in the place where the High Priest would enter once a year, barefoot after five plunges in the Mikveh [the ritual bath] ... but I was shod, armed and helmeted, and I said to myself: this is how the conquering generation looks.'

On the last day of the war, Israeli soldiers entered the Arab houses of the Mugrabi quarter next to the Western Wall and gave their inhabitants three hours to pack their belongings and leave. The houses were insanitary slums, the soldiers said, and they were going to be demolished. Days later there was a vast plaza where the houses had been, and crowds of celebrating Israelis. Just one piece of the old Mugrabi quarter survived the devastation: a cobbled ramp leading up to a door high in the wall. Deprived of the houses that once supported it on either side, the ramp looked insecure, but everyone decided to leave it as it was. It would be fine for now.

Eventually the United Nations condemned the occupation of Jerusalem and the destruction of the Mugrabi quarter, and in a gesture of reconciliation the Israelis returned the Haram e-Sharif to the jurisdiction of the Waqf. They kept the keys to the door at the top of the Mugrabi path, though – they still have them. As Teddy Kollek, the mayor of Jerusalem, said at the time, 'we need to establish facts on the ground'. Once you have those, international resolutions and condemnations carry all the weight of hot air.

The facts weren't just on the ground, but under it, too. On 27 June, the Israeli government announced that any antiquities found in any excavation whatsoever in Jerusalem belonged to the Israeli state. A month later they also declared that the whole of Jerusalem was an antiquity, and that no construction could proceed there without prior excavation. The combination of these orders neatly expropriated, de facto, the entire city.

And then the Israelis started digging. The destruction of the Mugrabi quarter was an obvious act of subjugation, but it was just the first of many. Benjamin Mazar's excavation of the Western Wall wasn't just an academic or even a historical exercise. Whether he intended it or not, the project was a strategic offensive. The tunnels that riddle the area are perforated with stairs and doors that allow the Israeli security forces to appear at will anywhere in the Muslim quarter at any time. The burgeoning Israeli presence brought about by the tunnels has also encouraged increasing numbers of Orthodox Jews who are buying properties in the Muslim quarter, establishing rabbinical schools and communes in the buildings there. Their yeshivas perch on the roofs of the Arab souk and survey the skyline of the Temple Mount; but they are also connected to the dark undercrofts of the medieval city, where the faithful pray at the buried foundations of the Kotel.

In 2000, right around the same time that the Israeli authorities placed their embargo on construction in the Haram, Yasser Arafat, head of the Palestinian Authority, and Ehud Barak, Prime Minister of Israel, met with Bill Clinton at Camp David for yet another peace conference. They weren't making much progress, and perhaps President Clinton wanted his guests to reflect on their intransigence. Noting that the Haram was built on top of the ground that the Israelis wanted to excavate, he proposed that in this area the border between Israel and the future Palestine should not be a vertical plane, but a horizontal one. That is to say, the surface of the Haram should belong to the Palestinian Authority, but the rock of the Temple Mount underneath it should belong to Israel. It was an absurd proposal, but in the context of Israel and Palestine nothing could have seemed more natural. Not, of course, that either side accepted the idea. The summit ended in failure, as everyone had expected.

After the collapse of the summit, the notoriously hawkish Ariel Sharon, then Israeli Minister for Defence, visited the Haram e-Sharif, although both sides in the conflict had begged him not to. He said to the waiting reporters: 'I came here as one who believes in coexistence between Jews and Arabs. I believe that we can build and develop together. This was a peaceful visit. Is it an instigation for Israeli Jews to come to the Jewish people's holiest site?' Then he walked off, surrounded by a thousand armed Israeli police. The next day, Muslims threw rocks down from the Haram onto the worshippers gathered at the Kotel below, and so began the second intifada.

Two years after Ariel Sharon's visit to the Temple Mount, Israeli architects Eyal Weizman and Rafi Segal mounted an exhibition for the World Congress of Architecture in Berlin. The key image in the show was a photomontage that showed a huge, hideous, concrete overpass crossing the Kidron

Valley between the Mount of Olives and the Haram e-Sharif. It was a proposal, Weizman and Segal baldly stated, to allow Palestinians to visit the Haram without encroaching on Israeli land, or even entering Jerusalem at all. It was a deliberately absurd response to show just how absurdly tangled the situation had become. Today, the closest that most Palestinians can get to their Noble Sanctuary is a concrete wall several miles away; and just as the Jews gather at the Kotel to mourn the loss of their holy place, so Palestinians go to this boundary to mourn the loss of theirs. In reference to that other infamous dividing wall, someone with a memory of Berlin has written on the concrete: 'Been there, done that.'

During the dispute about the Mugrabi path, the same cartoon kept on appearing in the Arab media: it showed a bulldozer marked with the Star of David undermining the Dome of the Rock. The Israeli authorities claim that all their work at the Mugrabi site is just archaeology, and that there is nothing to worry about. But the Palestinians have seen quite enough of Israeli archaeology not to believe them.

∗ ∗ ∗

But it wasn't the Israelis who started digging in this troubled ground, nor was it the Palestinians: the first excavators at the site of the ancient temple were Anglo-Saxon Protestants. Even today, the chief features of the Western Wall bear English names. At its southernmost end, a lump of stone indicates the broken remains of a bridge known as Robinson's Arch, surveyed by Edward Robinson, an American missionary who was sent to the Holy Land in the 1830s. Below the Mugrabi Gate, partially hidden by the infamous crumbling ramp, may be seen the gigantic lintel of Barclay's Gate, discovered by another American missionary in the 1840s. The largest chamber in the tunnels is vaulted by a Roman arch named for Major General Sir Charles Wilson, who surveyed Jerusalem in the 1860s for the British Royal Engineers.

Edward Robinson had come to the Holy Land as a missionary, but he was quite aware of the political dimensions of his work:

> The people in general in this part of the country were ready to give us information, so far as they could; and seemed not to distrust us ... The inhabitants everywhere appeared, for the most part, to desire that the Franks [i.e. Western Europeans] should send a force among them. They were formerly tired of the Turks; they were now still more heartily tired of the Egyptians; and were ready to welcome any Frank nation which should come, not to subdue, (for that would not be necessary), but to take possession of the land.

In 1865 the British established the Palestine Exploration Fund, which sought to know everything that could be known about that part of the world. For the devout Protestant Britons of the PEF, the Holy Land was no *terra incognita*. It was a region whose ancient history they already knew intimately from a Bible in which they believed absolutely. It was a place whose true and sacred geography lay dormant under the sleepy Arab villages and farms that had buried it for centuries. The excavation of this land was therefore a religious duty. Gathering knowledge of the Holy Land was not science, but an act of piety.

And dominion over the Holy Land would be an act of piety on a monumental scale. At the founding of the PEF, the Archbishop of York spoke with breathtaking confidence: 'The country of Palestine belongs to you and me. It is essentially ours. It is the land from which news came of our redemption. It is the land we turn to as the foundation of all our hopes. It is the land to which we look with as true a patriotism as we do for this dear old England.'

The Muslim authorities were well aware of the intentions of the British, and they consequently forbade them to make any excavations in the Haram. The explorers, of course, ignored the prohibition. Charles Warren, an officer in the British Royal Engineers (and later the chief of the London Metropolitan Police at the time of Jack the Ripper), rented properties around the south of the Haram e-Sharif and dug deep shafts through which he penetrated into the ancient vaults of the mount. Hidden among the rubble he found the 'Great Sea', a vast cistern carved into the rock, and numberless other caverns.

These exploits were more than imperial derring-do: they were pursued with true missionary zeal. Robinson and Warren had been appalled by the Christians that they found living in the land of Christ, sunk in Byzantine rituals and superstitions. The imperial powers hoped to save these Christians from their error and convert them to the more rational precepts of Protestantism. Impressing the locals with the scientific methods of history, archaeology, and geography would, the missionaries assumed, replace their childish cosmologies with a modern world view.

The British weren't too impressed with the religious practices of the other natives of the Holy Land either. They observed how the Jews used to stand before a ruined wall in the middle of Jerusalem, weeping and rocking with grief; and with amused detachment they called it the Wailing Wall.

* * *

The Jews weep at the wall because it is the only thing left of their Temple. Referring to the Muslim buildings of the Haram e-Sharif, the Spanish poet Yehuda al-Haziri wrote: 'What torment to see our Holy Courts turned into an alien temple! We tried to turn our faces away from this great and majestic church now raised on the site of the ancient tabernacle where once providence had its dwelling.' And the Jews weep, also, because the wall is the closest they will ever get to the place where the Temple once stood. This is not only the result of Islamic control of the site. Somewhere under the Haram on the Temple Mount is the site of the Holy of Holies; and the Holy of Holies is so sacred that it can only be entered by the High Priest, purified and barefoot, and then only once a year, on the day of Yom Kippur. Any Jew who enters the Haram runs the risk of treading accidentally on the sacred spot and committing a grave blasphemy. It is for this reason that most rabbis warn Jews against going into the sanctuary.

In 1850, Abdullah, a prominent Jew of Bombay, attempted to buy the wall from the Ottoman authorities, and in 1887 Baron Edmond de Rothschild tried to buy the whole quarter of houses that faced it. In both cases their requests were refused. The Waqf had no objections to the Jews praying at the foot of the wall, but it was part of the Noble Sanctuary, and that was that. Any attempt to make it into a permanent place of worship was quickly suppressed. At one point, when the Jews erected a screen to separate the women from the men at prayers, a riot ensued and several hundred people were killed in the violence; the screen was made of nothing more than a row of chairs. When the mood took them, Muslims would taunt the Jews as they prayed at the Kotel, dropping stones onto them from the Noble Sanctuary above. They still do, from time to time.

In 1902, a German Jew by the name of A.S. Hirschberg went to Jerusalem and visited the wall. He was a modern sort of man, and he found Jerusalem a squalid sort of place; but as he approached the stones he found himself dissolving into tears, overcome by a strange sorrow he never knew he possessed. He later wrote: 'All my private troubles mingled with our nation's consciousness to form a torrent.' There can be no greater symbol of the tenacity and the suffering of the Jewish people than the fact that they seek God by worshipping at a ruin that, they are told, does not even belong to them. No wonder they are so keen to excavate as much of it as possible.

* * *

Jews have been fascinated by the archaeology of their Temple for centuries – for longer, in fact, than the modern notion of archaeology has existed at all.

The idea that the stones of the Western Wall somehow tell the story of a whole people is an ancient one.

In 1524, David Reuveni, a tiny man wrapped in expensive oriental silks, arrived in Venice. His brother Joseph ruled over the ten lost tribes of Israel by the River Sambation, which is a torrent of stone and fire that stands still only on the Sabbath day. At least, that's what he told the merchants of Venice. That was the story he gave to the Pope in Rome, and to King John of Portugal, and to Keiser Karel at Regensburg. 'The King of the Jews', as they indulgently permitted him to style himself, was a man with a mission. Merchant, Pope, emperor, and king were all quite happy to help him, since Reuveni proposed to lead an army against the Sultan Suleiman of Constantinople, the ruler of Jerusalem and their avowed enemy. They received him at court, and offered him horse and cannon and men.

But Reuveni overplayed his hand, for he was less interested in the overthrow of the sultan than in the coming of the Messiah. There was a stone in the Western Wall, he said, that had been placed there by Jeroboam in the time of King Solomon. The stone was cursed, he said, for it had been taken from a pagan temple, and the Redeemer would not arrive until it had been removed. The military campaign against the sultan was merely the prelude to this great event. The Jews he met urged Reuveni to keep quiet about the true nature of his plan, for his Christian sponsors would not want to hear about the appearance of a Messiah. The Jews feared that the usual reprisals would be visited on them all, but they were lucky: only Reuveni was put on trial. Dispatched to Spain for disposal at the hands of the Inquisition, he was burned at the stake in 1535.

The sultan whose downfall Reuveni had plotted was in fact more sympathetic to the Jews than his Christian peers were. He observed the devotion of the Jews to the ancient Temple wall, the way they would stroke and kiss it, and he ordered his architect Sinan to make a space so that they could worship there. Sinan cleared a lane at the foot of the wall, excavating the ground to make the wall taller, and he built a low enclosure around it so that the Jews could say their prayers undisturbed. They later told one another that the sultan had purified the site by washing it with rose water with his own royal hands, just as if he were his namesake, King Solomon himself.

✶ ✶ ✶

The Messiah anticipated by David Reuveni did not arrive, and today the Western Wall forms but a tiny and unprepossessing part of the Haram e-Sharif, the Noble Sanctuary, which is the second most sacred place in the Islamic world. A beautiful grove of olives and cypresses surrounded by stone arcades, the Haram is studded with shrines, which are strange and wonderful retellings in architecture of the stories the Jews and Christians tell about the place. There is the Dome of the Chain where, it is said, King Daoud used to sit in judgement on the people of Israel. There is the Chair of Suleyman, in which the king rested after building the Temple, and the Cradle of 'Isa, from which the son of Maryam preached while still a baby. The upper part of the sanctuary is approached through arcaded gates where, they say, the souls of all mankind will be weighed on Judgement Day.

At the southern end of the sanctuary stands the Al-Aqsa Mosque, which, like a medieval cathedral, has been rebuilt again and again since it was first constructed in the seventh century. The ivory pulpit was installed by Saladin, the Gothic rose window in the eastern transept was built by the Crusaders, and the white marble columns under the dome were the gift of Mussolini.

In the centre of the sanctuary stands the Dome of the Rock, built in the late seventh century by the Caliph Abd Al-Malik. Covered in brilliant blue tiles, the gilded dome rests on two rows of antique columns of rich serpentine and porphyry. Beneath it, the holy rock itself, scarred with centuries of devotion and abuse, protrudes through a hole in the marble pavement.

Al-Aqsa means 'the farthest', and all the splendours of the mosque of that name and of the Dome beside it commemorate a single enigmatic sura of the Koran:

Glory be to He
Who carried His servant by night,
From the Holy Mosque
to the Farthest Mosque,
the precincts of which
We have blessed.
So that We might show him
Some of Our signs.
Surely He is the All-Hearing,
The All-Seeing.

Like the tomb at Gloucester or the tale of the Holy House, it started out as a simple story; but it has been told again and again, each retelling an elaboration of the last.

One night Muhammad had awoken and made his way through the streets of Mecca to the *Ka'aba*, where he started to pray. The angel Gabriel appeared to him and led him over to a white winged steed tethered nearby. This marvellous creature was named Al-Buraq. The angel grabbed him by his ear, and Muhammad mounted. They flew through the air at great speed, stopping to pray in Medina, in Sinai, and in Bethlehem. Soon they were hovering over a walled city, gazing down at domed churches and colonnaded streets and the courtyards of palaces becalmed in the silvery light of a crescent moon. The jumble of houses lapped at the walls of a rectangular platform that overlooked the town, empty of all habitation, like a plinth awaiting a statue. Al-Buraq swooped down, and Muhammad tethered the creature to an iron ring he found hanging from the western wall of the platform. He picked his way through ruinous rubble towards a low outcrop of rock.

Standing around the rock was a group of old men silhouetted against the night sky. Muhammad recognized them all. There was Adam: 'This is where I first stepped on the earth when God cast me out of Paradise,' he said to Muhammad. And Ibrahim added: 'It is where I offered up my son Ishaq in sacrifice.' And Jakoub said: 'It is where I saw a ladder between Heaven and Earth.' And Mousa spoke: 'It is where they laid the Ark of the Covenant to rest.' And Suleyman said: 'This is where I built the Temple.' And 'Isa added: 'This is the place of the Temple whose destruction I prophesied.' Then all the prophets moved aside to let Muhammad pass, and he led them in prayer.

And then Muhammad ascended from the rock through the seven circles of Heaven and was shown the Heavenly Throne. When he was finished in Heaven he returned to the Western Wall, and mounted Al-Buraq, and flew back to Mecca. The ring to which Muhammad tethered his miraculous beast is still there. It was uncovered in the 1930s, and Muslims named the wall in the honour of the winged horse who had borne the Prophet.

Some seventeen years after Muhammad's night journey, his successor Omar captured Jerusalem from the Byzantine Empire. The citizens sent a proud message out of the gates to their conquerors: 'Bring us your caliph, and we shall give him the keys to our city.' And so Omar, who was a humble, pious man, donned his goat's-hair shirt, mounted his camel, and waited for the Byzantine Patriarch Sophronius to emerge from the city in clouds of incense and stiff golden robes. 'Show me your city,' said the caliph; and not without trepidation the patriarch led him through the streets to the church of the Holy Sepulchre, where he invited him to pray. 'I will not pray here,' said Omar, 'lest I encourage my brethren to do so as well. You can keep your church. We shall not build our mosque here. Take me to Al-Aqsa.'

The patriarch was perplexed, for he did not know what Al-Aqsa was. 'I want to see the Mosque of Daoud,' said Omar. The patriarch thought he understood. He led the caliph up to Mount Zion, where King David is buried, but the caliph was not satisfied. 'I will not pray here,' said Omar. 'Take me to Al-Aqsa, as I said. Take me to the Mosque of Suleyman.'

'The Temple of Solomon?' asked the patriarch. 'But it is cursed and cast down. We leave our rubbish there in order to win merit in Heaven.' Omar nodded, and they went down to a place where the houses and the lanes were built against a mighty wall. The gateway in the wall had been blocked with all sorts of refuse; but Omar had his men remove it, and he made Sophronius go before him, scrambling up over the fallen stones onto the empty plateau above. Omar picked up a handful of dust and threw it over the wall to purify the desolate spot. Then he saw a low outcrop of rock that protruded from the filth littering the site, and he walked towards it. 'This is where it happened,' he said. 'We can pray here.'

Omar retreated to speak to his advisors. Among them was a certain Kaab ibn Ahbar, who had had once been a Jew. Ibn Ahbar told Omar the stories he could remember about the ruined mountaintop, and he reminded him that before Muhammad had chosen Mecca he had instructed Muslims to turn to Jerusalem in prayer. 'Build your mosque to the north of the mountain,' ibn Ahbar suggested, 'so that when we pray we can face the new *Qiblah* and the old at the same time.' But Omar turned on him: 'Are you not a true Muslim?' he said. 'Let us place the mosque to the south of the mountain, so that when we pray we face only Mecca. Mecca alone is the true *Qiblah* of the faithful.'

Omar's workmen began to build their Noble Sanctuary on top of the ruins of the Temple of the Jews. They almost succeeded in covering it completely, but in two places its remains are still visible. The living rock enshrined in mosaic splendour under the gilded dome and the crumbling stones of the Al-Buraq Wall remind both Muslim and Jew that, like it or not, the *Shekhinah*, the *Sakina*, the Glory of the Lord belongs to and eludes them both.

* * *

In the year 70, more than five centuries before Omar picked his way through its antique ruins, Titus, son of the Emperor of Rome, met with his generals to decide what to do with the Temple of the Jews. They were reaching the end of a long and bloody campaign. They had captured most of Palestine, and, indeed, most of the city of Jerusalem; but the rebels were holed up inside the Temple and showing no signs of surrender. Some of the aides, a general present at the meeting related, 'insisted that they should enforce the law of war' and destroy the building that the rebels were using as a fortress. 'Titus replied that even if the Jews did climb upon it for military purposes, he would not make war on inanimate objects instead of men, or, whatever happened, burn down such a work of art: it was the Romans who would lose thereby, just as their Empire would gain an ornament if it was preserved.'

But things didn't happen quite as Titus had planned: he hadn't reckoned with the tenacious attachment of the Jews to their Temple. His troops forced their way through the outermost walls that surrounded the sacred enclosure; but the Jewish rebels, instead of surrendering, retreated from the outer Court of the Gentiles into the Court of the Women. When the Romans fought their way into the Court of the Women, the rebels retreated into the Court of the Israelites. And when the Romans overran the Court of the Israelites, the Levites among the rebels retreated into the Court of the Priests, and the Jews who were not Levites fought to the death where they stood – refusing to retreat lest they defile the holy sanctuary of their Temple.

When the Romans forced their way into the Court of the Priests they found that 'around the altar the heap of corpses grew higher and higher, while down the sanctuary steps poured a river of blood'. And they saw that the few rebels who were still alive had climbed up onto the roof of the Temple, whence they bombarded the Romans with missiles torn from the building itself. The

Romans were so enraged that, despite Titus's prohibition, some of them set light to the shrine.

As the flames licked around the building Titus observed that the Jews themselves did nothing to put out the fire, and he knew the battle was over. He walked into the Temple, past the seven-branched candelabrum on the south side and the bread of sacrifice on the north, and up to the golden chains that veiled the Holy of Holies, the dwelling place of the *Shekhinah*. He wanted to see the thing which the Jews were prepared to die for, the thing they would rather destroy than surrender. He wanted to see if all the stories about the Holy of Holies were true. They were. There was absolutely nothing there.

✶ ✶ ✶

After he had defeated the rebels, Titus had the Jews rounded up and locked into the ruins of their Temple, where 11,000 of them died as they waited to hear their fate. Some starved to death, some were slain by the soldiers. Others, who were strong, were taken to the mines in Egypt; but the tallest and most beautiful were taken to Rome for the triumph. You can still see them there: they are carved on the Arch of Titus in the ruins of the Forum, bearing the seven-branched candelabrum of the Temple of God up to the temple of Jupiter the Best and Greatest.

The Jews who survived were exiled and scattered across the face of the earth. Their Temple had been cast down; but every year on Passover, wherever they were, as they celebrated their ancient liberation from slavery in Egypt, they turned to one another and said: 'Next year in Jerusalem.' They still do.

And they have for centuries, for the Israelites have long been in exile, and they have long yearned for Zion. Abraham, the father of them all, had left the city of Ur with its mighty ziggurat and followed the calling of the Lord into the land of Canaan. Having left his ancestral temple behind, he offered his only son Isaac in sacrifice to the Lord on an empty mountaintop. When his grandson Jacob wandered out into the wilderness, he laid himself down to sleep on the same empty rock, and he witnessed the angels climbing a ladder from Earth to Heaven. The Temple Mount has been a sacred place to the Jews, they say, from time immemorial.

But while they have nursed affection for this place, the Jews have also long rejected any notion of a material god of stone or wood or gold who might demand a physical home. When the sons of Jacob were in exile in Egypt they were forced to build the idolatrous temples of the Egyptians, and they longed to return to the empty mountain where their ancestors had communed with the divine. They went out from Egypt, just as Abraham their forefather had left the idolatrous ziggurat of Ur behind him; and they worshipped an immortal and invisible being, who told them:

I am the LORD thy God, which have brought thee out of the land of Egypt, out of the house of bondage.

Thou shalt have no other gods before me.

Thou shalt not make unto thee any graven image, or any likeness of any thing that is in Heaven above, or that is in the Earth beneath, or that is in the water under the Earth.

Their God led them out into the desert, and to transport the laws he gave them, the Israelites made a portable ark, carried on two poles and hung with the dyed pelts of rams and badgers. At night they would erect a tent over this ark; and the *Shekhinah* would rest there until morning, when she would lead them again out into the wilderness in the form of a pillar of fire and cloud.

Eventually, after many trials, the Israelites returned to the empty mountain where Abraham had offered his sacrifice and Jacob had seen the angels climb between Earth and Heaven. King David danced before the ark as it was carried up to its final resting place. His son Solomon prepared to build a temple to house it, sending to Lebanon for cedar to build the roof and to Sheba for spices to burn upon the altar of the Lord.

But the Lord, who had roamed the empty desert as a pillar of cloud and flame, and who had forbidden his people to make an image of him, was somewhat ambivalent about Solomon's Temple. He spoke to the king, saying: 'Concerning this house which thou art in building, if thou wilt walk in my statutes, and execute my judgements, and keep all my commandments to walk in them; then will I perform my word with thee, which I spake unto David thy father: and I will dwell among the children of Israel, and will not forsake my people Israel.'

It was only a conditional promise – more of a warning, perhaps – but Solomon went ahead and built his Temple. His successors filled it with splendours so copious that prophet after prophet warned them against their vanity, reminding them that the Lord did not want their hecatombs and their vain ceremonies:

When ye come to appear before me, who hath required this at your hand, to tread my courts?

Bring no more vain oblations; incense is an abomination unto me; the new moons and sabbaths, the calling of assemblies ...

Four centuries after Solomon had built it, the Temple was sacked and the Israelites were sent into exile in Babylon. There they sat down and wept for what they had left behind, saying: 'If I forget thee, O Jerusalem, let my right hand forget her cunning. If I do not remember thee, let my tongue cleave to the roof of my mouth; if I prefer not Jerusalem above my chief joy.' And when they returned from exile they rebuilt the Temple of God.

It was a poor affair built amid the ruins of lost Jerusalem, and so it was refurbished under King Herod the Great, who made it larger and more magnificent than it had ever been in the time of Solomon. The Jews were so concerned that the sacrifices and rituals of the Temple would not be interrupted during construction that Herod had to assemble all the building materials on the spot before work began, to reassure his people that the building would be completed as he planned. Not a single day of worship was missed during the century it took to renovate the Temple, and the Jews proudly said to one another: 'He who has not seen the Temple of Jerusalem has never seen a beautiful building.'

It was a moment of hubris. Titus destroyed Herod's Temple within a few years of its completion. After it had been destroyed, the Israelites said to one another that God must have forsaken them because they had not walked in his statutes and executed his judgements. God was a pillar of fire and cloud that swirled in the empty desert; he had forbidden his people from imprisoning him in a form of any kind. The Israelites had built him a home, a vessel for the formless *Shekhinah*, but they had ended up worshipping the temple they had made rather than the divinity it contained. The Temple of the Jews had begun as a building, but it had become an idol.

✳ ✳ ✳

Go to the Western Wall any Friday evening, look lost, and you may be invited back to someone's house for the Sabbath meal. At precisely eighteen minutes before sundown, two candles are placed on the dining table and lit. The father of the house blesses his family, and then everyone takes a glass of wine, which is also blessed; and then the family wash their hands. The father blesses the two loaves of plaited bread that have been laid upon the table, and then everyone sits down to eat the Sabbath meal.

It is a simple ritual; but it's an ancient one, which has been handed down,

Sabbath after Sabbath, from the rituals of the Temple. In fact, it is the Temple itself, whose vanished walls are reconstructed in the laying of the table with candles, bread, and wine. Rabbi Isaac de Luria wrote a poem about it in the sixteenth century:

> *To southward I set*
> *the mystical candelabrum,*
> *I make room in the north*
> *for the table with the loaves*
>
> *...*
>
> *Let the* Shekhinah *be surrounded*
> *by six Sabbath loaves*
> *connected on every side*
> *with the Heavenly Sanctuary.*

The *Shekhinah* appears every Sabbath eve and then flits away until she reappears the next week, as ephemeral as snow. The boundary of the Temple that was built to house her, on the other hand, has become – and always was – an architectural idol, the idolatry of which has led to its own ruin. The ownership and the archaeology of the Wailing Wall, the Kotel, the Al-Buraq Wall – call it what you will – has become an insoluble problem, whose fixed terms of revenge and offence are as hard and as heavy a burden as stone.

That is to take the short-term view of the dreaming architect, to whom buildings appear fixed and permanent. Over time, the wall, like all of the buildings whose secret lives have been recounted in this book, has been ruined by barbarians, appropriated by different faiths, and copied by the faithful. Its story has been retold in Hebrew and Latin, Arabic and English. It has been excavated and restored in prophecies, and has become a tourist spectacle. It has been evolving for centuries, and in all likelihood it always will be.

All of this has taken place in the blinking of an eye. Like all architecture, the Western Wall is nothing more than a miraculous blizzard that will have turned to rain by morning.

Notes

Introduction

4   *The cloud-capp'd towers ...*
Shakespeare, *The Tempest*, Act IV, scene i.

5–6 *an assemblage of structures ...*
William Cullen Bryant, 'A Funeral Oration Occasioned by the Death of Thomas
Cole, Delivered Before the National Academy of Design, New York, May 4th,
1848.'
http://books.google.com/books?id=OL4UAAAAYAAJ

7   *the problem of fixing standards ...*
Le Corbusier, *Vers un Architecture*, tr. Frederick Etchells (Academy Editions
1987), p. 133 (first published 1923).

8   *Full fathom five ...*
Shakespeare, *The Tempest*, Act I, scene ii.

9   *there are large palaces ...*
Aldo Rossi, *The Architecture of the City*, tr. Diane Ghirardo and Joan Ockman
(MIT Press 1982), p. 27.

11   *when a place is lifeless or unreal ...*
Christopher Alexander, *The Timeless Way of Building* (Oxford University Press
1979), p. 36.

11   *cannot be made ...*
      Alexander, *The Timeless Way of Building*, p. xi.

12   *Anyone can be creative ...*
      Quoted in Jane Milling and Graham Ley, *Modern Theories of Performance*
      (Palgrave 2001), p. 57.

13   *No building is ever perfect ...*
      Alexander, *The Timeless Way of Building*, p. 479.

—   *we assume we are going to transform it ...*
      Alexander, *The Timeless Way of Building*, p. 485.

The Parthenon, Athens

19   *Make your house ready ...*
      Roy George, *The Life of Proclus: Life in Athens* (1999).
      http://www.goddess-athena.org/Encyclopedia/Friends/Proclus/index.htm

21   *There is a sort of bloom of newness ...*
      Plutarch, *Life of Pericles*, tr. John Dryden.
      http://classics.mit.edu/Plutarch/pericles.html

23   *No-one is to go to the sanctuaries ...*
      Michael Routery, *The First Missionary War: The Church Take Over of the Roman
      Empire* (1997), ch. 4.
      http://www.vinland.org/scamp/grove/kreich/chapter4.html

27   *A fortunate shot ...*
      Helen Miller, *Greece Through the Ages* (Dent 1972), p. 12.

30   *It is very pleasant to walk the streets here ...*
      John Tomkinson, *Ottoman Athens II*.
      http://www.anagnosis.gr/index.php?pageID=218&la=eng

—   *Take away everything that you can ...*
      Comte de Choiseuil Gouffier to Louis Sebastien Fauvel, quoted in Brian Cooke,
      The Elgin Marbles (British Museum Publications 1997), p. 71.

31   *To enter freely within the walls of the citadel ...*
      Cooke, *The Elgin Marbles*, p. 71.

32   *In amassing these remains of antiquity ...*
      Cooke, *The Elgin Marbles*, p. 82.

—   *You have lost your labour ...*
    Cooke, *The Elgin Marbles*, p. 83.

—   *Cold is the heart, fair Greece! that looks on thee ...*
    George Gordon, *Lord Byron, Childe Harold's Pilgrimage*, Canto II, stanza 15.

36   *A charming midsummer night's dream*
    Mary Beard, *The Parthenon* (Harvard University Press 2003), p. 100.

37   *Your majesty stepped today ...*
    Beard, *The Parthenon*, p. 100.

The Basilica of San Marco, Venice

48   *Rome is no longer in Rome ...*
    Charles Freeman, *The Horses of San Marco* (Abacus 2005), p. 2.

62   *these barbarians, haters of the beautiful ...*
    Niketas Choniates, *Historia*, tr. Bente Bjørnholt. Corpus Fontium Historiae
    Byzantinae, vol. XI (De Gruyter 1975).
    http://www.kcl.ac.uk/kis/schools/hums/byzmodgreek/Z304/NicetasSignis.htm

65   *The murder of the commander of the Libérateur ...*
    Freeman, *The Horses of San Marco*, p. 193.

Ayasofya, Istanbul

74   *for the glory and elevation of the Romans ...*
    Constantini Pophyrogeniti Imperatoris de Ceremoniis Byzantini, quoted in:
    http://web.clas.ufl.edu/users/kapparis/byzantium/Coronation_Ceremony.doc

76   *'Solomon, I have outdone thee!'*
    Quoted in Heinz Kaehler and Cyril Mango, *Hagia Sophia* (Zwemmer 1967),
    p. 18.

—   *seems somehow to float in the air ...*
    Procopius, *De Aedis*, tr. H.B. Dewing (Loeb Classical Library 1940).
    http://penelope.uchicago.edu/Thayer/E/Roman/Texts/Procopius/Buildings/
    1A*.html

—   *Wondrous it is to see ...*
    Paul the Silentiary, *Descriptio S. Sophiae*, tr. W. Lethaby and H. Swainson
    (Macmillan and Co. 1894), p. 52.

77   *knew not whether we were in Heaven or earth ...*
      Quoted from *The Russian Primary Chronicle* in Rowland Mainstone, *Hagia Sophia: Architecture, Structure and Liturgy of Justinian's Great Church* (Thames and Hudson 1988) p. 11.

78   *guide his laden vessel ...*
      Paul the Silentiary, *Descriptio S. Sophiae*, p. 52.

—   *a large flame of fire issuing forth ...*
      Nestor Iskander, quoted in Roger Crowley, *Constantinople: The Last Great Siege 1453* (Faber 2005), p. 179.

79   *Hurl your javelins ...*
      Emperor Constantine XI Palaiologos addressing his forces on 28 May, *Chronicle of the Pseudo-Sphrantzes*, quoted in Judith Herrin, *Byzantium: The Surprising Life of a Medieval Empire* (Penguin 2007), p. 22.

—   *In the name of Allah ...*
      Crowley, *Constantinople*, p. 1.

85   *this ancient building ...*
      Kaehler and Mango, *Hagia Sophia*, p. 10.

—   *The victorious Shah of them all ...*
      Robert Mark and Ahmet Çakmak, eds., *Hagia Sophia from the Age of Justinian until the Present* (Cambridge University Press 1992), p. 22.

88   *What a travesty it is! ...*
      George Young, quoted in Lawrence Kelly, ed., *A Traveller's Companion to Istanbul* (Constable and Robinson 1987), p. 245.

—   *The Caliphate, your office ...*
      Harold Courtenay Armstrong, *Gray Wolf: The Life of Kemal Ataturk* (New York: Capricorn Books, 1961), p. 201.

The Santa Casa of Loreto

104   *In order that you may bear testimony ...*
      Sister Katherine Maria MICM, 'The Holy House of Loreto'.
      http://www.catholicism.org/loreto-house.html

110   *Beholde and se, ye goostly folkes all ...*
      Richard Pynson, Ballade of Walsingham (1490), stanzas 1, 2.
      http://www.walsinghamanglicanarchives.org.uk/pynsonballad.htm

111   *O daughter, consider ...*
      Pynson, *Ballade of Walsingham*, stanzas 4, 5.

112   *O gracyous Lady, glory of Jerusalem ...*
      Pynson, *Ballade of Walsingham*, stanza 21.

116   *'Twas in the moon of wintertime ...*
      Jean de Brebeuf, 'The Huron Carol' (ca. 1643), tr. Jesse Edgar Middleton (1926).
      http://www.angelfire.com/ca2/cmascorner/Huron.htm

Gloucester Cathedral

125   *In winter woe befell me ...*
      Alison Weir, *Isabella: She-Wolf of France, Queen of England* (Jonathan Cape 2005),
      p. 264.

126   *sitting at the table in the abbot's hall ...*
      Historia et Cartarium Monasterii Sancti Petri Gloucestriae, quoted in David
      Welander, *The History, Art and Architecture of Gloucester Cathedral* (Alan Sutton
      1991), p. 144.

128   *took much delight in working with his own hands ...*
      Historia et Cartarium Monasterii Sancti Petri Gloucestriae, quoted in Welander, *The
      History, Art and Architecture of Gloucester Cathedral*, p. 150.

129   *The offerings of the faithful ...*
      Historia et Cartarium Monasterii Sancti Petri Gloucestriae, quoted in Welander, *The
      History, Art and Architecture of Gloucester Cathedral*, p. 146.

134   *died without having done anything ...*
      Historia et Cartarium Monasterii Sancti Petri Gloucestriae, quoted in Welander, *The
      History, Art and Architecture of Gloucester Cathedral*, p. 236.

137   *John Gowere ...*
      Welander, *The History, Art and Architecture of Gloucester Cathedral*, p. 254.

138   *Hic incipient constituciones ...*
      http://freemasonry.bcy.ca/texts/regius.html

140   *In the name of the Lord ...*
      Weir, *Isabella: She-Wolf of France, Queen of England*, pp. 203–4.

The Alhambra, Granada

158   *Had I been he ...*
Robert Irwin, *The Alhambra* (Profile Books 2005), p. 63.

159   *a gate where the roads bifurcate ...*
Oleg Grabar, *The Alhambra* (Penguin 1978), p. 57.

—   *His throne comprises the Heaven and Earth ...*
Irwin, *The Alhambra*, p. 34.

—   *I am like a bride ...*
Grabar, *The Alhambra*, p. 141.

—   *with how many fine draperies ...*
Irwin, *The Alhambra*, p. 33.

160   *He is the all-mighty ...*
Irwin, *The Alhambra*, p. 44.

—   *In this garden I am an eye ...*
Irwin, *The Alhambra*, p. 151.

—   *a pearl which adorns ...*
Grabar, *The Alhambra*, p. 124.

161   *The hands of the Pleiades ...*
Irwin, *The Alhambra*, p. 126.

—   *'No victor but Allah.'*
Irwin, *The Alhambra*, p. 33.

—   *And how many infidel lands ...*
Grabar, *The Alhambra*, p. 140.

163   *The palace was furnished ...*
The Arabian Nights, quoted in Irwin, *The Alhambra*, p. 15.

The Tempio Malatestiano, Rimini

173   *Sigismondo Malatesta was an illegitimate member ...*
Pius II, *Commentarii Sinea*, quoted in Franco Borsi, *Leon Battista Alberti Complete Edition* (Phaidon 1975), p. 128.

174   *Before you blooms and grass lie down ...*
Hugh Bicheno, *Vendetta: High Art and Low Cunning at the Birth of the Renaissance*
(Weidenfeld and Nicolson 2008), p. 170.

175   *so full of pagan images ...*
Pius II, *Commentarii Sinea*, quoted in Alberti, *Leon Battista Alberti Complete
Edition*, p. 128.

181   *I bear the horn that all may see ...*
Bicheno, *Vendetta*, p. 176.

—   *Sigismondo Pandolfo Malatesta, the son of Pandolfo ...*
I. Pasini, 'Il Tempio Malatestiano', Exhibition Catalogue, *Sigismondo Malatesta e
suo tempo* (Rimini 1979), p. 134.

183   *Offer supreme honour to those ...*
Leon Battista Alberti, *Fatum et Fortuna*, from the *Intercoenales*, quoted in Mark
Jarzombek, *On Leon Battista Alberti: His Literary and Aesthetic Theories* (MIT
Press 1989), p. 132.

185   *What we have written ...*
Leon Battista Alberti, *On the Art of Building in Ten Books*, tr. Joseph Rykwert,
Neil Leach, and Robert Tavernor (MIT Press 1988), p. 155.

—   *Examples of ancient temples ...*
Alberti, *On the Art of Building*, p. 154.

187   *The greatest ornament to the forum ...*
Alberti, *On the Art of Building*, p. 265.

188   *I affirm again with Pythagoras ...*
Alberti, *On the Art of Building*, p. 301.

—   *Beauty is that reasoned harmony ...*
Alberti, *On the Art of Building*, p. 156.

189   *Greetings. Your letters ...*
Robert Tavernor, *On Alberti and the Art of Building* (Yale University Press 1998),
p. 61.

—   *As for the business of the pier ...*
Tavernor, *On Alberti and the Art of Building*, p. 61.

190   *If someone will come here ...*
Tavernor, *On Alberti and the Art of Building*, p. 61.

191   *wherever there was some noble stone ...*
Alberti, *Leon Battista Alberti Complete Edition*, p. 166.

192   *Divine Vespasian ...*
Alberti, *Leon Battista Alberti Complete Edition*, p. 166.

Sans Souci, Potsdam

201   *There was a nobility and harmony ...*
Franz Kugler, *Karl Friedrich Schinkel, Eine Characteristik siner kuenstlerishchen Wirksamheit* (Berlin 1842), first published in the *Hallesche Jahrbuecher*, 1838.

203   *The description of nature ...*
Quoted in Barry Bergdoll, *Karl Friedrich Schinkel: An Architecture for Prussia* (Rizzoli 1994), p. 156.

206   *If God made the world for me ...*
Nancy Mitford, *Frederick the Great* (Penguin 1970), p. 79.

–   *Quand je serai là ...*
Kunst-und Ausstellungshalle der Bundesrepublik Deutschland, *Filmreihe: Schätze der Welt – Erbe der Menschheit*, p. 11 (German, PDF).
http://www.kah-bonn.de/bibliothek/schaetze_pr.pdf

210   *ennobles all human relationships*
Michael Snodin, *Karl Friedrich Schinkel: A Universal Man* (Yale University Press 1991), p. 1.

211   *They consisted of a series of villas ...*
Diary entry of Field Marshal Alanbrooke, Chief of the General Staff, 15 July 1945, in *War Diaries 1939–1945: Field Marshal Lord Alanbrooke*, ed. Alex Danchev and Daniel Todman (Weidenfeld and Nicolson 2001), p. 705.

–   *All the Germans have of course ...*
Letter from Sir Alexander Cadogan, Permanent Under-Secretary, Foreign Office, to his wife, 15 July 1945, in *The Diaries of Sir Alexander Cadogan 1938–1945*, ed. David Dilks (Cassell 1971), pp. 761–2.

212   *I spared that beautiful country as far as possible ...*
Mitford, *Frederick the Great*, p. 200.

–   *Admit that war is a cruel thing ...*
Mitford, *Frederick the Great*, p. 145.

–   *in the end God will take pity on us ...*
Mitford, *Frederick the Great*, p. 215.

213   *Hats off, gentlemen!* ...
      Mitford, *Frederick the Great*, p. 291.

–   *disgraced by the stink of revolution* ...
      http://www.age-of-the-sage.org/history/1848/reaction.html

214   *Deep into the most distant jungles* ...
      Dr Annika Mombauer, 'Germany's Last Kaiser: Wilhelm II and Political
      Decision-making in Imperial Germany', *New Perspective*, vol. 4, no. 3 (Open
      University 1999).
      http://www.users.globalnet.co.uk/~semp/wilhelmii.htm

216   *Devastation of Potsdam terrible* ...
      Anthony Eden, *The Reckoning: The Eden Memoirs*, vol. 2 (Cassell 1965), p. 545.

–   *My hate had died with their surrender* ...
      Martin Gilbert, *Churchill: A Life* (Minerva 1991), p. 850.

Notre Dame de Paris

223   *The story of the arsonists* ...
      Guy Debord, *Sur la Commune* (Aux Poubelles d'Histoire 1962), tr. Ken Knabb
      2006.
      http://www.bopsecrets.org/SI/Pariscommune.htm

226   *The artist must efface himself* ...
      'L'artiste doit s'effacer entièrement, oublier ses goûts, ses instincts, pour
      étudier son sujet, pour retrouver et suivre la pensée qui a présidé à l'exécution
      de l'oeuvre qu'il veut restaurer.' Eugène-Emmanuel Viollet-le-Duc and Jean-
      Baptiste Lassus, *Projet de Restauration de Notre Dame de Paris* (Lacombe 1845), tr.
      by the author.
      http://www.gutenberg.org/files/18920/18920-h/18920-h.htm

–   *It was necessary to perform* ...
      'Il fallait que cette analyse minutieuse vint expliquer, compléter, et souvent
      même rectifier les opinions résultant de l'examen des textes seuls; car souvent
      un texte peut se prêter à des interprétations diverses, ou paraître inintelligible,
      tandis que les caractères archéologiques sont là, comme autant de dates irrécus-
      ables, gravées sur l'ensemble et jusque sur les moindres détails du monument.'
      Viollet-le-Duc and Lassus, *Projet de Restauration* (tr. by the author).

227   *It is impossible to conserve the form* ...
      'Car, en changeant la matière, il est impossible de conserver la forme; ainsi, la
      fonte ne peut pas plus reproduire l'aspect de la pierre que le fer ne peut se

prêter à rendre celui du bois.' Viollet-le-Duc and Lassus, *Projet de Restauration* (tr. by the author).

— *We think therefore that the replacement ...*
'Nous pensons donc que le remplacement de toutes les statues qui ornaient les portails, la galerie des rois, et les contreforts, ne peut être exécuté qu'à l'aide de copies de statues existantes dans d'autres monuments analogues, et de la même époque. Les modèles ne manquent pas à Chartres, à Rheims, à Amiens, et dans tant d'autres églises qui couvrent le sol de la France. Ces mêmes cathédrales nous offriront aussi les modèles des vitraux qu'il faudra replacer à Notre-Dame, modèles qu'il serait impossible d'imiter, et qu'il est beaucoup plus sage de copier.' Viollet-le-Duc and Lassus, *Projet de Restauration* (tr. by the author).

228 *The only espaliers he could conceive ...*
Victor Hugo, *Notre Dame of Paris*, tr. John Sturrock (Penguin 2004), p. 177.

229 *some goodwives, milk-jugs in hand ...*
Hugo, *Notre Dame of Paris*, p. 486.

229–30 *raised his eye to the gypsy ...*
Hugo, *Notre Dame of Paris*, p. 490.

231 *What a shame ...*
http://www.georgianindex.net/Napoleon/coronation/coronation.html

237 *Great buildings, like great mountains ...*
Hugo, *Notre Dame of Paris*, p. 129.

238 *that divine creation ...*
Hugo, *Notre Dame of Paris*, p. 124.

239 *the term* restoration *and the thing itself ...*
Viollet-le-Duc, *Dictionnaire Raisonné*, quoted in M.F. Hearn, ed., *The Architectural Theory of Viollet le Duc* (MIT Press 1990), p. 269.

— *a destruction accompanied ...*
John Ruskin, *Seven Lamps of Architecture: The Lamp of Memory*, quoted in Jukka Jokkilehto, *The History of Architectural Conservation* (Butterworth Heinemann 1999), p. 175.

240 *Surely it is a curious thing ...*
William Morris, *History and Architecture*, quoted in Chris Miele, ed., *William Morris on Architecture* (Sheffield Academic Press 1996), p. 118.

— *Watch an old building ...*
Ruskin, *Seven Lamps of Architecture*, quoted in Jokkilehto, *The History of Architectural Conservation*, p. 180.

– *If it has become inconvenient ...*
William Morris, *Manifesto of the SPAB*, quoted in Miele, *William Morris on Architecture*, p. 55.

– *We understand the rigour of these principles ...*
'Nous comprenons la rigueur de ces principes, nous les acceptons complètement, mais seulement, lorsqu'il s'agira d'une ruine curieuse, sans destination, et sans utilité actuelle.' Viollet-le-Duc and Lassus, *Projet de Restauration* (tr.by the author).

– *Gothic construction ...*
Viollet-le-Duc, *Rational Building*, from *Dictionnaire Raisonné*, quoted in Hearn, ed., *The Architectural Theory of Viollet le Duc*, p. 116.

The Hulme Crescents, Manchester

247 *Hello, good evening ...*
www.exhulme.co.uk/page2.php

248 *A MINI TOWN WITH ALL MOD CONS ...*
Manchester Evening News, 4 June 1969, quoted in Rob Ramwell and Hilary Saltburn, *Trick or Treat? City Challenge and the Regeneration of Hulme* (North British Housing Association and the Guinness Trust 1998), p. 5.

– *It is our endeavour at Hulme ...*
Quoted in Ramwell and Saltburn, *Trick or Treat?*, p. 5.

249 *In a rather deep hole ...*
Friedrich Engels, *Condition of the Working Class in England in 1844*, quoted in Ramwell and Saltburn, *Trick or Treat?*, p. 2.

250 *Abolition of property ...*
http://www.marxists.org/archive/marx/works/1848/communist-manifesto/index.htm

251 *Communists know only too well ...*
Friedrich Engels, *The Principles of Communism* (1847).
http://www.marxists.org/archive/marx/works/1847/11/prin-com.htm

– *We will sing of great crowds ...*
Filippo Tommaso Marinetti, *The Founding and Manifesto of Futurism* (1909).
http://www.cscs.umich.edu/~crshalizi/T4PM/futurist-manifesto.html

252 *We stand on the last promontory of the centuries ...*
Marinetti, *The Founding and Manifesto of Futurism.*

— *In spite of disease and death* …
Manchester Guardian, 10 January 1923, quoted in Ramwell and Saltburn, *Trick or Treat?*, p. 2.

253 *unlocks all the doors to the urbanism of modern times* …
Le Corbusier, *The Athens Charter* (Grossman 1973; 1st ed. Paris 1943), p. xiv.

— *An immense, total mutation* …
Le Corbusier, *The Athens Charter*, p. xiv.

— *the Charter must be placed* …
Le Corbusier, *The Athens Charter*, pp. 25–6.

254 *a three-dimensional, not a two-dimensional, science*
Le Corbusier, *The Athens Charter*, p. 105.

255 *Why are you showing me this desolation?* …
Miles Glendinning and Stephan Muthesius, *Tower Block: Modern Public Housing in England, Scotland, Wales and Northern Ireland* (Yale University Press 1994), p. 256.

256 *The planning brief for Hulme stage 5* …
Minutes of Meeting of Housing Committee, 6 July 1966, quoted in Manchester Housing Workshop, *Hulme Crescents: Council Housing Chaos in the 1970s* (Moss Side Community Press Women's Co-op 1980), p. 4.

257 *a high quality of finish* …
Minutes of Meeting of Housing Committee, 6 July 1966, quoted in Manchester Housing Workshop, *Hulme Crescents*, p. 5.

— *I was four* …
'Caroline', 15 November 2007, quoted in www.exhulme.co.uk

259 *A list to be drawn up* …
Ramwell and Saltburn, *Trick or Treat?*, p. 7.

260 *The day I moved in was 11th Dec.* …
Compost City 2: blog page on Hulme Crescents MySpace page, posted 18 December 2006.
http://www.myspace.com/index.cfm?fuseaction=blog.view&friendId=55432167&blogId=206922483

— *Moved to Hulme in 1982* …
'Karen', 22 April 2007, quoted in www.exhulme.co.uk

261 *Remember Queenie?* …
'Karen', 22 April 2007, quoted in www.exhulme.co.uk

262 *Punks, goths, ratios ...*
Hulme Crescents MySpace page, 'would like to meet'.

263 *My fondest memory ...*
'James', 10 February 2008, quoted in www.exhulme.co.uk

264 *Jamie taking a jackhammer ...*
'Mark/Bruce', 22 April 2007, quoted in www.exhulme.co.uk

— *There was a massive sound system ...*
'John Robb', quoted in www.exhulme.co.uk

265 *the memorable Hulme Demolition Sound System ...*
'Gonnie Rietveld', 18 April 2007, quoted in www.exhulme.co.uk

266 *safe, clean, and attractive ...*
Ramwell and Saltburn, *Trick or Treat?*, p. 19.

267 *Madchester City Council ...*
Ramwell and Saltburn, *Trick or Treat?*, p. 12.

268 *The oldest of us is thirty ...*
Marinetti, *The Founding and Manifesto of Futurism.*

The Berlin Wall

276 *Did the wall fall out of the sky? ...*
Calvin University German Propaganda Archive.
http://www.calvin.edu/academic/cas/gpa/wall.htm

285 *We know about this tendency in the population ...*
http://www.coldwarfiles.org/files/Documents/19891109_press%20conference.pdf

— *It comes into effect ...*
http://www.coldwarfiles.org/files/Documents/19891109_press%20conference.pdf

286 *This ninth of November is a historic day ...*
'Tagesthemen', broadcast on ARD, quoted in Frederick Taylor, *The Berlin Wall,
13 August 1961–9 November 1989* (Bloomsbury 2006), p. 427.

287 *a presentation and holding device ...*
http://www.google.com/patents?vid=USPAT6076675

The Venetian, Las Vegas

301 *A very regal-looking environment* ...
Connie Bruck, 'The Brass Ring: A Multibillionaire's Relentless Quest for
Global Influence,' *The New Yorker*, 30 June 2008.
http://www.newyorker.com/reporting/2008/06/30/080630fa_fact_bruck?current
Page=all

302 *Kublai Khan does not necessarily believe everything* ...
Italo Calvino, *Invisible Cities* (Harcourt Brace 1974), pp. 5–6.

308 *tailored to one lifestyle* – yours
http://www.wynnlasvegas.com/#Shopping/

— *Dream with your eyes open*
http://www.wynnlasvegas.com/#entertainment/

309 *Our goal was to build* ...
Steve Wynn, quoted in Las Vegas Strip Historical Site.
http://www.lvstriphistory.com/ie/sands66.htm

— *It's much more difficult to give a party* ...
Steve Wynn, quoted in http://thinkexist.com/quotes/steve_wynn/

310 *What was famous then* ...
Sands President Henri Lewin, quoted in Las Vegas Strip Historical Site.
http://www.lvstriphistory.com/ie/sands66.htm

312 *Authenticity is the basis for fantasy*
Wimberly Allison Tong and Goo, *Designing the World's Best Resorts* (Images
Publishing 2001), p. 110.

318 *Venice is not a hotel*
'Protests Against More Venice Hotels: Residents Group Fight Proposed New
Law', *Wanderlust Magazine*, 17 April 2004.
http://www.wanderlust.co.uk/article.php?page_id=1112

319 *presented as an immense accumulation of spectacles* ...
Guy Debord, *The Society of the Spectacle*, tr. Ken Knabb (Rebel Press 2006),
p. 7.

— *If I make other people feel good* ...
Bruck, 'The Brass Ring'.

— *We start with one question* ...
Steve Wynn, quoted in http://thinkexist.com/quotes/steve_wynn/

320 *Las Vegas is sort of like ...*
Steve Wynn, quoted in
http://www.woopidoo.com/business_quotes/authors/steve-wynn/index.htm

— *Even as this city moves forward ...*
Venetian Macao Brochure.
http://www.venetianmacao.com/uploads/media/download/brochures_english.pdf

— *Sire, now I have told you ...*
Calvino, *Invisible Cities*, pp. 86–7.

321 *The Venetian represents that first massive step ...*
Associated Press, 'Sands calls US$2.4b Casino Opening a "Massive Step" in
Macao', *International Herald Tribune*, 16 August 2007.

The Western Wall, Jerusalem

328 *The restoration of the Mugrabi path ...*
'Arabs Increase Threats at the Western Wall Plaza', *Israel Faxx*, Friday,
9 February 2007.
http://www.allbusiness.com/middle-east/israel/3954928-1.html

329 *Islam should show a serious reaction ...*
Associated Press, 'Ayatollah Blasts Construction Work by Temple Mt.',
Jerusalem Post, 7 February 2007.

— *nothing will work with Israel ...*
http://www.ynetnews.com/articles/0,7340,L-3364346,00.html

331 *Would anyone in the civilized world agree ...*
http://www.juf.org/news/israel.aspx?id=10300

— *has been done under the close supervision ...*
http://www.robat.scl.net/content/NAD/press/jerusalem/adnan_husseini.php

333 *the archeologists sold out to the enemy ...*
http://groups.yahoo.com/group/Bible_Codes/message/39738

— *The time has come to do ...*
www.keshev.org.il/FileUpload/20010101_Tample_Mount%20_Full_Text_Eng.doc

— *I stood there in the place where the High Priest ...*
Ehud Sprinzak, *The Ascendance of Israel's Radical Right* (Oxford University Press
1991), p. 44. Quoted in Karen Armstrong, *Jerusalem: One City, Three Faiths*
(Ballantine 1996), p. 400.

335   *I came here as one who believes in coexistence* ...
      http://www.mideastweb.org/Middle-East-Encyclopedia/second_intifada.htm

337   *The people in general* ...
      Edward Robinson, *Biblical Researches II*, quoted in Jay Williams, 'The Life and
      Times of Edward Robinson',
      http://www.bibleinterp.com/articles/robinson.shtml

—   *The country of Palestine belongs to you and me* ...
      Quoted in Armstrong, *Jerusalem*, p. 361.

338   *What torment to see our Holy Courts* ...
      Al-Haziri, quoted in Armstrong, *Jerusalem*, p. 229.

339   *All my private troubles mingled* ...
      Meri Ben Dov, *The Western Wall*, quoted in Armstrong, *Jerusalem*, p. 229.

342   *Glory be to He* ...
      Koran 17:1.

345   *insisted that they should enforce* ...
      Josephus, *The Jewish War*, tr. G.A. Williamson, rev. Mary Smallwood (Penguin
      1970), p. 356.

—   *around the altar* ...
      Josephus, *The Jewish War*, p. 358.

347   *I am the* LORD *thy God* ...
      Exodus 20:2–3 (King James version).

348   *Concerning this house* ...
      3 Kings 6:12, 13 (King James version).

—   *When ye come to appear before me* ...
      Isaiah 1:12, 13 (King James version).

—   *If I forget thee, O Jerusalem* ...
      Psalm 137 (King James version).

350   *To southward I set* ...
      Quoted in Armstrong, *Jerusalem*, p. 337.

Bibliography

Introduction

Alexander, Christopher. *The Timeless Way of Building*. Oxford University Press 1979.

Alexander, Christopher, et al. *The Oregon Experiment*. Oxford University Press 1975.

Alexander, Christopher, Ishikawa, Sara, and Silverstein, Murray. *A Pattern Language: Towns, Buildings, Construction*. Oxford University Press 1977.

Brand, Stewart. *How Buildings Learn*. Viking 1994.

Brooker, Graeme, and Stone, Sally. *Rereadings: Interior Architecture and the Design Principles of Remodeling Existing Buildings*. RIBA Press 2004.

Calasso, Roberto. *The Marriage of Cadmus and Harmony*. Vintage 1994.

Calasso, Roberto. *The Ruins of Kasch*. Vintage 1995.

Dal Co, Francesco, and Mazzarol, Guiseppe. *Carlo Scarpa, Complete Works*. Electa and Architectural Press 1990.

Darnton, Robert. *The Great Cat Massacre and Other Episodes in French Cultural History*. Allen Lane 1984.

Darnton, Robert. *The Great Cat Massacre and Other Essays*. Vintage 1985.

Fawcett, Jane, ed. *The Future of the Past*. Thames and Hudson 1976.

Frampton, Kenneth. *Studies in Tectonic Culture*. MIT Press 1995.

Hollis, Edward. 'Architecture about Architecture: Script and Performance.' Proceedings of the 5th Conference of the European Academy of Design, Barcelona, 2003, http://www.ub.es/5ead/princip5.htm

Hollis, Edward. 'Constructed Tradition: A Comparative Study of Carlo Scarpa's Castelvecchio and Geoffrey Bawa's garden at Lunuganga.' Paper delivered at the Mind the Map Conference, Istanbul Technical University, 2002.

Hyde, Lewis. *The Gift: How the Creative Spirit Transforms the World.* Canongate 2006 (1st ed. 1979).

Jokkilehto, Jukka. *A History of Architectural Conservation.* Butterworth Heinemann 1999.

Miele, Chris, ed. *William Morris on Architecture.* Sheffield Academic Press 1996.

Milling, Jane, and Ley, Graham. *Modern Theories of Performance.* Palgrave 2001.

Murphy, Richard. *Carlo Scarpa and Castelvecchio.* Butterworth Architecture 1990.

Norberg-Shulz, Christian. *Genius Loci: Towards a Phenomenology of Architecture.* Rizzoli 1979.

Perry, Gill, and Cunningham, Colin, eds. *Academies, Museums and Canons of Art.* Yale University Press and the Open University Press 1999.

Rossi, Aldo. *The Architecture of the City*, tr. Diane Ghirardo and Joan Ockman. MIT Press 1982.

Rowe, Colin, and Koetter, Fred. *Collage City.* MIT Press 1978.

Ruskin, John. *St Mark's Rest: The History of Venice.* 1885.

Schon, Donald. *The Reflective Practitioner: How Professionals Think in Action.* Basic Books 1983.

Scott, Fred. *On Altering Architecture.* Routledge 2008.

Scott Brown, Denise, and Venturi, Robert. *View from the Campidoglio: Selected Essays 1953–1984.* Harper and Row 1984.

Venturi, Robert. *Complexity and Contradiction in Architecture.* MOMA New York and Architectural Press 1966.

Viollet-le-Duc, Eugène-Emmanuel. *On Restoration*, tr. Charles Wethered. Sampson Low, Marston and Searle 1875.

Woodward, Christopher. *In Ruins.* Chatto and Windus 2001.

The Parthenon, Athens

Beard, Mary. *The Parthenon.* Harvard University Press 2003.

Cooke, Brian. *The Elgin Marbles.* British Museum Publications 1997.

Dontas, George. *The Acropolis and its Museum.* Clion Editions 1979.

Freeman, Charles. *AD 381: Heretics, Pagans, and the Christian State*. Pimlico 2008.

Herodotus. *The Histories*, tr. A. De Sélincourt. Penguin 1954.

Miller, Helen. *Greece Through the Ages*. Dent 1972.

Neils, Jenifer, ed. *The Parthenon: From Antiquity to the Present*. Cambridge University Press 2005.

Plutarch. *The Age of Alexander: Nine Greek Lives by Plutarch*, ed. Ian Scott Kilvert. Penguin 1973.

Plutarch. *Greek Lives*, tr. Robin Waterfield. Oxford University Press 1998.

Plutarch. *Lives*, tr. John Dryden. http://classics.mit.edu/Plutarch

Routery, Michael. *The First Missionary War: The Church Take Over the Roman Empire*, ch. 4 (1997). http://www.vinland.org/scamp/grove/kreich/chapter4.html

Thucydides. *The History of the Peloponnesian Wars*, tr. R. Warner. Penguin 1974.

Tomkinson, John. 'Ottoman Athens II.' http://www.anagnosis.gr/index.php?pageID= 218&la=eng

Wood, Gillen. 'The Strange Case of Lord Elgin's Nose: Or, a Study in the Pathology of Hellenism.' Columbia University, Prometheus Unplugged. http://prometheus.cc.emory.edu/panels/5E/G.Wood.html

The Basilica of San Marco, Venice

Basilica of San Marco, official site, www.basilicasanmarco.it

Freeman, Charles. *The Horses of San Marco*. Abacus 2005.

Gibbon, Edward. *Decline and Fall of the Roman Empire*. Wordsworth Publications 1998.

Goy, Richard. *Venice: The City and Its Architecture*. Phaidon 1997.

Grundy, Milton. *Venice Recorded*. Anthony Blond 1971.

Herrin, Judith. *Byzantium: The Surprising Life of a Medieval Empire*. Penguin 2007.

Howard, Deborah. *The Architectural History of Venice*. Yale University Press 1980.

Niketas Choniates. *Historia*, tr. Bente Bjørnholt. Corpus Fontium Historiae Byzantinae, vol. XI. De Gruyter 1975.

Norwich, John Julius. *A Short History of Byzantium*. Penguin 1998.

Ayasofya, Istanbul

Constantini Pophyrogeniti Imperatoris de Ceremoniis Byzantini, 2 vols., ed. J.J. Reiske. CSHB (1879).

Crowley, Roger. *Constantinople: The Last Great Siege 1453*. Faber 2005.

Herrin, Judith. *Byzantium: The Surprising Life of a Medieval Empire*. Penguin 2007.

Kaehler, Heinz, and Mango, Cyril. *Hagia Sophia*. Zwemmer 1967.

Kelly, Lawrence, ed. *A Traveller's Companion to Istanbul*. Constable and Robinson 1987.

Mainstone, Rowland. *Hagia Sophia: Architecture, Structure and Liturgy of Justinian's Great Church*. Thames and Hudson 1988.

Mark, Robert, and Çakmak, Ahmet, eds. *Hagia Sophia from the Age of Justinian until the Present*. Cambridge University Press 1992.

Procopius. *De Aedis*, tr. H.B. Dewing (Loeb Classical Library 1940).

Procopius. *The Secret History*, tr. G.A. Williamson. Penguin 1966.

The Santa Casa of Loreto

Coleman, Simon. 'Meanings of Movement, Place and Home at Walsingham.' *Culture and Religion*, vol. 1, no. 2 (November 2000), pp. 153–69.

Corbington, Robert. 'The Wondrous Flitting of the Kerk of Our Lady of Laureto.' Inscription in the Basilica di Santa Casa, Loreto.

Garatt, William. *Loreto: The New Nazareth and Its Centenary Jubilee*. Kessinger 2003.

Katherine Maria MICM, Sister. 'The Holy House of Loreto.' http://www.catholicism.org/loreto-house.html

Hollis, Christopher, and Brownrigg, Ronald. *Holy Places: Jewish, Christian and Muslim Monuments in the Holy Land*. Praeger 1969.

Santarelli, Guiseppe. *Loreto: Its History and Art*. Fotometalgrafica Emiliana 1983.

Phillips, G. *The Holy House*. Loreto Publications 2004.

Pynson, Richard. *Ballade of Walsingham*, 1490.

Roli, Renato. *Sanctuary of Santa Casa, Loreto*. Officine Graphiche Poligrafici il Resto di Carlino 1966.

Shapcote, Emily Mary. *Among the Lilies and Other Tales: With a Sketch of the Holy House of Nazareth and Loreto*. Kessinger 2008. 1st published 1881.

'Shrines of Our Lady – Walsingham.' www.shrinesofourlady.com/_eng/shrines/walsingham.asp

Vail, Anne. *Shrines of Our Lady in England*. Gracewing 2004.

Gloucester Cathedral

Braun, Mark. *Cathedral Architecture*. Faber 1972.

Duffy, Mark. *Royal Tombs of Medieval England*. Tempus 2003.

Gimpel, Jean. *The Cathedral Builders*, tr. Teresa Waugh. The Cresset Library 1983.

Harvey, John. *The Cathedrals of England and Wales*. Batsford 1950.

Harvey, John. *The Medieval Architect*. Wayland 1972.

Harvey, John. *The Perpendicular Style, 1330–1485*. Batsford 1978.

Morgan, Giles. *Freemasonry*. Pocket Essentials 2007.

Pevsner, Nikolaus, and Metcalf, Priscilla. *The Cathedrals of England: Midlands, Eastern and Northern England*. Viking 1985.

Saaler, Mary. *Edward II, 1307–1327*. Rubicon Press 1997.

Summerson, John. *Heavenly Mansions and Other Essays on Architecture*. Norton and Co. 1998.

Verey, David, and Welander, David. *Gloucester Cathedral*. Alan Sutton 1979.

Weir, Alison. Isabella: *She-Wolf of France, Queen of England*. Jonathan Cape 2005.

Welander, David. *The History, Art and Architecture of Gloucester Cathedral*. Alan Sutton 1991.

Westwood, Jennifer, and Simpson, Jacqueline. *The Lore of the Land: A Guide to England's Legends from Spring Heeled Jack to the Witches of Warboys*. Penguin 2005.

The Alhambra, Granada

Fletcher, Richard. *Moorish Spain*. Phoenix Press 1994.

Galera Andreu, Pedro, ed. *Carlos V y la Alhambra*. Patronato de la Alhambra 2000.

Goodwin, Godfrey. *Islamic Spain*. Penguin 1990.

Grabar, Oleg. *The Alhambra*. Penguin 1978.

Irvine, Washington. *Tales of the Alhambra*. Editorial Everest 2005.

Irwin, Robert. *The Alhambra*. Profile Books 2005.

Trevelyan, Raleigh. *Shades of the Alhambra*. Folio Society 1984.

The Tempio Malatestiano, Rimini

Alberti, Leon Battista. *On the Art of Building in Ten Books*, tr. Joseph Rykwert, Neil Leach, and Robert Tavernor. MIT Press 1988.

Bicheno, Hugh. *Vendetta: High Art and Low Cunning at the Birth of the Renaissance*. Weidenfeld and Nicolson 2008.

Borsi, Franco. *Leon Battista Alberti Complete Edition*. Phaidon 1975.

Burckhardt, Jacob. *The Civilization of the Renaissance*. Modern Library 2000.

Grafton, Anthony. *Leon Battista Alberti: Master Builder of the Italian Renaissance*. Penguin 2001.

Hutton, Edward. *The Mastiff of Rimini: Chronicles of the House of Malatesta*. Methuen 1926.

Jarzombek, Mark. *On Leon Battista Alberti: His Literary and Aesthetic Theories*. MIT Press 1989.

Il Potere, Le Arti, La Guerra: Lo Splendore dei Malatesta. Electa 2001.

Rainey, Laurence. *Ezra Pound and the Monument of Culture: Text, History, and the Malatesta Cantos*. University of Chicago Press 1991.

Tavernor, Robert. *On Alberti and the Art of Building*. Yale 1998.

Wittkower, Rudolf. *Architectural Principles in the Age of Humanism*. John Wiley and Sons 1998.

Sans Souci, Potsdam

Bergdoll, Barry. *Karl Friedrich Schinkel: An Architecture for Prussia*. Rizzoli 1994.

Boyd Whyte, Iain. 'Charlottenhof: The Prince, the Gardener, the Architect and the Writer.' *Architectural History*, vol. 43 (2000), pp. 1–23.

Danchev, Alex, and Todman, Daniel, eds. *War Diaries 1939–1945: Field Marshal Lord Alanbrooke*. Weidenfeld and Nicolson 2001.

Dilks, David, ed. *The Diaries of Sir Alexander Cadogan 1938–1945*. Cassell 1971.

Eden, Anthony. *The Reckoning: The Eden Memoirs*, vol. 2. Cassell 1965.

Gilbert, Martin. *Churchill: A Life*. Minerva, 1991.

Glad, Betty, ed. *Psychological Dimensions of War*. Sage Publications 1990.

Grisebach, August. *Karl Friedrich Schinkel: Architekt, Staedtebauer, Maler*. Im Insel Verlag 1982. 1st published Leipzig 1921.

Kugler, Franz. *Karl Friedrich Schinkel: Eine Characteristik siner kuenstlerishchen Wirksamheit*. Berlin 1842. 1st published in the *Hallesche Jahrbuecher* 1838.

Mielke, Friedrich. *Potsdamer Baukunst: Das Klässiche Potsdam.* Verlag Ullstein GmbH, Propyläen Verlag 1981.

Mitford, Nancy. *Frederick the Great.* Penguin 1970.

Pliny the Younger. *Letters.* Harvard University Press 1909–14.

Snodin, Michael. *Karl Friedrich Schinkel: A Universal Man.* Yale University Press 1991.

Van der Kiste, John. *Dearest Vicky, Darling Fritz.* Sutton Publishing 2002.

Watkin, David. *German Architecture and the Classical Ideal 1740–1840.* Thames and Hudson 1987.

Notre Dame de Paris

Bottinau, Yves. *Notre Dame de Paris and the Sainte-Chapelle.* George Allan and Unwin 1967.

Hearn, M.F., ed. *The Architectural Theory of Viollet le Duc: Readings and Commentary.* MIT Press 1990.

Hugo, Victor. *Notre Dame of Paris*, tr. John Sturrock. Penguin 2004.

Jokkilehto, Jukka. *The History of Architectural Conservation.* Butterworth Heinemann 1999.

Midant, Jean Paul. *Viollet le Duc and the French Gothic Revival.* L'Aventurine 2002.

Miele, Chris, ed. *William Morris on Architecture.* Sheffield Academic Press 1996.

Murray, Stephen. 'Notre Dame de Paris and the Appreciation of Gothic.' *The Art Bulletin*, vol. 80, no. 2 (July 1998).

Pevsner, Nikolaus. 'Ruskin and Viollet le Duc.' *Englishness and Frenchness in the Appreciation of Gothic Architecture.* Thames and Hudson 1969.

Temko, Allan. *Notre Dame of Paris.* Secker and Warburg 1956.

Viollet-le-Duc, Eugène-Emmanuel, and Lassus, Jean-Baptiste. *Projet de Restauration de Notre Dame de Paris.* Lacombe 1845.

Viollet-le-Duc, Eugène-Emmanuel. *Entretiens sur Architecture*, complete ed. P. Mardaga 1977.

The Hulme Crescents, Manchester

Department of the Environment. *Hulme Study Stage One: Initial Action Plan.* HMSO 1990.

Conrad, Peter. *Modern Times, Modern Places: Life and Art in the Twentieth Century.* Thames and Hudson 1999.

ExHulme: www.exhulme.co.uk

Glendinning, Miles, and Muthesius, Stephan. *Tower Block: Modern Public Housing in England, Scotland, Wales and Northern Ireland.* Yale University Press 1994.

Hulme Regeneration Limited. *Rebuilding the City: A Guide to Development in Hulme,* June 1994.

Hulme Views Project. *Hulme Views: Self Portraits.* Hulme Views Project 1990.

Le Corbusier. *The Athens Charter.* Grossman 1973. 1st published 1943.

Le Corbusier. *Towards a New Architecture,* tr. Frederick Etchells. Architectural Press 1991. 1st published 1923.

Le Corbusier. *The Radiant City: Elements of a Doctrine of Urbanism to be Used as the Basis of Our Machine-Age Civilization* (tr. of *La Ville Radieuse*). Orion Press 1967.

Makepeace, Chris. *Looking Back at Hulme, Moss Side, Chorlton on Medlock and Ardwick.* Willow Publishing 1995.

Manchester Corporation Housing Department. *A New Community: The Redevelopment of Hulme.* 1966.

Manchester Housing Workshop. *Hulme Crescents: Council Housing Chaos in the 1970s.* Moss Side Community Press Women's Co-op 1980.

Marinetti, Filippo. *The Founding and Manifesto of Futurism,* 1909. http://www.cscs.umich.edu/~crshalizi/T4PM/futurist-manifesto.html

Ramwell, Rob, and Saltburn, Hilary. *Trick or Treat? City Challenge and the Regeneration of Hulme.* North British Housing Association and the Guinness Trust 1998.

Reynolds, Simon. *Rip It Up and Start Again: Postpunk 1978–1984.* Faber 2005.

Wilson, Anthony. *24 Hour Party People.* Channel 4 Books 2002.

Wilson, Hugh, and Womersley, Lewis. *Hulme 5 Redevelopment: Report on Design.* City of Manchester, October 1965.

The Berlin Wall

Beevor, Anthony. *Berlin: The Downfall 1945.* Penguin 2002.

'The Berlin Wall: The Best and Sexiest Wall Ever Existed!!' http://berlin-wall.org/

Bernauerstraße Wall Museum. http://www.berlinermauerdokumentationszentrum.de/eng/index_dokz.html

Buckley, William. *The Fall of the Berlin Wall.* Wiley 2004.

Calvin University German Propaganda Archive. http://www.calvin.edu/academic/cas/gpa/wall.htm

City Guide to the Wall. http://www.stadtentwicklung.berlin.de/bauen/ wanderungen/en/ strecke4.shtml

East Side Gallery. http://www.eastsidegallery.com

Funder, Anna. *Stasiland: True Stories from Behind the Berlin Wall*. Granta 2003.

The Günther Schabowski Conference. http://www.coldwarfiles.org/files/Documents /1989-1109_press%20conference.pdf

Hensel, Jana. *After the Wall: Confessions of an East German Childhood and the Life that Came Next*. Public Affairs 2008.

Katona, Marianna. *Tales from the Berlin Wall*. Books on Demand GmbH 2004.

Ladd, Bryan. *Ghosts of Berlin: Confronting German History in the Urban Landscape*. University of Chicago Press 1998.

Petschull, Jürgen. *Die Mauer, von Anfang und vom Ende eines deutschen Bauwerks*. Stern Bücher 1990.

Schneider, Peter. *The Wall Jumper: A Berlin Story*. University of Chicago Press 1998.

Taylor, Frederick. *The Berlin Wall, 13 August 1961–9 November 1989*. Bloomsbury 2006.

The Venetian, Las Vegas

Bruck, Connie. 'The Brass Ring: A Multibillionaire's Relentless Quest for Global Influence.' *The New Yorker*, 30 June 2008. http://www.newyorker.com/reporting/ 2008/06/30/080630fa_fact_bruck?currentPage=all

Calvino, Italo. *Invisible Cities*. Harcourt Brace 1974.

Debord, Guy. *The Society of the Spectacle*, tr. Ken Knabb. Rebel Press 2006.

Earley, Pete. *Super Casino Inside the 'New' Las Vegas*. Bantam Books 2000.

Komroff, Manuel, ed. *The Travels of Marco Polo*. Liveright 2003.

Koolhaas, Rem. *Delirious New York*. Monacelli Press 1994.

Las Vegas Strip Historical Site. http://www.lvstriphistory.com/ie/sands66.htm

Moore, Rowan. *Vertigo: The Strange New World of the Contemporary City*. Laurence King 1999.

'Protests Against More Venice Hotels: Residents Group Fight Proposed New Law.' *Wanderlust Magazine* 17 (April 2004). http://www.wanderlust.co.uk/article.php? page_id=1112

Ruskin, John. *The Stones of Venice*, ed. Jan Morris. Faber 1981.

Sehlinger, Bob. *The Unofficial Guide to Las Vegas*. John Wiley and Sons 2008.

Sorkin, Michael, ed. *Variations on a Theme Park: The New American City and the End of Public Space*. Hill and Wang 1992.

Venetian Macao Brochure. http://www.venetianmacao.com/uploads/media/download/brochures_english.pdf

'Venice in Numbers.' http://www.myvenice.org/The-new-populations.html

Venturi, Robert, and Scott Brown, Denise. *Learning from Las Vegas*. MIT Press 1972.

Wimberly Allison Tong and Goo. *Designing the World's Best Resorts*. Images Publishing 2001.

Wynn interview with *Newsweek* 2006. http://www.podcastdirectory.com/podshows/1360547

The Western Wall, Jerusalem

Abu El-Haj, Nadia. *Facts on the Ground: Archaeological Practice and Territorial Self Fashioning in Israeli Society*. University of Chicago Press 2001.

Amico, Fra Bernardino. *Plans of the Sacred Edifices of the Holy Land*. Franciscan Printing Press 1997.

Armstrong, Karen. *Jerusalem: One City, Three Faiths*. Ballantine 1996.

Biesenbach, Klaus, ed. *Territories: Islands, Camps, and Other States of Utopia*. KW Institute for Contemporary Art 2003.

The Gaza Strip: One Big Prison. B'Tselem: The Israeli Information Center for Human Rights in the Occupied Territories 2005.

Gilbert, Martin. *Jerusalem in the Twentieth Century*. Pimlico 1996.

Goldhill, Simon. *Jerusalem, City of Longing*. Belknap Press 2008.

Jerusalem: Injustice in the Holy City. B'Tselem: The Israeli Information Center for Human Rights in the Occupied Territories 1999.

Josephus. *The Jewish War*, tr. G.A. Williamson and Mary Smallwood. Penguin 1970.

Kohn, Michael, et al. *Israel and the Occupied Territories*. Lonely Planet 2008.

Kroyanker, David. *Jerusalem Architecture Periods and Styles: The Jewish Quarters and Public Buildings Outside the Old City Walls 1860–1914*. Domino Press 1983.

Safdie, Moshe. *The Harvard Jerusalem Studio: Urban Designs for the Holy City*. MIT Press 1986.

A Wall in Jerusalem: Obstacles to Human Rights in the Holy City. B'Tselem: The Israeli Information Center for Human Rights in the Occupied Territories 2006.

Weizman, Eyal. *Hollow Land: Israel's Architecture of Occupation*. Verso 2007.

Williams, Jay. 'The Life and Times of Edward Robinson.' http://www.bibleinterp.com/articles/robinson.shtml

Illustration Credits

Page 2. *The Architect's Dream.* Thomas Cole, 1838. © Francis G. Mayer/CORBIS.

Page 16. *The destruction of the Grand Mosque of Athens.* G.M.K. Verneda, in F. Fanelli, *Atina Attica*, 1707. Mary Evans Picture Library.

Page 44. *A staging post for four horses.* Engraved by Onofrio Panvinio, *De Ludi Circensibus*, Venice, 1600, with creative commons licence, at flickr: http://www.flickr.com/photos/bibliodyssey/3442538337/sizes/o/

Page 70. *A Roman building seen through Muslim eyes.* Seyyid Loktun, Sehame-I Selim Han, MS T.K.S.A. 3595, fol. 156r, p. 214. Reproduced by permission of the Topkapi Palace Library.

Page 94. *The Holy House of Loreto carried by angels.* Mary Evans Picture Library/Interfoto Agentur.

Page 122. *The germ of a cathedral.* Engraving (b/w photo) by Hubert Gravelot (1699–1773). Private Collection/Bridgeman Art Library. Nationality/copyright status: French/out of copyright.

Page 144. *A contract of architectural marriage.* Biblioteca del Palacio Real, Madrid. Caja IX m 242 no. F2(1) (detail). Reproduced by Permission of the Patrimonio Nacional, Spain.

Page 170. *The emblem of a great man.* National Gallery of Art, Washington, DC.

Page 196. *Classical Ruins.* Engraving by Johann Friedrich Schleuen, c.1775. Wikimedia Commons: http://de.wikipedia.org/w/index.php?title=Datei:Ruinenberg.jpg&file timestamp=20061117165653.

Page 220. *A nineteenth-century fiction.* Frontispiece of 'Notre Dame de Paris' (1831) by Victor

Hugo (1802–85), engraved by Auguste François Garnier, 1844 (b/w photo) by François Joseph Aime de Lemud (1817–87) (after). Private Collection/Archives Charmet/Bridgeman Art Library. Nationality/copyright status: French/out of copyright.

Page 244. *Remember Tomorrow*. Reproduced by permissions of Joshua Bolchover and Shumon Basar (Newbetter).

Page 272. *History for Sale*. Photo by Berlin, Germany. © H.P. Stiebing/The Bridgeman Art Library.

Page 298. *Venice to Macao*. Reproduced by permission of Galleria Ravagnan, Venice.

Page 324. *The architecture of failed diplomacy*. Reproduced by permission of Eyal Weizman.

Index